Reimagining
the Moral Life

Reimagining
The Moral Life

On Lisa Sowle Cahill's Contributions
to Christian Ethics

Edited by

Ki Joo Choi
Sarah M. Moses
Andrea Vicini, SJ

ORBIS BOOKS
Maryknoll, New York 10545

Maryknoll, New York 10545

Founded in 1970, Orbis Books endeavors to publish works that enlighten the mind, nourish the spirit, and challenge the conscience. The publishing arm of the Maryknoll Fathers and Brothers, Orbis seeks to explore the global dimensions of the Christian faith and mission, to invite dialogue with diverse cultures and religious traditions, and to serve the cause of reconciliation and peace. The books published reflect the views of their authors and do not represent the official position of the Maryknoll Society. To learn more about Orbis Books, please visit our website at www.orbisbooks.com.

Copyright © 2020 by Ki Joo Choi, Sarah M. Moses, and Andrea Vicini, SJ.

Published by Orbis Books, Box 302, Maryknoll, NY 10545-0302.

All rights reserved.

No part of this publication may be reproduced or transmitted in any form or by any means, electronic or mechanical, including photocopying, recording, or any information storage or retrieval system, without prior permission in writing from the publisher.

Queries regarding rights and permissions should be addressed to: Orbis Books, P.O. Box 302, Maryknoll, NY 10545-0302.

Manufactured in the United States of America

Library of Congress Cataloging-in-Publication Data

Names: Choi, Ki Joo, editor. | Moses, Sarah, editor. | Vicini, Andrea, editor.
Title: Reimagining the moral life : on Lisa Sowle Cahill's contributions to Christian ethics / edited by Ki Joo Choi, Sarah Moses, Andrea Vicini.
Description: Maryknoll, NY : Orbis Books, 2020. | Includes bibliographical references and index. | Summary: This volume honors Lisa Cahill's 45 years of teaching Christian ethics at Boston College. With contributions from most of the doctoral students she directed during her career, it provides an interpretive overview of Cahill's specific contributions to Christian ethics.
Identifiers: LCCN 2020002309 (print) | LCCN 2020002310 (ebook) | ISBN 9781626983793 (trade paperback) | ISBN 9781608338436 (ebook)
Subjects: LCSH: Christian ethics. | Medical ethics. | Christian sociology. | Cahill, Lisa Sowle.
Classification: LCC BJ1251 .R435 2020 (print) | LCC BJ1251 (ebook) | DDC 241/.042092—dc23
LC record available at https://lccn.loc.gov/2020002309
LC ebook record available at https://lccn.loc.gov/2020002310

*To our gracious, creative, inspiring, and tireless mentor,
with gratitude and admiration.*

Contents

Acknowledgments — ix

Introduction — xi
   Transformative Engagement in Dialogue
   Andrea Vicini, SJ

Part I
Fundamental Christian Ethics

Natural Law, Moral Reasoning, and Common Morality: — 3
Toward a Liberationist Paradigm
   Ki Joo Choi

Experience, Embodiment, and Community — 17
   Maureen H. O'Connell

Christology and Christian Ethics — 30
   Marianne Tierney FitzGerald

"To the Church at Rome, All the Churches of Christ Greet You": — 40
A Catholic Feminist Correspondence
   Mary M. Doyle Roche

Method and the Use of Scripture — 54
   Sarah M. Moses

Part II
Christian Social Ethics

Catholic Social Teaching: Insights for a Fragmented U.S. Church — 71
   Raymond E. Ward

Just War, Peace, and Peacemaking: Moral Dilemmas — 83
   Kate Ann Jackson-Meyer

Lisa Sowle Cahill's Family Ethics *Matthew Sherman*	96
Theological Bioethics and Bridge Building *Virginia M. Ryan*	108
The Courageous "Middle Way": Lisa Sowle Cahill's Contribution to Healthcare Ethics *Hoa Trung Dinh, SJ, and Stephanie C. Edwards*	120
An Environmental Ethics of Hope and Creativity *Jill Brennan O'Brien*	133

Part III
The Future of Christian Ethics

Ethics from Marginalized Perspectives *Nichole M. Flores*	149
Doing Ethics in a Global Context *Joseph Loic Mben, SJ*	161
The Gift and Virtue of Presence: Catholic and Protestant Dialogue and the Future of Christian Ethics *Autumn Alcott Ridenour*	172
Living Vatican II's Vision of the Church in the World: Contributions of Lisa Sowle Cahill *Angela Senander*	187
Christian Ethics in the Public Sphere *Grégoire Catta, SJ*	197
Postscript *Ki Joo Choi*	209
Lisa Sowle Cahill: Selected Publications	213
Contributors	217
Index	221

Acknowledgments

As three coeditors, we greatly enjoyed working together, in very collaborative ways, on this volume reimagining theological ethics and honoring our mentor. Good humor, keen editorial skills, and enthusiastic fortitude were crucial in bringing this project into being, and we are very grateful for this opportunity. Definitely, the spirit of the Ethics Colloquium, which we experienced during our studies at Boston College, lives on.

KC is grateful to his colleagues and students at Seton Hall University who have generously tolerated the many, many days of not answering knocks on his office door and very late responses to emails in order to complete this project. And he is always thankful for his family, who had to put up with his frequent refrain of "I promise, I'm almost done working."

Sarah is grateful to the University of Mississippi for granting her the sabbatical time to work on this project. In addition, she is deeply grateful to Dean Ian Markham and Virginia Theological Seminary for hosting her as a Dean's Scholar during her sabbatical. The collegiality and hospitality she enjoyed with faculty, students, and the library staff created a fruitful environment in which to work.

Andrea is grateful for working on this volume a few steps away from Lisa, so often at her desk in her office, and for casually conversing with her in the hallway while this volume was in the making, and for Kristin Heyer's encouragement, sharing her experience and advice.

This volume would not be possible without, first, the expert commitment of our editor and contributor Jill Brennan O'Brien at Orbis Books—another of Lisa's graduates—and, second, the generous support of Gregory A. Kalschuer, SJ, dean of the Morrissey College of Arts and Sciences at Boston College. Our gratitude attempts to match their generosity.

Together, as coeditors, wholeheartedly we express our gratitude to Lisa Sowle Cahill for nurturing us, and many others, as scholars, believers, and citizens. Her model of thoughtful scholarship and generous mentorship informed by her engaged commitment to church and world continues to inspire (and prod!) us.

KC Choi, Sarah M. Moses, and Andrea Vicini, SJ

Introduction

Transformative Engagement in Dialogue

Andrea Vicini, SJ

We are transformed by any reality around us, and we contribute to the transformation of reality. Such a profoundly relational way to describe, understand, and experience our humanity is attentive to who human beings are, where we are located, and what we do. This threefold dimension of human agency—identity, context, and praxis—shapes and, at the same time, defines the character, location, and actions of a theological ethicist engaged in today's world. However, identity, context, and praxis require further explication.

Four Traits

In his 2014 book *Just Mercy: A Story of Justice and Redemption*, African American lawyer and activist Bryan Stevenson revisits encounters and experiences that profoundly transformed him; allowed him to unveil the complexity of multiple contemporary cultural, religious, and social contexts; and informed his future commitments and actions.[1] Four traits exemplify how he was transformed and how further transformation occurred.

First, *proximity with the poor*.[2] The faces, voices, stories, struggles, and hopes of those who are marginalized touch our hearts and minds. They affect us in our bodies and influence our thinking and critical analysis.

---

[1] Bryan Stevenson, *Just Mercy: A Story of Justice and Redemption* (New York: Spiegel and Grau, 2014). Stevenson is executive director of the Equal Justice Initiative in Montgomery, Alabama, a professor of law at New York University Law School, and a strenuous advocate fighting any bias against the poor and people of color.

[2] Ibid., 16, 18, 22.

The injustice and ordeals endured by too many persons in need haunt us, and outrage becomes vivid. Authentic proximity avoids clerical, patriarchal, and paternalistic biases that inform any rhetoric separating "us" from "them." Moreover, true proximity steers away from any discourse in which we, who live in the pockets of the developed Global North, presume to have all the answers and solutions to alleviate the suffering of the poor and relieve them of their pitiable condition. On the contrary, while it burdens us with the weighty suffering of the dispossessed, proximity implies togetherness: whoever we are, and wherever we are located, we might embrace the opportunity, even the privilege, of learning from the other, and we long for a shared engagement. We learn, share, and receive. We are changed, and the other is changed, too. Together we can work to transform any unjust dynamic that entraps those who are less advantaged; perpetuates racial discrimination; deprives persons of needed educational and working opportunities, safe living and working environments, and affordable, accessible, high-quality healthcare; and stifles chances for social and political empowerment and flourishing.

Second, we should work together to *change the narratives* that oppress, marginalize, discriminate, and alienate, and that, too often, are shaped by fear—whether it is fear of the other or of uncertainty.[3] We have the required ability and sufficient imagination to change any narrative that fosters racial inequality or caste discrimination. We need to change narratives of white supremacy and any other type of supremacy. The new narratives that we want are shaped by justice, equality, mutuality, collaboration, and participation.

Third, we need to *hope*.[4] Hope is essential. We should help one another to stay hopeful, to keep nourishing hope. Lack of hopefulness disempowers us. We need to hope. We should be able to find reasons to hope. With their own lives, passion, and commitments, many embody hope and they foster hope in us. With hope, we can engage to promote justice, and we can help others to hope. Moreover, many hope in us. We are part of their hopes for a better and more just future.

Fourth, we should be *willing to do things that are uncomfortable and inconvenient*.[5] This means neither to foster masochistic attitudes nor to promote a disordered sense of sacrifice. We know that there is a cost in caring for others, in helping them. Many helped us at their own expense, with their time, ingenuity, patience, and dedication. Naturally, we prefer comfort, quiet, relaxation, and rest. Without denying needed self-care and

---

[3]Ibid., 96, 184, 213, 259, 274.
[4]Ibid., 10, 22, 37, 57, 70, 92, 114, 191, 212, 255.
[5]Ibid., 103, 272.

the urgency of protecting ourselves and others from anything that might harm us, we see the value of empowering one another and many others across the planet, particularly those who cannot yet protect themselves. We want to support projects and initiatives that foster justice and embody mercy. We long to contribute to making our world a better place for everyone.

Choosing the demanding proximity with the poor, changing alienating narratives, hoping, and embodying a generosity that leads us to embrace even things that are uncomfortable and inconvenient: these four traits describe the concrete commitment for just mercy that informs Bryan Stevenson's life and activism. These same four traits might describe a way of being Christian ethicists in today's world and in churches where the ethicists' identity, context, and praxis are shaped by proximity with the poor, a commitment to change oppressive and discriminating narratives, a source of reasons to hope, and the call to do what may appear uncomfortable and inconvenient. *Reimagining the Moral Life* intends to celebrate this approach. These four traits are profoundly human. They are also rooted in the Christian experience informed by the gospel and lived in communal contexts across history and around the globe. Finally, for Catholics these four traits are strengthened by the ecclesial vision inspired by the Second Vatican Council of God's people discerning the signs of the times and sharing "the joys and the hopes, the griefs and the anxieties" of everyone, "especially those who are poor or in any way afflicted, [because] these are the joys and hopes, the griefs and anxieties of the followers of Christ."[6]

Among the many colleagues who, around the world, embody and live these four traits, what better way might we revisit the field of theological ethics than by focusing on one of them? Since 1976, in her forty-five years of teaching, lecturing, research, leadership,[7] and relational engagement in the Theology Department at Boston College as J. Donald Monan, SJ, Professor, in the academy, and in the Catholic Church and society at large, Lisa Sowle Cahill has embodied these traits and promoted the transformations they imply.

Throughout her career, Lisa Cahill has trained many scholars around the world by fostering their own personal and unique way of embodying these four traits and shaping their identity and praxis in their diverse contexts. The contributions of this volume, from a group of former doctoral

---

[6] Vatican Council II, Pastoral Constitution on the Church in the Modern World, *Gaudium et spes* (1965), no. 1, www.vatican.va.

[7] Within the academy, among many leadership positions, Lisa Cahill served as president of the Catholic Theological Society of America (1992–1993) and of the Society of Christian Ethics (1997–1998).

students whom she directed and are now colleagues spread throughout the United States and around the world, exemplify her mentorship and passion for a type of justice that is informed by equality, mutuality, reciprocity, and solidarity with the poor, and which aims at promoting concretely the common good in our world today. With passion, insight, dedication, and ingenuity, Cahill has influenced the field of theological ethics and empowered women and men, lay and religious, Catholic, Protestant, and Orthodox to find their own theological voices and join in transforming our world.

Theological Transformation

In his selection of influential voices in modern U.S. moral theology, Charles Curran discusses Lisa Cahill, together with Margaret A. Farley and Ada María Isasi-Díaz. He rightly identifies Cahill as "a prolific and very highly regarded moral theologian"[8] and he further stresses how "All have to admire the depth and breadth of her work."[9] While tracing the trajectory of Cahill's scholarship throughout her career, Curran highlights how transformation is a theological leitmotif in her work. For example, Cahill recognizes that the vision of sexuality lived by the early Christian communities empowers them to transform relationships within the surrounding, dominant social and cultural ethos of the time, "by reordering relations of dominance and violence toward greater compassion, mercy, and peace and by acting in solidarity with the poor."[10]

Moreover, transformation also affects Cahill's methodological approach by leading one to consider participation not merely as a strategic device instrumental to achieving consensus, but as a moral category that aims to change unjust social arrangements. In commenting on Cahill's theological ethics, Curran affirms, "The role of participatory Christian ethics is to promote social arrangements that are consistent with the values of human dignity, the alleviation of suffering, cooperative realities, and a preferential

---

[8]Charles E. Curran, *Diverse Voices in Modern US Moral Theology*, Moral Traditions, ed. David Cloutier, Kristin Heyer, and Andrea Vicini, SJ (Washington, DC: Georgetown University Press, 2018), 151.
[9]Ibid., 173.
[10]Ibid., 156. See also 157. In the present volume, Sarah M. Moses stresses how the idea of transformation is essential to understanding Cahill's scriptural hermeneutic.

option for the poor."[11] Practices,[12] experiences, symbols,[13] and narratives belonging to particular religious traditions—including Christianity—play a significant role in any social transformation that fosters participation and the promotion of the common good.[14] Transformation also informs social life in one of its essential components: family life. Hence, Curran highlights that, "The Christian family's threefold responsibility is to form children, to serve the Church, and to try to transform the world."[15]

Finally, transformation is needed even in the case of Catholic social teaching, particularly when it faces indeterminate and intractable issues—"wicked" problems, like climate change, and with it consequences for the quality of life on the planet for human beings, as well as for all living creatures and nonliving forms.[16] In particular, because of the lack of global authority, the difficulty of global governance and the absence of enforcement systems are added to the lack of political will, despite the

---

[11] Curran, *Diverse Voices*, 158. See also 164.

[12] For example, see Lisa Sowle Cahill, "The Bible and Christian Moral Practices," in *Christian Ethics: Problems and Prospects*, ed. Lisa Sowle Cahill and James Childress (Cleveland: Pilgrim Press, 1996), 3–17; Lisa Sowle Cahill, "*Laudato Si'*: Reframing Catholic Social Ethics," *Heythrop Journal* 59, no. 6 (2018): 887–900, at 894 and 897. For Alasdair MacIntyre, practices are "any coherent and complex form of socially established cooperative human activity through which goods natural to that form of activity are realized in the course of trying to achieve those standards of excellence which are appropriate to, and partially definitive of, that form of activity, with the result that human powers to achieve excellence, and human conceptions of the ends and goods involved, are systematically extended" (MacIntyre, *After Virtue: A Study in Moral Theory*, 3rd ed. [with prologue], Bloomsbury Revelations [London: Bloomsbury, 2007], 218).

[13] As examples, see Lisa Sowle Cahill, "'Playing God': Religious Symbols in Public Places," *Journal of Medicine and Philosophy* 20, no. 4 (1995): 341–46; Lisa Sowle Cahill, "Theology's Role in Public Bioethics," in *Handbook of Bioethics and Religion*, ed. David E. Guinn (Oxford: Oxford University Press, 2006), 37–57; Lisa Sowle Cahill, "Catholic Feminists and Traditions: Renewal, Reinvention, Replacement," *Journal of the Society of Christian Ethics* 34, no. 2 (2014): 27–51, at 39 and 45; and Lisa Sowle Cahill, "Bioethics, the Gospel, and Political Engagement," *Christian Bioethics* 21, no. 3 (2015): 247–61.

[14] "A participatory, theological ethics joins its narrative prophetic, ethical, and policy discourses to participatory intervention in social structures" (Curran, *Diverse Voices*, 162). See Lisa Sowle Cahill, "Global Health Justice: Love as Transformative Political Action," in *Love and Christian Ethics: Tradition, Theory, and Society*, ed. Frederick V. Simmons with Brian C. Sorrells, Moral Traditions, ed. David Cloutier, Kristin Heyer, and Andrea Vicini, SJ (Washington, DC: Georgetown University Press, 2016), 274–89. In this book, see Maureen H. O'Connell's chapter.

[15] Curran, *Diverse Voices*, 170. He refers to Lisa Sowle Cahill, *Family: A Christian Social Perspective* (Minneapolis: Augsburg Fortress, 2000), 4, 18–50.

[16] Cahill, "*Laudato Si'*: Reframing Catholic Social Ethics." On "wicked" problems, see Willis Jenkins, *The Future of Ethics: Sustainability, Social Justice, and Religious Creativity* (Washington, DC: Georgetown University Press, 2013), 20 and 149–89. On the origin of the term, see Gwin Prins, Isabel Galiana, Christopher Green, et al., *The Hartwell Paper: A New Direction for Climate Policy after the Crash of 2009* (University of Oxford and the London School of Economics, 2010), https://eprints.lse.ac.uk/27939/1/HartwellPaper_English_version.pdf.

urgent need to transform the patterns of economic development by making them globally sustainable and equitable. International agreements are necessary, but insufficient. Networking, and even alliances, involving multiple social entities—from communities to organizations—operating at the grassroots level are very promising.[17]

Hence, this transforming reality changes our ethical approach, and Cahill joins advocates of pragmatic solutions. She writes, "Willis Jenkins recommends 'a pragmatic sustainability ethic' as having some potential to overcome the 'dysfunctional and unjust moral culture' that inhibits the honest search for environmental solutions and the will to act for the common good."[18] For Cahill, "This strategy would not wait for a comprehensive analysis and action plan, but would attack limited and local cases of environmental injustice, where a potential remedy is both technically feasible and potentially able to command public support."[19] Pragmatic strategies and solutions aimed at concrete problem-solving promote cultural and social transformation; moreover, they might anticipate, follow, or implement needed political arrangements to address the urgency of the environmental issues that humanity is already facing.

About This Volume

Lisa Cahill is not retiring. As colleagues contributing to this volume, we are grateful for how she continues to stimulate and expand our reflection and scholarship with her creativity, expertise, and dedication. Hence, this volume is not a retirement gift that seals an impressive and long career. Instead, this book aims to show how a group of her former students and now colleagues—mentored, inspired, and trained by her—revisits the achievements and challenges of the recent forty-five years of theological ethics by focusing on the areas, and some of the topics, she has addressed. In the post–Vatican II era, while being profoundly rooted in the Christian tradition, Cahill contributed to transform the theoretical and practical approach of theological ethics. At the same time, she mentored and accompanied many scholars, and inspired them to renew their own ethical agenda and reflection. While we attempt to map her contributions, we will be further empowered and invited to continue joining her in addressing the pressing current and future ethical challenges in our world.

This volume joins other volumes that had a similar ambition, where

---

[17] Cahill, "*Laudato Si'*: Reframing Catholic Social Ethics," 894–95 and 897.
[18] Ibid., 893. She refers to Jenkins, *The Future of Ethics*, 150.
[19] Cahill, "*Laudato Si'*: Reframing Catholic Social Ethics," 893.

groups of scholars revisited theological ethics by focusing on how their mentor contributed to renew the field. We mention two of these books. Lisa Cahill coedited one of them, *Christian Ethics: Problems and Prospects*, dedicated to her mentor James Gustafson,[20] while the second—*Public Theology and the Global Common Good: The Contribution of David Hollenbach*—celebrated the influence of the scholarship of David Hollenbach, SJ, her colleague at Boston College for many years.[21]

A Theological Agenda

Within Christian ethics, the last four decades have seen many transformations and witnessed the overall strengthening of the field. Of note are the solid critical study of the Christian tradition; innovative methodological approaches to address complex problems; a constant commitment to engage the public arena; and the global contributions of scholars, particularly from the Global South and historically marginalized communities.

As a Catholic feminist theological ethicist, Cahill's remarkable contributions encompass many areas: first, the foundations of theological ethics, from Scripture and Christology to engaging natural law together with the study of major theological figures in the Christian ethical tradition (e.g., Augustine, Aquinas, Luther, and Calvin); and second, the major subfields of Christian ethics, including social ethics; the ethics of war, peace, and peacebuilding; theological bioethics; healthcare ethics; sexual ethics; and family ethics. Over four decades her work innovated and shaped the terms of debate in multiple areas of fundamental, social and sexual ethics, and bioethics. Working with both undergraduate and graduate students at Boston College and as visiting professor at Yale University and at Dharmaram College in Bangalore (India), she taught and mentored two generations of theological ethicists by empowering them to articulate the attentive and critical study of the Christian ethical tradition and to engage concrete areas of ethical concern.

Overview

Lisa Cahill's specific contributions to Christian ethics have shaped and enriched multiple areas of fundamental ethics and social ethics, while

---

[20]Lisa Sowle Cahill and James Childress, eds., *Christian Ethics: Problems and Prospects* (Cleveland: Pilgrim Press, 1996).
[21]Kevin Ahern, Meghan Clark, Kristin Heyer, and Laurie Johnston, eds., *Public Theology and the Global Common Good: The Contribution of David Hollenbach* (Maryknoll, NY: Orbis Books, 2016).

expressing her commitment to dialogue with authors and their ideas, and engaging diverse contexts within the public sphere and the ecclesial milieu. In its three parts, this volume provides an interpretive overview of theological ethics by highlighting how her work has advanced innovative approaches to address deeply contested methodological questions and ethical topics.

Part I focuses on the foundations of Christian theological ethics and highlights how Cahill's original contributions enrich the discipline. Ki Joo Choi examines natural law, moral reasoning, and common morality by stressing how Cahill's Thomist, feminist, and pragmatic approaches to natural law are framed by liberation theology and aim at radical transformation of any unjust structure, dynamic, or relationship.

Both Maureen O'Connell and Mary M. Doyle Roche revisit the fourfold typology that helped Cahill map the field of Christian ethics and, particularly, feminist scholarship: the Thomist, Augustinian, Neo-Franciscan, and the biblically inspired Junian.[22] O'Connell relies on those typologies to frame the import of embodiment and the role of communities and practices in moral reasoning. In emblematic ways, she also articulates the tension between the local and the particular, as well as the global and the universal in a racialized world where whiteness still dominates and oppresses.

Doyle Roche highlights how these four approaches of feminist ethical theory and praxis inform Cahill's own theological contributions on sex and gender in Christian ethics. Moreover, for Doyle Roche, Cahill's ability to appreciate theological contributions differing from her own is combined with an attentive and respectful hermeneutic of suspicion, and it engages the concrete practices of the marginalized who are left voiceless and powerless. The result is a sexual ethics that encompasses nature and culture, norms and discernment, and that is capable of suggesting future directions for human flourishing centered on empowerment and inclusiveness.

Christian ethics is profoundly and radically centered on Jesus's Incarnation, on his table fellowship with the downtrodden and outcast, and on the good news of the coming of God's kingdom of justice and peace. Marianne Tierney FitzGerald explores the relevance of a liberationist Christology in Christian ethics that fosters solidarity with the marginalized and makes a preferential option for the poor. The crucified Jesus is on the cross in loving solidarity with today's crucified people and calls us to speak against any violence, injustice, and discrimination, and to act with the poor for justice and liberation, longing for the gift of the Resurrection here and now.

---

[22]Lisa Sowle Cahill, "Catholic Feminists and Traditions: Renewal, Reinvention, Replacement," *Journal of the Society of Christian Ethics* 34, no. 2 (2014): 27–51.

Scripture is the heart and soul of Christian ethics. Since the Second Vatican Council, theological ethicists more explicitly articulated their ethical reasoning, and their attention to practices, informed by the richness of the biblical witness. In examining the role of Scripture in theological ethics, Sarah M. Moses discusses Cahill's methodological hermeneutic of transformation. Without dismissing the diverse biblical texts, Cahill aims to identify patterns of moral practice that transform society, culture, and ecclesial communities by challenging existing entrenched dynamics and by welcoming the gift of conversion. Concretely, Moses shows how Cahill's family ethics is framed by her critical reading of New Testament sources, in a collaborative, ecumenical dialogue with socio-historical-critical biblical scholarship. Finally, for Cahill, the existing diverse communities in the global context demand careful attention to how each community, within global Christianity, discerns and lives their discipleship.

Part II, on Christian social ethics, shows how the tenets of Catholic social teaching and thought shape Cahill's approach to each specific area of theological ethics. Raymond E. Ward revisits the essential elements of Catholic social ethics and how Cahill relies on them constantly, by stressing the social relevance and feasibility of the Catholic social agenda focused on relentlessly promoting the common good and social justice, participation, solidarity, and subsidiarity, within civil society and in ecclesial contexts. In light of Cahill's contributions, he highlights three strategies that inform Catholic social teaching: dialogue (seeking common ground), advocacy (fighting for structural change), and shared action (building communities aimed at promoting justice).

In our world plagued by what seem like unstoppable, unsolvable violence and prolonged conflicts, Kate Ann Jackson-Meyer turns to the irreducible ethical dilemmas that shake our moral lives, are sadly too common in war, and challenge pacifism and peacemaking. Moral dilemmas, and the strategies proposed to address them (e.g., the principle of double effect), stretch the limits, or fracture the possibilities of virtuous behavior both in warfare and in the demanding process of peacebuilding and peacemaking. Jackson-Meyer highlights how recent developments in official Catholic teaching, among scholars, and in Cahill's theological reasoning point toward an increasingly dominant, pragmatic tendency to avoid considering war as the ethical way of addressing and solving international and local conflicts. While just war, with its well-articulated and traditional limiting criteria, is not entirely dismissed as a tragic possibility, peacebuilding and peacemaking seem to be better able to embody the radical faithfulness to the gospel and to the demands of the love command.

As Matthew Sherman highlights, social ethics also informs Cahill's family ethics. To flourish and to promote the common good in familial contexts, in light of the biblical witness critically examined, and in dialogue with Roman Catholic Magisterial teaching (from the U.S. Catholic Bishops to John Paul II and Pope Francis) and with theological scholarship, Cahill engages diverse and composite experiences of families in multicultural contexts, arguing for inclusion, promotion, accompaniment, and liberation. For Sherman, Cahill's methodology and practical reasoning provide guidance in continuing to address ongoing challenges by examining familial practices and by focusing on specific areas of concern: from children's agency to parenthood, from pervasive consumerism to families as domestic churches.

Virginia M. Ryan highlights Cahill's innovative approach to theological bioethics that stresses the value of participation, justice, and change. Cahill has been critical of any narrow approach to moral reasoning that would aim at too rapid a simplification of the complexity of the issues, that would not rely on the rich ethical tradition by privileging short lists of narrowly interpreted principles, and that would favor individualistic emphases. Assuming that any bioethical issue is a social issue, since the beginning of her career Cahill has relied on the ethical resources offered by the Catholic social tradition to address a large spectrum of bioethical concerns, from the more traditional issues (e.g., at the beginning and the end of human life) to universal healthcare, genetics, biotechnology, and global issues like the HIV/AIDS pandemic. Her articulated approach has become mainstream, as confirmed by recent scholarship.[23]

Hoa Trung Dinh, SJ, and Stephanie C. Edwards focus on healthcare by stressing how, in the current increasingly divisive political, cultural, and religious global context, Cahill has chosen a middle way that engages in dialogue and aims at finding any possible common ground. Providing access to healthcare services universally should address people's health needs, privileging the most vulnerable. Moreover, solving controversial and divisive ethical cases, which periodically dominate public imagination and debates, is urgent and requires dedicated efforts and generous commitments. Participation facilitates the pursuit of the social good that is represented by available and affordable healthcare services. Dinh and Edwards show how Cahill's methodology—informed by her dialogic attitude, participative methodology, and collaborative pursuit—is congruent with the overall goal of promoting healthcare services and access as belonging to the common good agenda in the public arena, both on the world scale and on the North American scene.

---

[23] M. Therese Lysaught and Michael McCarthy, eds., *Catholic Bioethics and Social Justice: The Praxis of US Health Care in a Globalized World* (Collegeville: Liturgical Press, 2018). In her foreword (xiii–xvi), Cahill stresses how the bioethical approach offered by the volume "is not only grounded and practical, it is hopeful and transformative" (xvi).

At the moment of this writing, while Lisa Cahill has not yet fully articulated her interest in environmental ethics,[24] Jill Brennan O'Brien anticipates this forthcoming development. She explores Cahill's methodology and scholarship to propose, first, that the scholarship and practical engagement for promoting sustainability needs a fruitful, reciprocal interaction between theoretical reasoning and practical initiatives. Second, participatory reflection and action are remarkably inclusive, in a context where divisions and particular interests hinder successful commitments and efficacious actions to address both the global climate crisis and many other multifaceted challenges to sustainability and resilience. Faithful to Cahill's attention to Scripture, and inspired by the critical biblical scholarship on the creation stories in the book of Genesis, O'Brien stresses the moral obligation to protect creation and to care for it with creativity and hope.

Cahill's wide-ranging scholarly corpus not only reflects the kinds of questions that Christian ethics has debated over the past four decades, but also, more importantly, indicates the future directions and growing edges of Christian ethics. How should we reimagine the task of Christian ethics in an increasingly globalizing yet also particularizing economic, political, and cultural landscape?

In response, Part III reflects on the future of Christian ethics. In light of Cahill's work, Nichole M. Flores highlights that such a future is marked by the empowerment of those who are marginalized, while being aware of one's own social-cultural-religious location and, because of that, of one's possible marginalization. The transformative character of articulating an ethics from marginalized perspectives informed Cahill's scholarship in family ethics, Christology, and theological bioethics, as well as the type of leadership, accompaniment, and mentorship that Cahill has provided throughout her career. As Flores argues, a Christian ethics from the margins transforms society, culture, and the Church, and promotes a pedagogy of solidarity nourished by the virtues of faith, love, hope, and humility.

Joseph Loic Mben, SJ, recognizes in Cahill's scholarship ethical reflection situated in today's global and pluralist context that does not shy away from seeing and naming the pervasive evil in the social fabric. Such a theology of personal, social, and structural sin, however, demands the constructive and hopeful contributions that Mben finds in Cahill's realist commitment to promote the common good for the whole of humanity, while trusting in the possibility of ethical transformation that the Thomistic natural law tradition suggests.

For Autumn Alcott Ridenour, constructive and collaborative Catholic-Protestant dialogue and the training of Protestant colleagues further

---

[24]However, see Cahill, "*Laudato Si*': Reframing Catholic Social Ethics."

define Cahill's Christian ethics. Cahill's familiarity with major figures of the Christian tradition—Augustine, Martin Luther, John Calvin, and Reinhold Niebuhr—centers her scholarship in dialogue with the concerns, strengths, and limits of their historically dependent contributions. Integrating the insights of these major figures with feminist scholarship, with theological voices from the Global South, and with modern and contemporary Protestant scholars, a few relevant themes emerge. Among them, Ridenour highlights the believers' union with Christ, the gifts of the Spirit within the community, the virtue of presence, and the importance of the community and its practices. The resulting portrayal further confirms the importance of identity, context, and praxis in Christian ethics and in Cahill's scholarship.

Angela Senander enriches the ecclesial dimension of Cahill's theological location and engagement by highlighting how Cahill's contributions exemplify, embrace, and develop the ethical commitment that informs the vision of the Church articulated by the Second Vatican Council, echoing the summons formulated in *Gaudium et spes*. Being part of God's people, and caring for those in greater need within humankind, promotes ecclesial ethical dynamics with even more urgency while the Catholic Church struggles to deal with the tragic sexual abuse scandal.

In the book's conclusion, Grégoire Catta, SJ, describes Cahill's commitment to a Christian ethics situated within, and in dialogue with, the public social context in a globalized world that many characterize as a liquid and secular society challenged by the ecological crisis. Inspired by Cahill's scholarship and commitment, Catta stresses the need to listen to the poor, while being grounded in the living ecclesial tradition that incorporates the experiences of those at the periphery. The chapter also stresses being engaged in inclusive dialogue and announcing the coming of God's kingdom as a radical, transformative liberation for anyone oppressed, and even for the oppressors.

Conclusion

Transformative engagement that promotes dialogue has a moral authority not dependent on power over against others, but rather an authority that continues to learn, promotes reciprocity, and empowers the powerless and the excluded, including women, children, persons who are poor, and those who are suffering from what limits their abilities. Lisa Cahill rightly avoids any limiting label that boxes scholars into rigid, predetermined caricatures that oversimplify one's nuanced theological methodology, faith commitment, social persona, and praxis.[25] The biblical literature and the Christian tradition, however, do not hesitate to define this transformative dynamism as prophetic, because it embodies a vision of the good to be pursued and creates opportunities to welcome and embrace transformation.[26] This volume attempts to nourish this prophetic transformative engagement in dialogue with the academy, the Church, and society.

---

[25]William Bole, "No Labels, Please: Lisa Sowle Cahill's Middle Way," *Commonweal* 138, no. 1 (January 14, 2011): 9–15.

[26]James F. Keenan, SJ, "Prophetic Pragmatism and Descending to Matters of Detail," *Theological Studies* 79, no. 1 (March 2018): 128–45.

Part I

Fundamental Christian Ethics

While it is generally agreed that theory and praxis are inseparable facets of Christian ethics, there is less consensus on how their interrelation is to be understood. One distinguishing characteristic of Lisa Sowle Cahill's vast scholarship is its sustained vision of how theory and praxis are to be brought together and the enduring impact of this vision in the development of contemporary Christian ethics.

Authors in this first part of the book call attention to central methodological priorities that shape Cahill's theological and social ethics. Included are essays on the reciprocal relationship between Cahill's moral commitments and the natural law tradition; Cahill's attunement to embodiment, experience, and relationality as nonnegotiable dimensions of human existence and agency; her insistence on the Christological shape of Christian moral values; her retrieval of Scripture as an integral source in moral discernment; and her advocacy of feminism as a necessary vantage point for the goal of universal human liberation. Together, these essays offer a multiperspectival view into how Cahill envisions the role of theological reflection in informing moral practice and, more particularly, how she links moral theorizing with practical agency.

All in all, while Cahill's scholarship represents the critical and constructive salience of Christian social ethics for religious and nonreligious publics alike, the essays in Part I underscore the extent to which her work as a Christian social ethicist finds its grounding in her contributions as a fundamental moral theologian.

Natural Law, Moral Reasoning, and Common Morality

Toward a Liberationist Paradigm

Ki Joo Choi

Whether a moral theologian's natural law theory leans more toward a kind of physicalist, rationalist, or historicist conception is, to be sure, a familiar way of characterizing one's approach to the natural law. Another way of assessing such leanings would be to determine the extent to which one's natural law theory is authentically Thomistic, that is, in keeping with not only the spirit but also the letter of Aquinas's statements on natural law. Accordingly, one's natural law theory can be characterized as deviating from Thomas or maybe even a refinement, if not a contemporary appropriation, of his thought, perhaps in the mold of the neo-Scholasticism of John Finnis and Germain Grisez or the neo-Aristotelianism of Alasdair MacIntyre. Or, a particular natural law theory might draw from other sources—namely, Protestant ones—and move perhaps in very different directions from the general family of Thomistic discourse on the natural law.

With these familiar and prevailing categorizations of the natural law in mind, how might we situate Lisa Sowle Cahill's approach to the natural law in contemporary theological ethics? That she relies on a natural law theory is not in dispute, but how to categorize her natural law theory eludes precision. In this chapter, rather than simply providing a detailed accounting of how Cahill's natural law theory defies standard, prevailing categories, I aim for an *interpretation* of her natural law theory that emphasizes the larger contexts or social concerns within which she conceptualizes natural law and employs it in her theological-ethical thinking.

Zeroing in on these social concerns—particularly, her feminist commitments—not only aids in explaining why Cahill's natural law theory cannot be situated neatly in any one of the prevailing paradigms of natural law theorizing, but it also sets the framework for appraising and, ultimately, appreciating what I propose here are the radical implications of her dialogical and dialectical model of moral reasoning. The import of her account of moral reasoning goes beyond debates about the prospects for natural law and extends, more radically, to a reappraisal of the very task of contemporary theological ethics as one that depends on the pluralism of theological discourses, especially from the margins. With this proposal in mind, I conclude this chapter by suggesting that one reason why Cahill's natural law theory cannot be situated neatly in any one of the prevailing paradigms of natural law is that what we have with her natural law theory is a new paradigm, one that we might call a *liberationist conception of the natural law*.

Cahill's Thomism

Before mapping out how her social commitments inform her natural law theory, it will be helpful to provide a brief sketch of how Cahill's natural law theory enters the landscape of interpretative debates on Aquinas's natural law. To this end, her 2002 article "Toward Global Ethics" is particularly instructive and serves as a useful template through which to engage Cahill's other numerous works on the natural law, some of which will be considered in sections to follow.[1] In this article she proposes a reinterpretation of Thomas's natural law theory that focuses on the culturally contingent or historically bounded nature of practical reason. Thus, the natural law project that Cahill pursues is one that begins with a strong nod to the particularist turn that has prevailed in many sectors of contemporary philosophy and theology. Cahill sees such a turn as clarifying an integral dimension to practical reason, that is, to the reality of how it works. In short, practical reason does not operate despite time and circumstance but rather operates within and through them. (On this point, she cites favorably Pamela Hall's and Daniel Westburg's work on the narrative character of the natural law.[2])

With respect to Thomas more specifically, Cahill observes that practical reason "deals with the truth in contingent matters" such that "moral

---

[1] Lisa Sowle Cahill, "Toward Global Ethics," *Theological Studies* 63, no. 2 (2002): 324–44.

[2] Ibid., 332. See Pamela Hall, *Narrative and Natural Law: An Interpretation of Thomistic Ethics* (Notre Dame, IN: University of Notre Dame Press, 1994); Daniel Westburg, *Right Practical Reason: Aristotle, Action, and Prudence in Aquinas*, Oxford Theological Monographs (Oxford: Clarendon, 1994).

reasoning always takes place within ongoing patterns of action."[3] And, if moral reasoning does not take place outside the thickness of human affairs, then the apprehension of moral truth is only possible through rational reflection on experience. As she asserts, "The issue is not so much whether moral truth exists at all, but how it emerges from the relation between agents or knowers and their contexts."[4] This point is developed more specifically through an interpretation of Thomas's account of the virtues, especially prudence:

> The intellectual virtues, including prudence, are "directed to the apprehension of truth" (see 1, q. 79, a. 11, ad 2). But truth and reason in moral contexts have to be understood as integrally bound to action, indeed as emerging within action, not only as "leading to" it as their effect. Since prudence is "right reason about things to be done" (*ST* 1-2, q. 57, a. 4), "practical truth," the truth of practical reason, "arises only within contingent states of affairs," and by means of an "inevitable choice between competing options." Aquinas thus generalizes the basic principles of the natural law from inclinations and patterns of behavior that all societies experience as contributing to human flourishing (preserving life, rearing young, cooperating socially) (*ST* 1-2, q. 94, a. 2), with applications depending in part on circumstances and cultural settings.[5]

In calling attention to the work of practical reason in tight conjunction with the intellectual virtues, a key premise for Cahill is that while moral truth is discernible—specifically, the kind of goods that are needed for human well-being and flourishing—disagreements about the ordering of such goods are to be expected given the vast variability and diverse expressions of our culturally constitutive existence. As such, the virtue of prudence, for instance, is critical to facilitating discernment and, hopefully, consensus on how such goods are to be ordered.[6] But Cahill's larger point is that moral truth—its discernment of general principles and their application—is made possible through a dynamic process, "realized inductively, experientially, interactively, and in the midst of concrete human problems and projects."[7]

In specifying the process of moral reasoning as inductive, Cahill makes explicit that her reading of Thomas's account of natural law stands against

---

[3]Cahill, "Toward Global Ethics," 333.
[4]Ibid., 329.
[5]Ibid., 324.
[6]Ibid., 338–39.
[7]Ibid., 334.

the deductivism of neo-Scholastic accounts of the natural law that display high confidence in the "self-evident" knowledge of universal and absolute moral truths, both general and particular.[8] Yet Cahill is committed to moral realism in the same way that these deductive approaches are, too. However, this commitment to moral realism is cast critically, which is to say, developed in such a way as to signal the veracity of alternative interpretations of Thomistic rationality that are linked to "tradition-bound and even revelation-dependent exercise of practical reason."[9] Thus, for Cahill, Thomas's inductive account of moral reasoning allows for the successful navigation between the poles of foundationalist and antifoundationalist approaches to moral truth without forsaking moral objectivity, even though she thinks that the basic insights of the postmodern (and, more specifically, the philosophical-pragmatist) turn to particularity are right.[10]

Cahill's Feminism

The inductive nature of moral reasoning is a refrain throughout her vast corpus of writings, and it allows Cahill to engage in both critique and appreciation of opposing Thomistic approaches to the natural law.[11] Hence, there is a genuine challenge in defining the kind of natural law theory that Cahill represents. But it would be too simplistic to say that Cahill's impulse to critique and appreciate contrasting Thomisms is for the sake of being irenic or theologically nonpartisan.[12] It would be too simplistic as well to say that her inductive moral theory emerges solely from her reading of Thomas. Just as important is the need to consider the kind of social concerns and commitments that inform Cahill's approach to the natural law and confidence in common morality. What are those social concerns and commitments?

Consider again her explicit nod to the cultural boundedness and historicity of practical reasoning. Arguably, such a nod is made more assertively

---

[8] Ibid., 333.
[9] Ibid., 331.
[10] Ibid., 329.
[11] A notable and more recent example is Lisa Sowle Cahill, "The Natural Law, Global Justice, and Equality," in John Berkman and William C. Mattison III, eds., *Searching for a Universal Ethic: Multidisciplinary, Ecumenical, and Interfaith Responses to the Catholic Natural Law Tradition* (Grand Rapids: William B. Eerdmans, 2014), 239–49.
[12] See, for instance, William Bole, "No Labels, Please: Lisa Sowle Cahill's Middle Way," *Commonweal* 138, no. 1 (January 14, 2011): 9–15. Assessments of her work such as Bole's give the impression that Cahill's work navigates poles of discourse as a kind of methodological priority. That is true, but only to an extent; there is a larger *telos* at work in her "middle way," or so I am proposing, at least with her natural law theory.

in her influential 2005 book *Theological Bioethics: Participation, Justice, and Change*, where she argues for the prophetic importance of particularistic theological discourse in policy debates on medicine and healthcare.[13] The particularistic character of moral reasoning is further emphasized in her sweeping 2013 book *Global Justice, Christology, and Christian Ethics*.[14] Yet Cahill has consistently resisted what others, such as Jean Porter, have proposed are the dim prospects for global, universal ethics.[15] But what warrants such resistance? It is striking that while she considers neo-Scholastic deductivism flat-out untenable given the contextuality of moral reasoning, for Cahill, the logical conclusion of that observation is not that moral reasoning is consequently particular all the way down, nor is she tempted to consider such a conclusion a reasonable possibility. Note the extent to which she is willing to read Aquinas as supporting the particularity of moral norms and conclusions. "A point to be stressed perhaps more strongly," she argues, "is that human nature, its ends, its flourishing, and its moral standards are not 'discovered' as already existent and unchanging entities. They too are 'contingent' and perhaps in some degree mutable."[16] However, she adds a key qualification: "the extent to which [the mutability and contingency of moral norms] is the case is a matter of debate."[17] The larger point underlying this qualification has been a consistent and defining feature of Cahill's theological and social ethics, reflected in her critically measured acceptance of the postmodern assessment of truth.

To some extent, such measured acceptance can be explained by her concern over the susceptibility of sectarianism in tradition-centered accounts of truth, especially in Christian theology, a position she stakes out forcefully in her landmark 1996 book *Sex, Gender, and Christian Ethics*.[18] While this position is perhaps moderated to a degree in her *Theological Bioethics* book, which I alluded to above, in *Sex, Gender, and Christian Ethics*, at least, Cahill lays out clearly the stakes of sectarian overtures in

---

[13]Lisa Sowle Cahill, *Theological Bioethics: Participation, Justice, and Change*, Moral Traditions, ed. James F. Keenan, SJ (Washington, DC: Georgetown University Press, 2005), 13, 22.

[14]Lisa Sowle Cahill, *Global Justice, Christology, and Christian Ethics* (Cambridge: Cambridge University Press, 2013), esp. chapters 1 and 7. See also note 39.

[15]See, for instance, Jean Porter, "Does the Natural Law Provide a Universally Valid Morality?" in *Intractable Disputes about the Natural Law: Alasdair MacIntyre and Critics*, ed. Lawrence Cunningham (Notre Dame, IN: Notre Dame University Press, 2009), 53–96, at 55–56.

[16]Cahill, "Toward Global Ethics," 334.

[17]Ibid.

[18]Lisa Sowle Cahill, *Sex, Gender, and Christian Ethics*, New Studies in Christian Ethics, ed. Robin Gill (Cambridge: Cambridge University Press, 1996).

Christian theological discourse. An unqualified turn to theological particularism complicates the prospects for the salience and effectiveness of Christian witness in the public sphere by constricting opportunities for the public receptivity and intelligibility of Christian truth claims, or so she argues.[19] Such a concern, she notes, is not simply an ethical one but also a feminist one.[20] A feminist concern over sectarianism is not distinct from an ethical one; sectarianism does not serve the interest of justice, which in turn does not advance the well-being of women.

As Mark S. Massa has mapped out in detail, one key trajectory in Cahill's account of practical reason is her attempt at responding to critiques of the natural law as reinforcing cultural and social hegemony. Globalization not only threatens the distinctiveness of local cultural expressions and forms of life, but from a more explicit feminist perspective, the uniformity that globalization imposes on communities is the threat of maintaining unjust patterns of social relationships. Likewise is the threat that emerges from the universality of moral norms emanating from a natural law account of truth. As Massa notes, for Cahill, feminist scholars are not wrong to distrust "*supposedly* universal laws of nature" since they "usually turned out to be the 'mothers of all oppression,'" and a "set of values that was always true almost inevitably turned out to offer decidedly male, Western, and profoundly oppressive directions that took no account at all of cultural difference, political loyalties, or gender concerns."[21] This is why Cahill warns that even Thomas, from a feminist perspective, must be approached with caution: "Aquinas's own perspective on matters of sex and gender is quite limited by his cultural setting, and by his tendency in these areas to forget that the most distinctive human capacities are intellect and will."[22]

Yet for Cahill, Thomas's own limitations do not mean that Thomas's overall natural law project is wholly suspect. In fact, feminist concerns demand the moral realism of Thomas's natural law theory, which provides a surer ground to securing the kind of goods that women and, by extension, all persons require for their well-being and flourishing beyond what is possible through liberalism's "mere formal or procedural guarantees

---

[19]Ibid., 68, 70.
[20]Ibid., 69.
[21]Mark S. Massa, SJ, *The Structure of Theological Revolutions: How the Fight over Birth Control Transformed American Catholicism* (New York: Oxford University Press, 2018), 154 (emphasis in the original). He draws from Lisa Sowle Cahill, "Natural Law: A Feminist Reassessment," in Leroy S. Rouner, ed., *Is There a Human Nature?*, Boston University Studies in Philosophy and Religion 18 (Notre Dame, IN: Notre Dame University Press, 1997), 80–93.
[22]Cahill, *Sex, Gender, and Christian Ethics*, 50.

like the right to equal protection under the law."[23] In practice, such liberal rights and proceduralism too easily amount to resorting to power politics to advance human well-being. Such a resort to power, while understandable, would amount to adopting a method of persuasion that is tenuous at best; more sure-footed is rational, intellectual (and affective) persuasion:

> If feminist ethics is to base social change on anything other than the acquisition of enough power to shove aside those who formerly monopolized it, we will have to rediscover or reinvent a reasonable account of knowledge and truth, and of the "universals" in human experience. This is what the "Catholic" (Aristotelian-Thomistic) ethical tradition is essentially about: a confidence that reasonable reflection on human existence can lead us not only to recognize and condemn injustice, but to persuade others that they can recognize and condemn it on more or less the same terms we do.[24]

Cahill's Pragmatism

Just as Cahill's feminist-rooted commitment to justice underwrites her advocacy for moral realism and universality even as she recognizes the mutability and contingency of moral reasoning, her feminism, by the same token, also leads her to an account of particularity that *serves the goal of* moral realism and common morality. So, while Cahill makes clear that "Even a very modestly realistic ethic must . . . [grant] that truth is integrally related to the social and historical context of the knower and hence to community experiences and practice," she asks whether such a postmodern philosophical-pragmatist insight necessarily means that "individual subjects or groups create disparate realities and truths through idiosyncratic practices, languages, and self-understandings?" Further, "is 'rational justification' radically particular to specific traditions, or is there such a thing as reasonable evidence upon which different communities can agree?"[25] Unless we simply believe that persons of different cultural backgrounds and linguistic communities are unable—not just in theory but also in practice—to engage in meaningful conversation and maybe even undergo a change in mind by way of reasonable persuasion, then we need to respond to those questions with a resounding no. However, Cahill opts for the optimism of Catholic social teaching, which "typically

---

[23] Massa, *The Structure of Theological Revolutions*, 154.
[24] Cahill, *Sex, Gender, and Christian Ethics*, 69.
[25] Cahill, "Toward Global Ethics," 329.

works on the assumption that any two traditions with the occasion for conversation can have a meaningful exchange. When a matter of justice is at stake, criticism, argument, judgment, and action are required to transform specific situations toward objectively greater human well-being."[26] Likewise, "feminists and other liberation theologians approach 'foreign' traditions and engage them in moral exchange toward political results."[27]

That intercultural exchange, cross-contextual conversation, and moral agreement are possible is, for Cahill, indicative of what she often refers to as the dialogical and dialectical nature of practical reason. *Dialogical* and *dialectical* specify the essential inductive nature of moral reasoning, as we discussed earlier. Truth may be inferred from particular experiences, not in some straightforward or obvious manner, but in a manner that is attuned to complexity and ambiguity. For instance, consider a 2010 essay titled "Nature, Change, and Justice," where Cahill reflects on whether human nature provides uncontested moral insight. Making the distinction between descriptions of human nature and normative judgments about nature, nature at the descriptive level, she observes, is hardly simply good. As she notes, "Speaking in purely factual terms, there is a *natural* human disposition to evil as well as to good."[28] Moreover, "Competition, violence, and destruction are part of human nature."[29] The polyvalence of human nature, therefore, complicates the kind of normative judgments we can make about what human nature implies about morally appropriate actions. What kind of human activities and inclinations contribute to human flourishing and happiness, and what are considered as vice or sin? Both involve contingent judgments, which vary based on time and circumstance. But rather than concluding that the ambiguity of human nature means certain basic goods cannot be generally known,[30] Cahill recasts such ambiguity as the grounds for an epistemology that is always mindful of the need for humility and constant self-correction. The "process of discerning human goods and normative human relationships" is "never free from error and bias."[31] Accordingly, for Cahill, conversation across cultures is not simply for the sake of cultural sensitivity and appreciation, though that is certainly valuable; an additional if not more important value to such exchange is its potential to identify and respond

---

[26]Cahill, *Sex, Gender, and Christian Ethics*, 70.
[27]Ibid.
[28]Lisa Sowle Cahill, "Nature, Change, and Justice," in David Albertson and Cabell King, eds., *Without Nature? A New Condition for Theology* (New York: Fordham University Press, 2010), 282–303, at 293. Emphasis in the original.
[29]Ibid.
[30]This is a rewording of a line from ibid., 291.
[31]Ibid.

to cultural "blind spots" and, ultimately, to refine or in some cases change our viewpoints in a manner that serves justice.[32] In sum, "Defining the line between justice and injustice is obviously a challenge; decreasing the latter in favor of the former is an even more massive one. To do that, we must confront the totality of human nature—and confront it honestly."[33]

Inasmuch as moral truth emerges dialogically and dialectically, Cahill claims that the discernment of truth will necessarily have to be pragmatic or practical, that is, whether it can pass the test of justice.[34] In that way, the dialogical and dialectical discernment of truth must be provisional.[35] One question that arises, then, is whether the proviso of provisionality is indeterminate. In other words, are definitive or absolute truth claims (even exception-less moral norms) possible? The following is suggestive of a negative or at least a chastened response to the question: "practical evidence for a global convergence of moral values cannot be conclusive and final."[36] Also suggestive is her reference to the Vietnamese Catholic theologian Peter Phan, who claims, "'The pendulum of cognition never comes to a dead stop.'"[37]

One can wonder—legitimately, I think—whether a moral truth claim can ever be counted as universal and absolute or, more specifically, whether a moral truth claim *can ever be known* for certain as universal and absolute. Does not the proviso that the dialectical and dialogical discernment of truth is provisional, then, end up playing into the hands of those who doubt that there is such a thing as a universally valid morality? This is not to say that moral consensus is impossible, but only that whatever moral consensus is present between persons and communities is not indicative of global ethics or common morality; it is indicative simply of the fact that moral consensus is possible only on an ad hoc basis.[38] It would seem, then, that Cahill can be read as inadvertently providing more rather than less reason to support the trajectories of interlocutors she aims to correct.

Cahill's advocacy for a pragmatic and provisional account of truth is, I think, susceptible to such a predicament. And it raises the question of the extent to which Thomas can provide the kind of natural law theory she is looking for. In this respect, her explicit and sustained turn to "the

---

[32]Ibid.
[33]Ibid., 293.
[34]Cahill, "Toward Global Ethics," 335.
[35]Ibid., 329.
[36]Ibid., 335.
[37]Ibid., and Peter C. Phan, SJ, "Method in Liberation Theologies," *Theological Studies* 61, no. 1 (2000): 40–63, at 61.
[38]This is Jean Porter's conclusion in her "The Search for a Global Ethic," *Theological Studies* 62, no. 1 (2001): 105–21.

American philosophical tradition of pragmatism" and reference to it as her "own cultural heritage" in *Global Justice, Christology, and Christian Ethics* is striking.[39] Thus, we have good reason to ask whether the kind of natural law theory she advocates is possible not because of Thomas but primarily because of her feminist and, more broadly, liberationist commitments that are undergirded conceptually by a particular philosophical approach to the epistemological question of realism versus antirealism. That does not necessarily diminish the value and insight of a natural law theory that underscores the provisionality of truth, but it does underscore the difficulty of pinpointing the kind of natural law theory Cahill ultimately adopts. It is Thomistic, but also much more than that. In the following and concluding section, I propose an important implication of this complexity to Cahill's natural law.

While Cahill's stress on the provisionality of truth confronts important conceptual challenges (whether it responds successfully to the kind of moral particularism that others such as Jean Porter advances), what cannot be ignored is her suggestion that how we assess the provisionality of truth is a deeply consequential matter of perspective. To some large extent, we can see Cahill as mapping out two choices: either interpret pluralistic moral judgments and responses to questions of justice "as testifying to their fragmented and ultimately incommensurable nature," or interpret them as "evidence of a remarkable convergence of ethically motivated action."[40] Cahill of course opts for the latter choice, explicitly stating that the former interpretation "is a mistake" in part by arguing that pluralistic moral responses to questions of justice are the manner through which universal truths are discerned; in other words, moral pluralism is not proof of moral balkanization but indicative of the "dialectical nature of ethical knowledge, commitment, action, and truth."[41] And for Cahill, such indications can be found in numerous examples of diverse individuals, groups, nongovernmental organizations, and states coming together to solve problems at the international level, even if they disagree on what the solutions ought to be (e.g., the work of the United Nations

---

[39]Cahill, *Global Justice, Christology, and Christian Ethics*, 4. For her discussion on philosophical pragmatism, see ibid., 10–18, 273–80.

[40]Cahill, "Toward Global Ethics, 342, 343.

[41]Ibid., 342. She invokes Stephen Pope in this argument: "Stephen Pope, writing on the use in ethics of scientific descriptions of human nature, affirms that moral evaluation is not given immediately in human experience, whether rendered via personal accounts or scientific description. . . . Natural law ethics is, then, best 'conceived as an ongoing tradition of moral reflection with plural expressions'" (Cahill, "Natural Law: A Feminist Reassessment," 88). She refers to Stephen J. Pope, "Scientific and Natural Law Analyses of Homosexuality: A Methodological Study." *The Journal of Religious Ethics* 25, no. 1 (1997): 89–126 at 117.

on matters of global health, war and peace, and climate change). Differences in this context do not necessarily amount to negation of universal moral values but, more specifically, to disagreements on their realization. As Cahill remarks, "What is at stake in cultural differences over ethical issues like gender equality, debt relief, health inequities, and politically motivated violence is not so much disagreement about what is good for human 'flourishing' but about who exactly is entitled to flourish."[42]

For Cahill, the costs are too high to see moral pluralism as simply self-referential moral expressions; it is global ethics that allows for a moral standard and platform by which persons, communities, and nations can be held accountable to a higher, more equitable, and just standard of relationality.[43] It can be an effective tool "to prod 'society at large' into rescinding its denial of 'shared' humanity."[44] More forcefully, it can be a powerful means of moral shaming.[45] The challenge, as Cahill sees it, is to figure out ways to promote the virtue of solidarity so that moral pluralism—and thus the "dialectical nature of ethical knowledge, commitment, action and truth"—serves to secure the material, social, and spiritual needs of all persons.[46]

Conclusion: Cahill's Distinctive Radicalism

In a 1997 essay titled "Natural Law: A Feminist Reassessment," the connection between Cahill's feminist commitments, on the one hand, and natural law as a dialectical, dialogical mode of moral reasoning and discernment, on the other hand, are drawn explicitly: "An understanding of natural law as discovered within an ongoing process of action and reflection converges with the feminist accent on experience, on differences mediated by reciprocity, and on practice as a test of theory."[47] In drawing this connection between feminism and natural law, Cahill makes clear that what feminist theory does for natural law theory is to underscore the importance of experience as a source of illuminating what it means to be human. More specifically, feminist theory illumines those dimensions of the human condition that have been either ignored out of ignorance or abused out of a perverse interest in domination.

---

[42]Cahill, "Toward Global Ethics," 337.
[43]Ibid.
[44]Cahill, "Natural Law: A Feminist Reassessment," 82.
[45]Cahill, "Toward Global Ethics," 337.
[46]Ibid., 342.
[47]Cahill, "Natural Law: A Feminist Reassessment," 79.

What is novel about contemporary appeals to experience—feminist and otherwise—is not their existence as such, nor the fact that they aim to accomplish social and political goals, but their self-conscious quality and their attentiveness to diversity of experience and to the social location of the one who experiences and interprets. Appeals to experience are used constructively in feminist moral argument to shift the balance within given patterns of interpretation of the human condition. *An appeal to "experience" introduces some dimension of women's situation which an existing construct diminishes or leaves out of account.*[48]

What is important to especially appreciate in the italicized lines above is how Cahill sees feminist appeals to experience as *adding to and correcting* what it means to be human (the goods that human well-being requires). This is why she thinks that feminist appeals to experience are reflective of an account of moral reasoning that is dialogical and dialectical. As Cahill states further, "While the reference point of experience does not amount to a universal paradigm or structure, neither is it lacking in normativity, as relevant only to the standpoint of the speaker. Rather, it functions as a testimony to the communal, dialectical and practical qualities of moral knowledge and judgment."[49] Thus, feminist appeals to experience are not simply an assertion of difference and demand for recognition qua female identity but part and parcel of advancing moral truth dialectically via practical experience.

With that said, the distinctiveness of Cahill's natural law theory can be articulated as follows. Part of what makes Cahill's natural law theory strikingly distinctive is the role her feminist commitments play in her reinterpretation of Thomistic epistemology. What is more significant, however, is how her feminism demands a natural law that prioritizes particularized appeals to experience without which the discernment and pursuit of the goods requisite for human well-being and flourishing are necessarily frustrated. In her own words, "What the feminist debate about difference brings to [natural law] theory, or emphasizes within it, is that mutual understanding and agreement on goods is not achieved in some sphere above or beyond difference, but only from reflection which begins within determinate historical communities with particular experiences of goods and evils, and particular visions or hopes of change."[50] In

---
[48] Ibid., 86 (emphasis added).
[49] Ibid.
[50] Ibid., 82.

short, particularity is the necessary condition for the discernment of the "objectivity of values."[51]

The distinctive contribution that Cahill's feminism makes to the tradition of natural law, therefore, is more accurately a *radical* contribution. But the radicalness of this contribution extends to the task of theological ethics more generally and, thus, well beyond the specific internecine debates between natural law theorists. If, as Cahill notes, "The task of ethics is to specify as clearly and in as detailed a manner as possible the nature of [human] goods, what they mean in the concrete, and what kinds of actions will or will not attain them,"[52] then Cahill's approach to the natural law requires that we pay attention to whether accounts of human well-being and flourishing are adequate or deficient. The nuance of this claim is in how her conception of moral reasoning as dialogical and dialectical requires taking seriously theological-ethical discourses that make appeals to experience in very particular, localized ways. That of course must include paying special attention to feminist theological discourses, but one can imagine that for Cahill, that cannot mean only being concerned for feminist theological discourses. If moral objectivity is only possible through the particular, then the radicalness of Cahill's natural law theory resides in the fact that theological ethics fails in its task unless it resolutely seeks out the insights of other marginalized discourse or—perhaps, more accurately—a diversity of liberationist theological discourses. Appeals to experience by African American theological ethics, Latinx theological ethics, and Asian American theological ethics—as well as voices from Africa, Asia, and Latin America—and their specific demands for liberation are just as critical as appeals to experience by feminist theory and theology.

What Cahill's natural law theory accomplishes in its dialectical and pluralistic emphases is no small feat. Her natural law theory amounts to a conceptual-epistemological basis for casting particular theological discourses or appeals to experience not as indicating thoroughgoing social constructivist and antiessentialist standpoints with respect to identity and experience but rather as positioning particular theological discourses as publicly accessible—that is, critical and constructive—theologies that are essential to the emancipatory *telos* of theological ethics as a discipline.

Thus, for theological ethics, Cahill demonstrates how a commitment to natural law, of all the conceptual moral frameworks or theories available to contemporary ethicists, opens up a way of thinking about theological-

---

[51]Ibid., 89.
[52]Ibid., 84.

ethical pluralism not as a function of identity politics in theological garb but as essential to the task of theological ethics itself. The very point of her natural law theory is, to state the obvious, to advance universal ethics, but the universal ethics that emerges will be only as good as we are willing to be challenged by a diversity of appeals to experience, whether racial, ethnic, gender, queer, postcolonial, and so forth. It would be a mistake, therefore, to consider such particular theological discourses matters of difference in perspective or opinion or simply "subdisciplines," which could imply that they are ancillary discourses to the more central discourse of theological ethics. Instead, from Cahill's natural law perspective, theological discourses from the margins are parts of a whole, or, more strongly, integral pathways into a view of the whole.

For theological discourses arising from marginalized communities, especially communities of color, Cahill's natural law theory, then, means that far from being an anachronistic mode of theological reflection, natural law can be imagined and employed—and perhaps *must be* imagined and employed—for the theological-ethical end of emancipation of all persons. As she remarks, "The inspiration of feminism is precisely an incredulous, justly angry reaction to [unjust] ideas" that have been uncritically accepted as true, distorting moral reflection.[53] But such anger is attributable as *just* anger—anger that is morally unavoidable or necessarily demanding of due recognition and consideration—in other words, a nonnegotiable source of moral reflection and judgment, if ethics is taken as primarily an emancipatory task that depends on pluralistic moral analysis. Cahill's natural law theory offers that pathway, and in that respect, it moves well beyond the conventional concerns that define the tradition of natural law theorizing. As such, Cahill's approach to the natural law controverts any attempts to define it within typical natural law paradigms. Cahill's theory, perhaps more accurately, establishes a new paradigm, one that sees the natural law as a liberationist discourse, or as *grounding* the need to listen to and advocate for theological discourses of liberation.

---

[53] Ibid., 86.

Experience, Embodiment, and Community

Maureen H. O'Connell

On a crisp November morning a few years ago, colleagues and I went on a walking tour of the neighborhood surrounding our university in the northwest corner of Philadelphia. We wanted to encounter Belfield on its own terms rather than as it is too often framed by people who pass through it on the way to somewhere else, especially those coming to and from our campus. We had invited Dr. Mindy Fullilove, professor of urban policy and health at the Parsons School of Design and cofounder of Orange University in New Jersey, to lead us on a pilgrimage. Fullilove, a board-certified clinical psychologist, sees placemaking as an effective antidote to the "mad plagues" of poverty. These plagues arise from external forces that have sifted and sorted urban populations and act on people living in neighborhoods like ours rather than through collaboration with them. They often come in the form of interventions motivated by assumptions of lack rather than innovations sparked by visions of abundance.

In order to answer her explicit question, "How can we make the sorted-out city whole again?" Fullilove first had to shake us out of our deficit mind-sets when it came to "the neighborhood." We began to realize that framing Belfield in terms of what it lacked came naturally to us as a Catholic university. We started to see ourselves as one of those sorting and sifting forces in the neighborhood with our proclivity to "fix" people and things through our charitable interventions. To interrupt this mind-set, we used Fullilove's "nine elements of urban restoration"[1] and wandered through Belfield looking for the latent joy all around us.

"The aim," Fullilove explained at one of our stops, "is to allow yourself to fall in love." She intently gazed around what appeared to be an aban-

---

[1] Mindy Thompson Fullilove, *Urban Alchemy: Restoring Joy in America's Sorted-Out Cities* (New York: New Village Press, 2013).

doned lot and then settled her gaze back on us. "And then you agitate for your beloved."

I was struck by her choice of words, which have since become a mantra. "*Agitate for your beloved.*" As a Christian ethicist and emerging community organizer, the words were at once both familiar and strange to me. I rifled through paradigms of justice looking for the most fitting analogue. How to turn a neighborhood, and the people in it, into my beloved? How to be more than a voyeur or voluntourist passing through Belfield, or even an ally or missionary serving the needs of the people living here? How to become an accomplice in our collective liberation?[2]

In what follows, I identify elements of Lisa Sowle Cahill's approach to Christian ethics that uniquely position me, a teaching and researching theological ethicist, to receive and apply Fullilove's imperative—and social change commissionings by others like her—in the context of my Catholic university and its neighborhood. Although Cahill's approach to justice is more often global than local in scope, I contend that her theological development of the concepts of experience, embodiment, and community can be applied to approaches to social change in the hyperlocal particularities of a specific zip code. Placing her thought in dialogue with those engaged in social change movements, I also agitate for continued growth in the trajectories of Cahill's work in these same areas.

Foundations for Agitating for the Beloved

Generally speaking, there are several aspects of Cahill's own self-understanding and method that encourage effective work for social change. First, Cahill unapologetically claims that our purpose as Christian ethicists is to remain deeply rooted in the story of Christ and his vision of the kingdom of God, while at the same time branching out into the world around us with a commitment to human flourishing. She suggests that the link between the story in which we are rooted and the vision that beckons us beyond ourselves is the imperative to love: to love God and to love as God loves, essentially with a particular attention to—dare I say agitation for—the marginalized and oppressed. She is motivated by a vision of abundance, inclusivity, and flourishing and not simply by the need to reject and deconstruct the antithesis of these things.

---

[2] Adapted from "Opportunities for White People in the Fight for Racial Justice," https://www.whiteaccomplices.org/; and Colleen Clemens, "Ally or Accomplice: The Language of Activism," https://www.tolerance.org/magazine/ally-or-accomplice-the-language-of-activism.

Secondly, for Cahill the gospel imperative to love is not a private affair between God and the believer, nor the believer and her beloved. Rather, it is a story of justice to be repeatedly encountered, proclaimed, and lived. As such, the work of theological ethics is public and political. It is public in that it spurs us to risk sharing our unique stories and visions with others in our tradition, and more importantly to insist on Christianity's contributions to storytelling and dreaming communities beyond the boundaries of this tradition. The point, she says, is to make "religiously inspired, theologically grounded, practically located, yet normatively comprehensive judgments that can break cross-cultural and interreligious moral action."[3] She has witnessed to this in her own vocational life, working with peacebuilders and bioethicists, editors on international and regional projects, Catholics seeking a prophetic agenda in American politics, and people of various faiths committed to peace and justice.

Similarly, in Cahill I also find support for the claim that living the gospel is political in that it calls us to examine systems, structures, and power dynamics that deny the full humanity of individuals and communities. To be sure, in keeping with a commitment to historical consciousness, she acknowledges that Jesus was not a "social reformer" who aimed "to make large-scale structural changes favoring disadvantaged groups."[4] Yet she also insists that "if Jesus' counsels about love of neighbor, compassion for the marginalized, and willingness to suffer for these ideals were taken seriously, the social and political ramifications today would be far-reaching."[5] Her interpretation of Christ's reading of the two sides of the coin of the realm is unequivocal. Rendering unto Caesar what is Caesar's "means acknowledging that social and political structures provide the essential conditions of human identity, agency, and association; and believing that those who live in God's image and under God's rule can give a different moral quality to practices, structures, and politics."[6]

Ultimately, the point of this public and political loving agitation is social transformation of persons, systems, or communities. To that end, justice is certainly much more than unilateral transactions between those who enjoy the goods of life and those without access to them. Rather, in Cahill we find a model in the academy of one who insists that agitating for the beloved entails diagnosing with them and others the systems and structures that preclude human flourishing. These foundational ideas

---

[3]Lisa Sowle Cahill, *Global Justice, Christology, and Christian Ethics*, New Studies in Christian Ethics, ed. Robin Gill (New York: Cambridge University Press, 2013), 21–22.
[4]Lisa Sowle Cahill, "Bioethics, the Gospel, and Political Engagement," *Christian Bioethics* 21, no. 3 (2015): 247–61, at 253.
[5]Ibid.
[6]Cahill, *Global Justice, Christology, and Christian Ethics*, 67.

come into even clearer focus if we consider the dimensions of community, embodiment, and experience, and the relationship among them, in her feminist, neopragmatist, and universal common method. Hers is a method that lends itself to the kind of "urban alchemy" Fullilove practices—a way of aligning values, creating possibilities amid the impossible, and celebrating instances and conditions when life prevails.

Feminism Anchored in Experience

Although not originally an explicit component of her method, the centrality of experience in the theological and ethical dimensions of Cahill's method point to her innate feminist orientation. In her 2014 plenary address to the Society of Christian Ethics, Cahill identified a three-part hermeneutic that Christian feminist ethicists bring to what she sees as a multiplicity of "traditions" under the umbrella of Christianity, itself an inflection of experience. By acknowledging the complex landscape of feminist ethics, Cahill lifts up the diversity of women's experiences within it. She also proposes four paradigms by which Christian feminist ethicists apply the feminist hermeneutic of appreciation, suspicion, and praxis. Dimensions of women's experience serve as inflection points of difference among them. The Augustinian privileges the experiences of women in the "special roles" we play in "family and society." The neo-Thomistic brings historical consciousness to an examination of women's experience of the goodness of creation and unfolding revelation of truth. The neo-Franciscan orbits around women's experiences with and reflections on the call to radical discipleship. And the Junian relies on the experiences of women marginalized by colonialism and neocolonialism to decenter Eurocentrism in Christian ethics.[7]

Her own engagement with experience places her in the neo-Thomistic paradigm and provides the linchpin between what she calls the "neopragmatic" dimension of her method, in which she acknowledges the limits of human capacity to know and do the good, and her "universalist" method, through which she persists in claiming that truths can be known and acted upon through and not in spite of contextual particularities. "Unlike Aquinas and most of the Catholic tradition," she notes, "contemporary feminist theological ethics must pay more attention to women's concrete experiences of embodiment, to the interdependence of relationships and moral knowledge, and to the perspective of the excluded in deciding what constitutes the common good."[8]

---

[7]Lisa Sowle Cahill, "Catholic Feminists and Traditions: Renewal, Reinvention, Replacement," *Journal of the Society of Christian Ethics* 34, no. 2 (2014): 27–51.
[8]Ibid., 34.

As a white cisgender female ensconced in the academy but oriented toward the people in the neighborhood, I find this paradigm of feminism most appropriate and effective when it comes to contributing to social change movements. I resonate with the value that Cahill places on "engagement and learning—perhaps most visibly from the natural and social sciences," since these sources of wisdom can clarify moral visions and strategies for achieving it with others. This is an endorsement for interdisciplinary teaching, participatory-action research, and "paracademic" affiliation with social movements. I suspect Cahill would agree with faith-based organizers who suggest that "moral authority is at its most powerful when it is wielded together by people who are the most vulnerable in intimate solidarity with those who could easily walk away."[9] Moreover, her commitment to cross-cultural discernment of truth and basic goods encourages curiosity and humility, dispositions essential for accomplices in intersectional movements for justice.

Cahill also warns against a Eurocentric tendency to distance ourselves with intellectualizing or abstracting when we are confronted by others entangled in profound suffering. "To be practically effective, theology and ethical ideals must grip people and communities at more than the intellectual or theoretical level," she writes.[10] To that end, she regularly endorses the emotional intelligence of empathy, compassion, imagination, memory, and hope. This opens her up to engagement with thinkers associated with social change movements who recognize the power of emotion in perceiving reality with precision and in building trust and endurance. For example, indigenous change leader Eve Tuck notes that intellectualizing can lead us in the direction of "damage-centered research" on communities impacted by social injustice. Such an approach focuses on individual pain and deprivation rather than on broken systems and structures. It fails to perceive the ways in which racism and colonization contribute to conditions of injustice and limits responses to injustice to material or political gains alone. Moreover, people within marginalized communities rarely see themselves as damaged. Tuck demands "desire-centered research" that focuses instead on the experiential wisdom and tangible hope within the community. Leading with desire turns decision-making power over to the people most impacted by injustice. This desire is fueled by a longing enriched by gut insights into the dynamics of racism and colonialization in the past and a vision of a future in which those dynamics are no longer in play. "Desire is not mere wanting but our informed seeking," explains

---

[9]Alexia Salvatierra and Peter Heltzel, *Faith-Rooted Organizing: Mobilizing the Church in Service to the World* (Downers Grove, IL: IVP Books, 2014), 99.
[10]Cahill, *Global Justice, Christology, and Christian Ethics*, 6.

Tuck.[11] "Desire is both the part of us that *hankers* for the desired and at the same time the part that *learns* to desire. It is closely tied to, or may even be, our wisdom."[12]

Emotional wisdom is not only for those closest to the pain of injustice. Gordon Whitman of the national interfaith organizing network Faith in Action suggests that all who seek social change would do well to tap into the "social-change superpower" of the emotions in order to stay rooted in our purpose, and attract others to the work.[13] "We can use this power not only to shape how we're feeling ourselves but also to shift the emotional state in a room or in a relationship," he writes.[14] "We can create human environments that make people more open to reflect on their purpose, learn, grow, and develop strong and trusting relationships with one another. This makes it possible for people to take risks together."[15] Cahill recognizes this too. Returning to that warning against intellectualizing, she says that theological and ethical ideals "must have imaginative and affective appeal."[16] Cahill's own turn toward desire, imagination, and affection becomes more evident when we consider the role of embodiment in her method.

Neopragmatism Tethered to Embodiment

While acknowledging that "natural law ethics no doubt need to be updated and revised in a global, post-modern context," Cahill nevertheless insists that "the moral realism at its center is worthy of a vigorous defense."[17] As one aware that the capacity for moral goodness and moral wrongdoing often unfold simultaneously and on parallel tracks, she joins a cadre of feminist ethicists who bring a hermeneutic of appreciation, suspicion, and praxis where the Thomistic tradition is concerned.[18] Her distinct contributions include an affirmation of the applicability of Thomistic natural law to ever-changing contexts via its practical, experiential, and historically conscious potentialities. She also contends that

---

[11] Eve Tuck, "Suspending Damage: A Letter to Communities," *Harvard Education Review* 79, no. 3 (2009): 409–27, at 418.

[12] Ibid. (emphasis in the original).

[13] Gordon Whitman, *Stand Up! How to Get Involved, Speak Out, and Win in a World on Fire* (Oakland, CA: Berrett-Koehler Publishers, 2018), 56.

[14] Ibid.

[15] Ibid.

[16] Cahill, *Global Ethics, Christology, and Christian Ethics*, 6.

[17] Ibid., 250.

[18] Lisa Sowle Cahill, "Natural Law: A Feminist Reassessment," in *Is There a Human Nature?*, ed. Leroy S. Rouner, Boston University Studies in Philosophy and Religion 18 (Notre Dame, IN: University of Notre Dame Press, 1997), 78–91. See also Ki Joo Choi's chapter in the present volume.

these potentialities can be unleashed when we embrace somatic sources of insight and embodied ways of knowing.

Three dimensions of her neopragmatism have roots in experience as well as embodiment. First, our embodied selves are socially constituted through interaction with other embodied selves. Our worldviews may be entrenched in our systems and even in our bodies, but they are also malleable so long as we are actively engaged in ever-expanding circles of "collective belonging."[19] Second, the search for truth is an active correspondence, at once individual and collective, between knowers and reality to be known. This exchange happens through embodied investigation and dialogue. In other words, our bodies make universal and global knowing and doing possible. Third, truth claims have recognizable universal implications, which impact real and embodied people regardless of socially constructed difference. Once again, Whitman helps me see the application of Cahill's insight about the role of embodied knowing for social change movements, which prioritize embodied encounters at every stage of the work. "[Face-to-face] experiences help us realize that we're up against other human beings, and human-created rules, rather than fixed truths," he explains.[20] Humanizing systems of oppression makes them easier to dismantle.

Cahill also contends that paying attention to embodiment in Thomistic thought clarifies what it means to be human and the basic goods required to uphold human dignity. "Human embodiment both sets conditions on and enables human knowing and choosing," she affirms.[21] Moreover, it is through our "corporeal existence" in communities that we come to know our relational and social natures, which she thinks "might be *more* constitutively human than characteristics ascribable to human individuals, such as rational intellect and free will."[22] Her understanding of "corporeal" includes the psychological.[23] She recognizes that exclusive focus on conditions for physical survival that fails to take into consideration equally the psychosocial dimensions will hardly yield a vision of full flourishing toward which we should aim. This would certainly resonate with social change leaders attempting to translate practices of trauma-informed care into trauma-informed practices of social justice education or trauma-informed justice work, given the psychological impact of either being marginalized or of the work of bridging that marginalizing gap.[24]

---

[19]Cahill, *Global Ethics, Christology, and Christian Ethics*, 12.
[20]Whitman, *Stand Up!*, 135.
[21]Cahill, *Global Ethics, Christology, and Christian Ethics*, 254.
[22]Ibid. (emphasis added).
[23]Ibid., 15.
[24]For trauma-informed teaching, see David E. Kirkland, *A Search Past Silence: The Literacy of Young Black Men*, Language and Literacy (New York: Teachers College Press,

Finally, her acknowledgment of human embodiment allows Cahill to pivot toward ecological concerns, which provide the literal common ground and wellspring for all social change movements. She notes that "in our human nature, rational self-consciousness and voluntary decisions are involved with and dependent on the corporal existence we share with animals and other beings."[25] The more aware we become of our existence "as material, embodied, evolved, living, and social only in [our] ecological niches,"[26] we will realize our interdependence and agitate for our ecological kin, especially by "interfacing and networking" at local, national, and transnational levels with religious and nonreligious, grassroots, governmental, and nongovernmental entities.[27]

Universalism Arising from Community

Cahill is equally preoccupied with the goods of human relationship, which is a fundamental way she understands the common good: "Inclusive community with other human beings is a constitutive dimension of community with God."[28] Her approach to ethics certainly cultivates the common good through her implicit acknowledgment of the capacity of social capital to effect social change. Relational goods of shared experience, story, vision, norms, strategies—whether among otherwise sorted and distant people, or within fractured communities themselves—are both an experience of and a prerequisite for justice. For example, her engagement with the Aristotelian political philosopher Martha C. Nussbaum points to her desire to put fundamentals of Catholic ethics at the disposal of cross-cultural conversations beyond the scope of theology or religious identity, and about commitments to living distinctively human lives. To that end, she falls into what she calls the "universal common good ethics" paradigm of post-Conciliar ethics.[29]

Moreover, her work is also increasingly viable for intrareligious dia-

---

2013); for trauma-informed justice work, see adrienne maree brown, *Emergent Strategy: Shaping Change, Changing Worlds* (Chico, CA: AK Press, 2017), and Jardana Peacock, *Practice Showing Up: A Guidebook for White People Working for Racial Justice* (Mountain View, CA: Jardana Peacock, 2018).

[25]Cahill, *Global Justice, Christology, and Christian Ethics*, 254. See Jill Brennan O'Brien's chapter in this volume.

[26]Ibid., 287.

[27]Lisa Sowle Cahill, "*Laudato Si'*: Reframing Catholic Social Ethics," *Heythrop Journal* 59, no. 6 (2018): 887–900.

[28]Cahill, *Global Justice, Christology, and Christian Ethics*, 1.

[29]Lisa Sowle Cahill, "Catholic Theological Ethics beyond Vatican II," *Concilium: Journeys of Liberation: Joys and Hopes for the Future*, ed. Maria Clara Bingemer and Luiz Carlos Susin, no. 1 (2016): 93–103.

logue among those with strong ties to their own traditions. Not only is Cahill confident in the link between these two but also in our ability to remain simultaneously grounded in and oriented toward the particularities of the Christian story and vision while collaborating with others with different stories and visions, to cultivate full flourishing for all people. She insists that knowing and doing the good are best achieved in pluralistic communities anchored in values, motivated by visions, and achieved through virtuous practice. She implicitly endorses that most effective social change movements embrace relational goods of "inclusiveness, equality and solidarity" by "display[ing] a unity of moral vision and common commitment of redressing imbalances of power and well-being so that marginal persons, groups, and nature can flourish."[30] When it comes to the environmental crisis, she suggests it may be time to move beyond interreligious dialogue toward alliances rooted in moral visions and virtues.[31]

These dialogues and alliances can also be internal, fostering a kind of bonding social capital within fractured communities. For Cahill, the focus is not being right, but getting it right by being authentic to the gospel story, especially as it continues to be told and heard in different contexts. This is a particular kind of faithfulness that is more than fidelity to specific moral prescriptions—it fosters a fidelity to tellers and hearers of stories of life and purpose, whether the gospel or otherwise. Faithfulness is critical to community and to the vocation of the socially engaged ethicist in the same way that Natalia Imperatori-Lee spells it out for ecclesiologists. Imperatori-Lee calls for a return to narrative as the central praxis of the Church, but in the plural sense of that term given the distinct biographies that make up the people of God.

> Ultimately, ecclesiologists seem to have realized that in trying to tell a single story that encapsulates everyone's experience generally, only the experience of the powerful shines through. If, however, ecclesiology shifts toward *narratives*, and a dialogue among narratives, power relationships are laid bare, marginalized voices can be included, and through dialogue unity can emerge where uniformity was once imposed.[32]

Cahill speaks this language of listening when she prioritizes authenticity in Christian ethics, noting "authenticity goes beyond theoretical claims

---

[30]Cahill, *Global Justice, Christology, and Christian Ethics*, 275.
[31]Cahill, "*Laudato Si'*: Reframing Catholic Social Ethics."
[32]Natalia Imperatori-Lee, *Cuéntame: Narrative in the Ecclesial Present* (Maryknoll, NY: Orbis Books, 2018), 15.

and positions to the living of the gospel."[33] Ethics is not "injunctions or proscriptions but a narrative and communal embodiment of resurrection life by the power of the Spirit in the name of Jesus Christ."[34] When rooted in the telling of the gospel, especially in contexts where embodied and cultural distinctiveness are celebrated, Christians can bring to the public square a sense of being formed in a vision, virtues, and practical commitments to those gospel values, which Cahill sees as nothing less than "life for the world."[35]

Some Agitations

If I join others in considering Cahill's body of work a beloved corpus, then I am compelled to agitate for some of its limitations. These have become evident in my ongoing learning how to become an "accomplice" in the collective liberation of all, thanks to the mentorship and leadership of people closest to the pain of social injustice.

First, the centrality of experience in her thought provides an opportunity for a deepening of her notion of sin. To be sure, sin is at the center of her approach. She insists that theology reflects on the experience of salvation, which implies being healed or made whole from the wounds of sin, which in turn animates a similar commitment to the wholeness and healing in and for the world. By reflecting on human experiences of this kind of wounding, Cahill certainly moves us beyond thinking about sin as a personal reality and toward more structural frameworks that better describe overlapping layers of oppression. However, persistence of particular kinds of wounding by the sins of things like racism or sexism—or in the case of the planet, anthropocentrism—suggests that we may need to begin to think of sin as a cultural reality. Here, Bryan N. Massingale's work on cultural racism provides a helpful analogue.[36] A shift to a cultural framework allows us to see ways in which conditions form and inform us and ways that those same conditions can be deconstructed and rebuilt—healed, shall we say.

Likewise, the role of power in Cahill's concept of sin can lead to further reflections on power itself, which social change thinkers define as "the capacity to act or influence others to act" and set as the focal point

---

[33] Cahill, "Bioethics, the Gospel, and Political Engagement," 254.
[34] Ibid.
[35] Ibid. See also Robert Song, "Christian Bioethics and the Church's Political Worship," *Christian Bioethics* 11, no. 3 (2005): 333–48.
[36] Bryan N. Massingale, *Racial Justice and the Catholic Church* (Maryknoll, NY: Orbis Books, 2010).

of both social analysis and social action.[37] In her exegesis of Genesis she notes that "sin consists not in wanting to know good and evil, but in seeking undue control over the conditions and results of this knowledge, without humility about the scope of one's power or the justice of one's vision."[38] We can look to systematic theologian Jeannine Hill Fletcher in naming the historical and contemporary contributions of Christians and Catholics to the "racial project" of white supremacy, to sharpen our ethical focus on particular forms of power that undergird injustice.[39] Similarly, Katie Walker Grimes exposes the power of antiblackness, particularly in Catholic thought, and American Catholic social teaching and practice.[40]

In addition, diagnosing power more precisely requires more precise responses to its abuses. In her work in peacebuilding, Cahill certainly recognizes the efficacy of nonviolent witness. Organizers call it "dove power"—the ability to persuade through the claims that we are all rooted in the image and likeness of God, confidence in the work of the Holy Spirit to do great things in and among people, moral visions of the good life, or the disruptive nature of forgiveness. And yet those of us who operate universalist common good or neopragmatic paradigms, often as a result of our own proximity to sources of power, must also be attentive to what organizers call "serpent power," or our ability to use public goods like force, wealth, control of resources, and influence toward just or unjust ends.[41] We need to own our roles as gatekeepers to these public goods and be attentive to how we deploy the power awarded us as a result.

Second, in terms of embodiment, we can continue to deepen the connection between universal claims and particular realities. While Cahill's commitment to facing unjust suffering from her social location as a white North American cisgender female may situate her in the "universal common good" paradigm, she trends toward the liberationist paradigm given her attention to experiences of marginalized persons and groups. A variety of black scholars remind us that we can further attune that liberationist attention by remembering that injustices happen to particular bodies marked as particular by systems and cultures—in other words, that particular bodies matter. We see this with M. Shawn Copeland's insistence that we read the preferential option for the poor, to which Cahill is so drawn, in terms of Jesus's preference for bodies marked by the wounds

---

[37]Salvatierra and Heltzel, *Faith-Rooted Organizing*, 73.

[38]Cahill, *Global Justice, Christology, and Christian Ethics*, 61.

[39]Jeannine Hill Fletcher, *The Sin of White Supremacy: Christianity, Racism and Religious Diversity in America* (Maryknoll, NY: Orbis Books, 2017).

[40]Katie Walker Grimes, *Christ Divided: Antiblackness as Corporate Vice* (Minneapolis: Fortress Press, 2017).

[41]Salvatierra and Heltzel, *Faith-Rooted Organizing*, 73–74.

of empire in his day. To resist tendencies toward domination inherent in Eurocentric frameworks, Copeland insists that solidarity cannot reduce the particularities of others in their otherness, nor expect them to assimilate to dominant cultures and frameworks. This suggests that her empowerment framework of ethics may be optimal for Christian ethicists engaged in social change movements. This stance might ensure the kind of solidarity Cahill believes will allow us "intersubjectively, linguistically, practically, prayerfully to communicate who we are, and for what and for whom we struggle"[42] or a kind of solidarity that "sets the dynamics of love against the dynamics of domination."[43]

Third and finally, while community is undoubtedly central to Cahill's vocation as a theologian, she also acknowledges that it holds the thorniest challenge to Christian ethics. "The central quandary of Christian and political ethics is not the achievement of agreement on basic human goods," she warns.[44] Rather, "it is the expansion of the circle of solidarity in which basic goods are shared in practice."[45] Through her work in the ethics of nonviolence, for example, she insists on the power of reconciliation to extend that circle of solidarity to those who have been victims of violence. Yet some point to the limits of reconciliation to build truly transformed communities and call instead for more comprehensive expansion of access to basic social goods—like education, housing, and political participation—through structural and cultural remedies or reparations.[46] Too many others to mention here have taken Cahill at her word and turned a focus to the reluctance of the Catholic community to expand its circle of concern. That said, in light of the locus from which most of us do our work as Christian ethicists, Gerald J. Beyer's contribution is particularly interruptive in this regard. He highlights the ways in which Catholic communities in higher education have yet to extend adequately our circles of solidarity to a variety of people within our campus communities, denying goods such as fair compensation, healthcare, access to multicultural education to the people we rub shoulders with every day, or the goods of ecological sustainability to the web of life in which our

---

[42]M. Shawn Copeland, *Enfleshing Freedom: Body, Race, and Being*, Innovations: African American Religious Thought, ed. Anthony B. Pinn and Katie G. Cannon (Minneapolis: Fortress Press, 2010), 94.

[43]Ibid.

[44]Lisa Sowle Cahill, "Goods for Whom? Defining Goods and Expanding Solidarity in Catholic Approaches to Violence," *Journal of Religious Ethics* 25, no. 3 (1997): 183–219, at 183.

[45]Ibid.

[46]Massingale, *Racial Justice and the Catholic Church*, 96–102; Grimes, *Christ Divided*, 254–58.

campus communities are enmeshed.[47] The invitation to look within, to agitate for what Jeremy V. Cruz calls an "ecclesial reconstruction,"[48] is as urgent as any we hear calling to us from beyond the Catholic communities that sustain our ongoing theological reflection and action.

Conclusion: Why Are You Here?

Cahill provides an analogue for that imperative Mindy Fullilove imparted to me and my colleagues that November afternoon. Cahill puts it this way: "Christian transformation in community is the proving ground of theological reflections."[49] Her pairing of transformation and community provides a helpful departure from voluntouristic or missionary approaches to theological reflection and the social responsibility that can arise from it, which tend to be private, unilateral, transactional, intellectual, damage-focused, and power-blind. Cahill's evolving turn to experience, embodiment, and community ensures that private reflections go public, that unilateral exchanges become dialogical and corporeal allegiances, that intellectualizing incorporates emotions and imagination, that we do not lose sight of desires when responding to the damages of injustice, and that power over or for others becomes power with them. In short, with Cahill as a guide, Christian ethics will be nothing short of falling in love and agitating for our beloved.

---

[47] Gerald J. Beyer, *Just Universities: Catholic Social Teaching Confronts Corporatized Higher Education* (New York: Fordham University Press, 2021).
[48] Jeremy V. Cruz, "Catholic Education and Sexual Violence: From Complicity to Ecclesial Reconstruction," *American Catholic Studies*, 130, no. 2 (2019): 12–15.
[49] Cahill, *Global Justice, Christology, and Christian Ethics*, 7.

Christology and Christian Ethics

Marianne Tierney FitzGerald

In her 2013 book *Global Justice, Christology, and Christian Ethics*, Lisa Sowle Cahill writes, "In the face of the evils of poverty, war, gender-based violence, and environmental destruction, Christians must proclaim in deed and word the cosmic span of God's creating power and the transformative possibilities of redemption."[1] This path toward redemption is made available in how the figure of Jesus, his life and ministry, relays the call to attend to those suffering on the margins. This chapter aims to unpack how Scripture's witness to Jesus's life and ministry lays out the centrality of solidarity with the marginalized as a driving moral principle. As such, three themes central to Cahill's Christology are considered: Jesus's teachings on the reign of God, the cross, and the Resurrection. I conclude with a few reflections on the significance of these three Christological themes for contemporary Christian ethics.

The Reign of God: A New Way of Being in the World *Now*

The gospel narratives provide us with at least two key insights into the centrality of the proclamation of the reign of God in Jesus's life and ministry. First, Jesus ushers the reign of God into the world through his unique ministry and service to the marginalized; thus, the reign of God is not simply something Jesus preaches about, but it is also a reality that Jesus practices and embodies. For instance, God's reign can be seen through the miracles that Jesus performs[2] and, more strikingly, through the out-

---

[1] Lisa Sowle Cahill, *Global Justice, Christology, and Christian Ethics*, New Studies in Christian Ethics, ed. Robin Gill (Cambridge: Cambridge University Press, 2013), 3.

[2] See Mt 8:1–4 as an example of Jesus healing a leper, or Mt 9:2–8 as an example of Jesus healing a paralytic.

casts Jesus befriends.[3] Cahill highlights that "Jesus is especially critical of those who exploit the vulnerable."[4] By examining the teachings of Jesus and observing how he treated those who were seen as "outsiders," we can see "a radically different basis for a community ethic."[5] Accordingly, "the normative content of Christian practices is defined primarily by the fact that Jesus proclaimed and actively embodied the kingdom of God."[6]

Second, the reign of God refers to the reality that God is present in our midst "in and through Jesus' ministry."[7] The emphasis on presence signals the this-worldliness of God's kingdom. More specifically, Jesus's life and ministry demonstrate that the reign of God is both a possibility for the future and a historic reality in the present. In this latter sense, Cahill asserts that the most fundamental aspect of Jesus's historical experience is his role as "the prophet of God's kingdom or reign."[8] Through his interactions with outcasts and his example of compassion toward the marginalized, Jesus models for others what God's reign "looks like."[9] Jesus's idea of the kingdom of God is open to "sinners, the poor, women and 'outsiders' (Gentiles),"[10] and this openness teaches Christians to consider seriously those whom society often scorns.

Liberation theologian Jon Sobrino, whose work informs Cahill's Christological reflections, describes the reign of God in the following way: "God's 'Kingdom' is what comes to pass in this world when God truly reigns: a history, a society, a people transformed according to the will of God. . . . The Kingdom of God is . . . a highly positive reality, good news but also a reality highly critical of the bad and unjust present."[11] He argues that what is important about Jesus's earthly life is the commitment he shows to those who have been cast out to the margins. The reign of God offers something for which humans can strive in the here and now. We can live with the knowledge that the kingdom is both something to reach for in the future but is also available in the world right in our very own lives. Cahill concurs, explaining that "Jesus understood God's kingdom to be a future reality that is nonetheless accessible in a practical

---

[3] See Lk 7:36–50 as an example of Jesus showing compassion to a woman who was scorned by others in society, or Mk 2:13–17 as an example of Jesus eating with tax collectors and sinners.

[4] Cahill, *Global Justice, Christology, and Christian Ethics*, 101.

[5] Ibid., 97. Bible passages (Mt 5:43–48; Lk 6:27–28, 32–36) are cited.

[6] Cahill, *Global Justice, Christology, and Christian Ethics*, 79.

[7] Ibid., 96.

[8] Ibid., 76.

[9] Ibid., 247.

[10] Ibid., 77.

[11] Jon Sobrino, *Jesus the Liberator: A Historical-Theological Reading of Jesus of Nazareth* (Maryknoll, NY: Orbis Books, 1993), 71.

way within the limits of history."[12] And like Sobrino, Cahill underscores the reign of God as a radical reality, a rejection of the status quo. More specifically, Jesus's ministry highlights the ways that God is present in the world already, but also indicates the need for more dramatic change in order for the reign of God to become more concrete. "People can enter God's reign now," explains Cahill, "by seeing and living in a new way; the fullness of the reign, which depends on God's decisive action, is a future reality which our present action anticipates."[13] Theologian Roger Haight, another of Cahill's important interlocutors, agrees that "in Jesus this kingdom of God is not far off or unrelated to this world."[14] Jesus illustrates how the kingdom of God is a historic possibility through his teachings and actions, as he both preaches about the kingdom and embodies its reality. Cahill adds that "it is widely accepted that God's reign for Jesus entailed a *reversal* of worldly values, including an upset of standard social and religious criteria of worthiness and acceptability."[15] Such a reversal of worldly values, however, is not something to be hoped for simply in the future, but it is a reality at work now inasmuch as the kingdom of God calls us to a new, robust ethics to be lived in the present time. As a consequence, the moral salience of the reign of God moves well beyond the historical specificity of Jesus's life and ministry to our present time. In short, Christians are called to discern how to address contemporary issues—war, poverty, gender violence—through an examination of "the center of Jesus' ministry . . . the imminent reign or 'kingdom of God.'"[16]

The Cross: Being in Solidarity with the Victims of Injustice

In addition to the events of Jesus's life, his death also offers valuable lessons and insights into Christian ethics. Jesus's death is often represented in the Christian tradition by the symbol of the cross, but the tradition of the cross of Jesus has many complexities from a Christological perspective. For Cahill, the cross symbolizes both the turmoil Jesus experiences and the idea of God's solidarity with those who are suffering. Through the cross, we can see that God is present in the midst of despair and angst; as

---

[12]Cahill, *Global Justice, Christology, and Christian Ethics*, 77.
[13]Lisa Sowle Cahill, "The Bible and Christian Moral Practices," in *Christian Ethics: Problems and Prospects*, ed. Lisa Sowle Cahill and James F. Childress (Cleveland: Pilgrim Press, 1996), 9.
[14]Roger Haight, *Jesus: Symbol of God* (Maryknoll, NY: Orbis Books, 1999), 80.
[15]Cahill, "The Bible and Christian Moral Practices," 8 (emphasis added).
[16]Ibid., 7.

Cahill asserts, "The cross represents God's initiative and compassionate presence in human suffering and evil."[17]

Cahill observes that Christians often think of the cross as either a "historical consequence of Jesus' life and ministry" or as a "symbol of God's solidarity with the innocent victims of injustice,"[18] but neither of these positions is entirely adequate on its own. As a result of Jesus's experience on the cross, humans are saved. However, no simple theory of satisfaction explains the salvific nature of the cross. Although one predominant interpretation of the cross asserts that Jesus suffers in our place and, therefore, satisfies whatever need God has to rebalance the sins of the world, this interpretation of Jesus's Resurrection allows violence and torment to be God's desire for him. The idea of a satisfaction-oriented "Anselmian theory of Christ's death as atoning for sinful humanity"[19] is problematic for those who argue that this type of thinking valorizes violence. Feminist theologians as well as liberation theologians assert that, especially in a contemporary world that struggles with different types of violence, Jesus's suffering should not be turned into something to be glorified.[20] For Cahill, it is "very problematic" to understand Christian ethics as working within "the notion that God purposively inflicts suffering, that our 'perfection' depends on suffering, and that obedient submission to the 'test' of suffering is the path to Christ-like existence."[21] Jesus's suffering should not be viewed as redeeming in and of itself.

An alternative view of the cross asserts that God does not desire violence and that the Resurrection indicates that Jesus lives "a life in union with God and in dedication to all whom society rejects."[22] This notion of the cross as something other than a tool used for violence has gained deep resonance particularly among communities that have been on the receiving end of social and political violence. "If violence is the means of redemption," Cahill asserts, "then violence is God's will."[23] But theologically, a God who promotes violence is inconsistent with what the Christian tradition proclaims about God. Cahill, therefore, stresses the importance

---

[17] Lisa Sowle Cahill, "Jesus, Christ, and Ethics," in *Who Do You Say That I Am? Essays on Christology*, ed. Mark Allan Powell and David R. Bauer (Louisville, KY: Westminster John Knox Press, 1999), 236.

[18] Cahill, *Global Justice, Christology, and Christian Ethics*, 206.

[19] Ibid., 204.

[20] Liberation theologians such as Jon Sobrino, Gustavo Gutiérrez, and Leonardo Boff, and feminist theologians such as Nancy Pineda-Madrid, Ivone Gebara, and Delores Williams make similar assertions about how Jesus's suffering is not redemptive in and of itself.

[21] Cahill, *Global Justice, Christology, and Christian Ethics*, 215.

[22] Ibid., 56.

[23] Ibid.

of the cross's contextualization within other structures and experiences of violence, suggesting that "the cross is never salvific alone" but must be understood "as a human, historical event of unjust accusation, state torture and capital punishment."[24] In other words, Jesus is the victim of a corrupted system of justice.

Consider the days leading up to his death: Jesus's flawed human relationships revealed his friends as vulnerable and easily persuaded to reject him. Judas betrays Jesus for thirty pieces of silver (Mt 26:15), and even though Jesus warns Peter that he will deny their friendship (Mt 26:35), Peter still denies Jesus three times (Mt 26:69–75). Jesus's human experience of being rejected by his friends helps us to further compare his suffering and loneliness to the despair felt by those who have been marginalized and excluded.

The suffering that Jesus experiences illustrates his humanity and lets us know that Jesus truly understands human suffering. "Christ lives and dies in complete solidarity with human beings," writes Cahill.[25] Jesus experiences the same anguish that humans experience, and he understands suffering, ridicule, anguish, and torment. But Cahill again insists that "a suffering death is not the major point of the incarnation,"[26] but rather that through his experience of crucifixion, we might know that God, through the person of Jesus, also experiences some of the darkest moments of humanity. As a result, we can assert that Jesus stands with those who are oppressed by violent situations in our world today. This ability to identify with victims is expressed through the violence on the cross.

Consider, further, Jesus's trial, when Pontius Pilate states multiple times that he has found no reason to sentence Jesus to death (Lk 23:4, 14, 22). Pilate says, "I have examined him in your presence and have not found this man guilty of any of your charges against him" (Lk 23:14 NRSV). But the crowds nevertheless insist that Jesus is guilty and should be put to death. In Matthew's Gospel, Pilate washes his hands (Mt 27:24), indicating that he disagrees with Jesus's death sentence and wants to be cleared of this responsibility. The injustice that Jesus endures is comparable to the many unjust systems that continue to oppress humans around the world today. As a result, Cahill notes that "the life of Jesus and his death on the cross condemn historical injustice and reveal God's compassion for victims."[27] Jesus's experience as someone who is targeted and unjustly

---

[24]Ibid., 207.
[25]Lisa Sowle Cahill, "Salvation and the Cross," *Concilium: Jesus as Christ*, ed. Andrés Torres Queiruga, Lisa Sowle Cahill, Maria Clara Bingemer, and Erik Borgman, no. 3 (2008): 53–63, at 60.
[26]Cahill, *Global Justice, Christology, and Christian Ethics*, 212.
[27]Lisa Sowle Cahill, "Christology, Ethics, and Spirituality," in *Thinking of Christ: Proc-*

victimized relates to the experiences of so many who are suffering in our world and who are forced to work against a system that was designed to oppress them. "The cross," notes Cahill, "especially as God's transforming solidarity with those who suffer, calls Christians to act on behalf of the poor" and others who suffer under unjust conditions.[28] Jesus's "suffering death was not the major point of the incarnation,"[29] but rather that through his experience of crucifixion, we might know that God, through the person of Jesus, also experiences some of the darkest moments of humanity. The cross is "a powerful religious symbol of divine solidarity with suffering humanity."[30]

The Resurrection of Jesus: Liberating the Oppressed

Although the cross highlights the suffering of Jesus, the Resurrection event following the crucifixion completes Christ's journey and offers liberation for the oppressed. The cross and the Resurrection are deeply connected to one another in Jesus's story, and as Cahill says, "the cross is endowed with salvific meaning because it is always already understood from the perspective of faith in the risen Lord in the Christian community."[31] Thinking about the salvific nature of the cross, Cahill says, "The cross saves within a process of incarnation, resurrection, and the sending of Christ's spirit."[32]

What is the salvific meaning of the cross from the perspective of the Resurrection? Through the Resurrection of Christ, we determine that hope for the victims of injustice is possible. Like those who have been victims of gender-based violence, war, poverty, racism, and genocide, Jesus was the victim of an unjust system. But just "as Jesus' resurrection is a historically 'impossible' act of God," Cahill explains, "the resurrection life of Christians in history must express what is 'historically possible.'"[33] The Resurrection insists that those who have been treated unjustly can hope for a better outcome. Those who work for justice as peacebuilders and grassroots organizers serve as examples of individuals who are making the Resurrection a reality. As Cahill elaborates, "The resurrection is a premise of the cross, the guarantee of our assurance that solidarity in

---

lamation, Explanation, Meaning, ed. Tatha Wiley (New York: Continuum, 2003), 198.
[28]Cahill, *Global Justice, Christology, and Christian Ethics*, 237.
[29]Ibid., 212.
[30]Ibid., 245.
[31]Ibid., 234.
[32]Cahill, "Salvation and the Cross," 62.
[33]Cahill, *Global Justice, Christology, and Christian Ethics*, 292.

Jesus' suffering will not be in vain."[34] Within the fullness of Jesus's story, we see that his death on the cross is not the end of the story. Beyond Jesus's suffering is the Resurrection, which allows him to overcome the burdens of the cross. As Cahill notes, "God's purposes aim beyond suffering to liberation."[35]

According to Sobrino, the Resurrection of Christ proves that there will be justice for those who have been treated inhumanely. He writes, "*Resurrection . . . means first and foremost doing justice to a victim*, not merely *giving new life to a corpse*."[36] For Sobrino and other liberation theologians, Resurrection symbolizes a restoration of power both to Jesus and to those who have been powerless. The story about Jesus's Resurrection again highlights for us the fact that Jesus has been on the side of those who have been oppressed throughout history. A notable example is found in the Gospel of Matthew in its narration of the Resurrection witnessed by Mary Magdalene and "the other Mary" (Mt 28). When we see that the women in this story were the first to witness the Resurrection of Jesus, this narrative continues to prioritize the experiences of those who are considered often "less than" by wider society. Women are at the tomb first, and they encounter the angel and then see the risen Jesus. This narrative shows that the risen Christ appears alongside women and also illumines the critical role that Mary Magdalene, who had a particular reputation as a sinner, played in sharing the news of Jesus's Resurrection. Jesus does not exclude her in life or in death.

But Jesus's solidarity with the oppressed is not only historical but also present; the Resurrection helps us see that Jesus stands with those who are suffering right now. Jesus is present to those who are experiencing their own types of crucifixion, and offers the consolation of solidarity and compassion. Cahill writes that, through his Resurrection, "Jesus embodies and communicates the decisive transformation of violence, suffering and death."[37] The Resurrection event provides a historical moment in the life of the Church, but it also gives Christians the opportunity to consider how Jesus played a role in their lives through God's presence. For Cahill, the Resurrection is "God's act of compassion and renewal of life. . . . As an ethical model, the cross inspires resistance, not acquiescence."[38]

---

[34] Ibid., 234.
[35] Cahill, "Jesus, Christ, and Ethics," 239.
[36] Jon Sobrino, "The Resurrection of One Crucified: Hope and a Way of Living," *Concilium: The Resurrection of the Dead*, ed. Andrés Torres Queiruga, Luiz Carlos Susin, and Jon Sobrino, no. 5 (2006): 100–109, at 102.
[37] Cahill, *Global Justice, Christology, and Christian Ethics*, 123.
[38] Ibid., 235.

Conclusion: A Realistic Hope

Although there are many other aspects of Christology to explore, focusing on the ministry of Jesus through the reign of God, Jesus's suffering on the cross, and his Resurrection allows us to see how Cahill establishes a Christological foundation for Christian ethics. As Cahill so directly puts it, not only do "Christians have the *obligation* to challenge sinful social structures. . . . Christians can [also] *hope* that social transformation is really possible in light of what God has done in Christ."[39] Accordingly, Christian hope is not an unrealistic but very much a realistic hope. That hope is "really possible" is underscored in Jesus's life and ministry, in the kind of relationships he fosters and pursues. The narrative of the cross and the Resurrection confirms the essential truthfulness of Jesus's embodiment and enactment of God's kingdom, one defined by solidarity with the least in society.

That Cahill finds the Christological themes of the reign of God, the cross, and the Resurrection as establishing the moral priority of solidarity and the option for the poor underscores the extent to which she adheres to a "Christology from below." Such a Christology places theological-ethical import on the kind of social relationships and practices he engaged; it requires, as Cahill suggests, that we "see the events in the life of Jesus of Nazareth as a constant resource and referent for Christian spirituality and ethics,"[40] an approach that Cahill contrasts with a "Christology from above," which is "focused not on the earthly career of Jesus Christ, but on a vision of Christ identified with the preexistent Logos (as in the Gospel of John)" as well as other theological doctrines.[41] It is a Christology that elevates the human Jesus in his solidarity with the marginalized—that inaugurates the Christian tradition of challenging those in power. And yet it does so without rendering Jesus into simply a "historical" Jesus, a Jesus to simply admire or to observe. Instead, given what the reign of God, the cross, and the Resurrection signify, the human Jesus of solidarity and the option for the poor presents himself as a realistic, practical moral imperative in the present. In other words, Jesus grounds the theological-ethical hope of liberation.

But what exactly does it mean to work for justice in the image of Jesus's solidarity with the marginalized, the poor, the suffering? In what way ought we to consider the events of Jesus of Nazareth as moral resources

---

[39]Cahill, "Christology, Ethics, and Spirituality," 194.
[40]Ibid., 195.
[41]Ibid.

for the obligation to resist and transform sinful social structures *today*? Such questions pertain, in part, to how Scripture, more broadly, ought to be taken as a relevant guide to contemporary life and moral questions. Using Scripture to inform Christian ethics is of course a given, but it does require special care when working with the text. Cahill suggests that "relating Scripture to ethics is a complex interpretive process"[42] that can include many different dimensions of the text depending on what ends are being determined. But with this complexity in mind, Cahill explains, "Even if not every moral command in the New Testament is relevant today, we can still aim to form communities whose moral practices, *though different in some aspects*, embody the 'reign of God' *in recognizably similar ways*."[43] Hence, "The framework of the cross allows us to name, confront, and identify emphatically with suffering,"[44] and the cross pushes us to assess how far we still have to go in terms of treating others with love and compassion. Furthermore, the Resurrection offers the hope that this task of justice will ultimately prevail.

Not every moral practice recorded in Scripture is meant to be or can be reinscribed in contemporary times. How then should the person of Jesus impact Christian ethics? For Cahill, "In and through Jesus Christ, humans are reunited to God, healed from sinfulness, and empowered for life in a community of forgiveness, reformation, and solidarity."[45] In that vein, Scripture is less a moral manual than a call to embody sustained practices of solidarity that witness to the transformative power of God's justice in the person of Christ. For Cahill, it is partly her Christology that informs an approach to Jesus's life as generating models of practice. In other words, in her Christology, what we have is a *theological* account of how to interpret Scripture and, in turn, how to be faithful to Jesus in our present time. As theologian Lúcás Chan suggested, Cahill's writing highlights how "biblical narratives of Jesus contour Christian social ethics, while key christological formations provide its inspiration and reasoning."[46]

The significance of Cahill's Christology for Christian ethics is reflected in her own commitment to speaking out against violence, sexism, and ecological deterioration and in her advocacy for peace and the well-being of women, especially in the Global South. Her insistence on the need to

---

[42] Cahill, "The Bible and Christian Moral Practices," 5. In this volume, see the chapter by Sarah M. Moses for an extended analysis of Cahill's methodology regarding Scripture.
[43] Ibid. (emphases added).
[44] Cahill, "Jesus, Christ, and Ethics," 239.
[45] Cahill, *Global Justice, Christology, and Christian Ethics*, 76.
[46] Lúcás Chan, SJ, "Biblical Ethics: 3D," *Theological Studies* 65, no. 1 (2015): 112–28, at 126.

resist and disrupt unjust power and social relationships help create a "shared conclusion that Jesus shattered the standard status markers of his world and overturned barriers to inclusion in a community characterized by forgiveness, compassion, and mutual service."[47] In Cahill's own writings, Christology is not an abstract theological concept but very much a morally consequential one; it obligates Christians to make choices that serve others in a world in which the marginalized and oppressed continue to suffer under unjust systems. As Cahill puts it, "Inasmuch as Christ is still suffering in the suffering of the victims of history, Christian faith and theology furnish a powerful motivation to change the historical situation of needless human misery."[48]

---

[47]Cahill, "Jesus, Christ, and Ethics," 230–31.
[48]Cahill, "Christology, Ethics, and Spirituality," 197.

"To the Church at Rome, All the Churches of Christ Greet You"

A Catholic Feminist Correspondence

Mary M. Doyle Roche

At the heart of the feminist Christian vision is neither complaint nor criticism, but hope—hope that change is possible and that justice and love can be realized more completely in society and in the church.[1]

In 2014 Lisa Sowle Cahill delivered a plenary address at the Annual Meeting of the Society of Christian Ethics (SCE) titled "Catholic Feminists and Traditions: Renewal, Reinvention, Replacement."[2] In that address she surveyed the landscape of Catholic feminist ethics. Rather than outlining the various waves of feminist thought as is commonly done, Cahill mapped the work of forerunners, longtime colleagues, and emerging scholars onto enduring schools of thought and spiritual charisms in the theological traditions of Catholicism: Augustinian, Thomistic, and Franciscan. The addition of a fourth school, *Junian*, is the fruit of Cahill's deep attention to Scripture and the experience of the earliest Christian communities as a discipleship of equals.

The address is emblematic of Cahill's way of proceeding in theological conversation and makes explicit the qualities her students and readers have long admired: postures of appreciation and suspicion, and a commitment to highlighting lived practices. The honor of delivering a plenary address

---

[1] Lisa Sowle Cahill, "Feminist Theology and a Participatory Church," in *Common Calling: The Laity and Governance of the Catholic Church*, ed. Stephen J. Pope (Washington, DC: Georgetown University Press, 2004), 127–50, at 129.

[2] Lisa Sowle Cahill, "Catholic Feminists and Traditions: Renewal, Reinvention, Replacement," *Journal of the Society of Christian Ethics* 34, no. 2 (Fall/Winter 2014): 27–51.

on the sweeping topic of Catholic feminist ethics and tradition is surely recognition of Cahill's expertise and distinctive contribution to the field. Yet one consequence is that the demands of modesty and humility leave that very contribution in the shadows—clear to everyone in attendance, but left unsaid. In this chapter I would like to remedy that. Since Cahill herself defies easy categorization, I instead attempt to highlight the ways in which her work has drawn on and shaped the discourse in each of the four schools of feminist ethical theory and praxis examined in the address. Though I hope to show how Cahill's feminist approach has moved into multiple arenas of ethical concern, most notably bioethics and the problem of violence, I focus on sexual ethics as an illustration of her contribution and its future possibilities. Finally, as I have thought about Cahill's legacy, I have been drawn into deeper engagement with Junia, the distinguished apostle greeted by Paul in Romans 16, and patron saint, if you will, of Junian feminists. I share my reflections as a way of gesturing toward hopes for the future of Catholic feminist ethics.

Appreciation, Suspicion, Praxis

Therefore traditions should always be discerned with a threefold hermeneutics of appreciation, suspicion, and praxis: How does wisdom from the past give life today? (appreciation); how do traditions mediate dominant ideologies that continue to oppress some community members? (suspicion); and how can our traditions be embodied in just relationships now? (praxis).[3]

Before mapping out Cahill's survey of the four schools of Christian feminist thought and her particular contributions, it will be helpful to first note briefly the threefold posture that Cahill adopts with respect to thinking about, with, and through the Christian tradition: appreciation, suspicion, and praxis.

Appreciation

After nearly forty-five years of teaching at a Jesuit university, it comes as no surprise that Cahill's posture toward dialogue could easily be characterized by the Ignatian presupposition of goodwill among interlocutors. Her work is marked by appreciation, not only for the tradition but for the work of those whose perspectives, experiences, and conclusions are

---
[3] Ibid., 28.

different from her own. Early in her career, Cahill was attuned to this kind of self- and other-awareness when she wrote, "Perhaps the best advice for the ethicist is to recognize her or his own presuppositions and implicit hypotheses, and so consider most seriously the impact that evidence unfavorable to them would have on his or her agenda."[4] Even when common ground might only be found at the most abstract levels—for example, that all human beings have intrinsic dignity and that Christian discipleship is ultimately about love and life—this is the ground on which Cahill stands, where she sows and reaps a harvest of authentic argument in search of the good. This posture of appreciation has the advantage of squarely locating feminist thought in the flow of tradition even as it presses the development of that tradition in new directions. Cahill holds things together—in tension—compassionately, reverently, and realistically.

Suspicion

Cahill places ethical issues in the context of fundamental questions about nature and grace, autonomy and relationality, freedom and moral responsibility, and so her feminist ethics can at once appreciate the tradition's enduring commitments, abide in paradox, and offer incisive critiques of sexist and gendered assumptions operating in Church teaching about these values. Her feminist hermeneutic of suspicion marshals the work of biblical scholars, theologians, and historians to ask and answer questions about women's presence among the first disciples but absence from much of the record, their leadership in Church and society, and the marginalization of their experiences in theological reflection. Constructively, Cahill retrieves lost memories for Christian ethics and highlights examples of women's enduring gospel witness, from the likes of Junia, whom we will consider shortly, down to networks of women acting in the present moment.

Praxis

In answering the question "How can traditions be embodied in just relationships now?" Cahill illuminates the possibilities by shining a light on particular communities and practices. I name but a few examples: solidarity among African American families as domestic churches;[5] the

---

[4] Lisa Sowle Cahill, *Between the Sexes: Foundations for a Christian Ethics of Sexuality* (Philadelphia: Fortress Press, 1985), 90.

[5] Lisa Sowle Cahill, *Family: A Christian Social Perspective* (Minneapolis: Fortress Press, 2000), 111–29.

workshops, training, and advanced theological education provided by the All-Africa Conference: Sister to Sister;[6] the work of women peacebuilders in places from Colombia to Burundi to Bosnia and Herzegovina;[7] networks of empowerment among women confronting the HIV and AIDS epidemic;[8] and the women leaders of organized protest and resistance in the #BlackLivesMatter movement.[9] In her 2006 lecture "Moral Theology: From Evolutionary to Revolutionary Change," given at the Catholic Theological Ethics in the World Church conference in Padua, Cahill notes, "One positive legacy of our natural law tradition is to give a basis on which to commit ourselves to dialogue about what divides us, on the assumption that our shared humanity will support practical agreements about how to resolve specific threats to the common good."[10] The threats are numerous and include racism, poverty, violence, and gender discrimination. Our "access to Christian narratives and practices that provide pathways to conversion of the imagination, the emotions, and the moral dispositions" will help "sustain hope at the practical level."[11] She has held up feminists for being "ahead of the curve" in connecting "theories and worldviews to cooperative social action, combatting systemic social distortions with reformist or revolutionary practices that create or join coalitions in civil society."[12] By focusing on praxis and lived experience, Cahill is able to claim that human struggles and initiatives, across a wide variety of historical and social contexts, as well as other forms of difference, are "relevant and revelatory to one another."[13]

---

[6] Lisa Sowle Cahill, "Feminist Theology and Sexual Ethics," in *A Just and True Love, Feminism at the Frontiers of Theological Ethics: Essays in Honor of Margaret A. Farley*, ed. Maura A. Ryan and Brian F. Linnane, SJ (Notre Dame, IN: University of Notre Dame Press, 2007), 20–46, at 41–42.

[7] Lisa Sowle Cahill, *Blessed Are the Peacemakers: Pacifism, Just War, and Peacebuilding* (Minneapolis: Fortress Press, 2019), 325–63.

[8] Lisa Sowle Cahill, "AIDS, Women, and Empowerment," in *Calling for Justice throughout the World: Catholic Women Theologians on the HIV/AIDS Pandemic*, ed. Mary Jo Iozzio, Mary M. Doyle Roche, and Elsie Miranda (New York: Continuum, 2009), 25–30.

[9] Cahill, *Blessed Are the Peacemakers*, 325–63.

[10] Lisa Sowle Cahill, "Moral Theology: From Evolutionary to Revolutionary Change," in *Catholic Theological Ethics in the World Church: The Plenary Papers from the First Cross-Cultural Conference on Catholic Theological Ethics*, ed. James F. Keenan, SJ (New York: Continuum, 2007), 221–27, at 223–24.

[11] Cahill, "Moral Theology," 225 and 227.

[12] Lisa Sowle Cahill, *Theological Bioethics: Participation, Justice, Change*, Moral Traditions, ed. James F. Kennan, SJ (Washington, DC: Georgetown University Press, 2005), 40.

[13] Lisa Sowle Cahill, *Sex, Gender, and Christian Ethics* (Cambridge: Cambridge University Press, 1996), 11.

Augustinian, Neo-Thomist, Franciscan, and Junian Feminisms

In her SCE plenary, Cahill describes major strands in Catholic ethics (each with their own appreciations, suspicions, and praxes) and how they take shape in Catholic feminist thought. My intention here is not to categorize Cahill's work in one of these four schools but rather to demonstrate how her work weaves strands together. It is also not to claim that a torch is being passed as if the schools emerge in a linear chronological or generational order. Each moves in and among the others. Each will bring distinctive and much-needed strengths in addressing particular moral challenges. On the issues of gender, gender identity, gender performance, and building an LGBTQ+-inclusive Church, the time is ripe for a Junian approach to take the lead.

Those in the Augustinian trajectory "see the Church as a haven of grace in a sinful world" and "embody the experience of a real but transcendent God in an increasingly secular world." Being "faithful to the distinctive moral and religious practices that set them apart, they can evangelize modern culture and attract more people to the faith."[14] In this school, Cahill locates scholars like Mary Ann Glendon and others who employ John Paul II's "theology of the body" to address women's social and familial roles and the ethics of reproduction.[15]

By contrast, the neo-Thomist school "stressed the created goodness of the world, history, politics, and the sciences and affirmed that grace is already present in these spheres." This school considers the "concrete reality of persons" and "recognize[s] historical consciousness," holding that human knowledge of truth is "constantly emerging" and not a finished product that has already been revealed, known, and taught.[16] Neo-Thomists place a high priority on "engagement and learning—perhaps most visibly from the natural and social sciences—in areas such as sex and gender, economics, evolution, and the environment."[17] These scholars, including Cristina Traina, Lisa Fullam, Barbara H. Andolsen, Christine Firer Hinze, and Margaret A. Farley, turn to the tradition of Catholic social thought to articulate norms for gender justice and pursuit of the common good.

Among the neo-Thomists we might find the most resonance with Cahill's own work on sex and gender, which is deeply indebted to the natural law idiom. She notes, "Gender understood as a moral project entails the

---

[14]Cahill, "Catholic Feminists and Traditions," 29.
[15]Ibid., 31.
[16]Ibid., 32, 34–35.
[17]Ibid., 33.

social humanization of biological tendencies, capacities, and differences, including the social ties that they, by their very nature, are inclined to create."[18] While she critiques "sexual and reproductive behavior, gender expectation, and family forms that dominate women," she also notes that human sexual differentiation and sexual reproduction "do stand as experiences which begin in humanity's primal bodily existence, and which all cultures institutionalize (differently) as gender, marriage, and family."[19] And yet, there are hints too of the Augustinian strand winding through the neo-Thomist cord. A realist about the pervasiveness of human sinfulness and its manifestation in the oppression of women throughout history and culture, Cahill espouses that "Christian sex and gender ethics, as a transformative ethics of discipleship, builds on but reforms human cultural practices so that they better represent the Christian values of incarnation, community, solidarity, fidelity, compassion, and hope that moral and social change are possible."[20]

The Franciscan view rounds out Catholic feminist ethics insofar as it grows out of and beyond traditional theological approaches. Cahill sees in these scholars, who may not explicitly reference Saints Francis and Clare to support their positions on social issues, an approach infused with a spirituality akin to the Franciscan charism. According to Cahill, "A contemporary neo-Franciscan approach would stress a countercultural evangelical identity in the world" and "would be strong on Christian spirituality, prayer, and ritual, but—consistent with Catholic tradition and with the new Pope Francis—it would not represent a sect-type church."[21] While this school tends to emphasize less the need for institutional and structural change for gender justice, "a strength of neo-Franciscan ethics for gender equality is its attention to the way communities of faith, solidarity, and practice can shape relationships in different ways from the ground up, locally, lending conviction and momentum to what may become larger trends of reform."[22] Here we find scholars like Julie Hanlon Rubio writing on the ethics of family life and highlighting the transformative practices of family meals, charitable giving, service and justice work, and sexual intimacy. Cahill's work too has moved from the grassroots, as noted previously in her attention to praxis, in ever-expanding circles of solidarity toward higher levels of social and structural organization. This kind of neo-Franciscan impulse leads us toward the school of Catholic feminism that Cahill calls *Junian*.

---

[18] Cahill, *Sex, Gender, and Christian Ethics*, 89.
[19] Ibid., 1, 109–10.
[20] Ibid., 257.
[21] Cahill, "Catholic Feminists and Traditions," 36.
[22] Ibid., 37.

In describing the Junians Cahill writes, "Today Catholic women are united internationally in action that hands on this message in practical ways, through Catholic infrastructures such as women's religious congregations, Catholic universities, associations of scholars, networks of activists, and Catholic nongovernmental organizations."[23] Like their foremother in Paul's letter to the Romans, Junians are transmitting the gospel message in small communities of faith that are linked to and open out upon the universal church. As was likely the case for Junia, "Catholic feminists have to hand on traditions about Christ, . . . within a church that already incorporates well-established norms of gender subordination."[24] This process of transmission is aided by the Junian's "most interesting move," the "turn to non-elite Western traditions and non-Western traditions, especially traditions from the cultures in the Global South."[25] Junians lead feminism to the "growing global edge" of theological ethics.[26] Cahill highlights the work of Ada María Isasi-Díaz and Agnes M. Brazal, though there are a multitude of theological ethicists who could be cited, as several collections of international scholars attest.[27] Though Cahill's social location places her in the halls of the "elite" Western academy, she has consistently used the access this affords her to both learn from the Junians and introduce the world church to their work. One might say she has brought the margins to the center, though it may be better to say that she has taken up the challenge of decentering the locus of moral authority.[28] In the proceeding sections I suggest that the Junian approach be expanded to include LGBTQ+ scholars and the moral wisdom found outside of the cis- and heteronormative traditions, in diverse experiences of gender identity and sexual orientation.

Cahill leads Catholic theological feminism today in appreciating the reality of sin and its "original-ness" in structures of oppression and violence, the roles of reason and theological reflection in discerning ethical action, the good of human interdependence amid pluralism and diversity, and the crucial contributions to be made to the common good at every level of social organization from the most intimate in the family to international networks of solidarity. Her appreciation of each school provides,

---

[23] Ibid., 39.
[24] Ibid.
[25] Ibid., 41.
[26] Ibid., 35.
[27] Ibid., 40–41. See Iozzio, Roche, and Miranda, eds., *Calling for Justice throughout the World*; and Linda Hogan and Agbonkhianmeghe E. Orobator, eds., *Feminist Catholic Theological Ethics: Conversations in the World Church*, Catholic Theological Ethics in the World Church (Maryknoll, NY: Orbis Books, 2014).
[28] On this decentering, see also Nichole Flores's chapter in this volume.

rather than inhibits, a vantage point from which to raise suspicions about narrow views of the nature of human sinfulness, the limits of our ability to get things right as we "descend to particulars," and the tendency for patriarchy and other forms of gender injustice to be perpetuated in families and larger institutions across cultures. Matching the hermeneutic of suspicion with one of generosity also allows Cahill to be a "detective of grace" in the lived practices of communities of Christians.[29]

Ethics of Sex and Gender

Cahill's feminism infuses her work on the wide array of ethical issues about which she has taught and written. All Catholic feminisms, whether in the Augustinian, Thomistic, Franciscan, or Junian register, are committed to "difference in unity, moral realism, social meliorism, human equality, preferential option for the poor, and interreligious dialogue."[30] Though Cahill's arguments flow primarily from a Thomistic/natural law frame, her illustrations of what is possible to accomplish gesture toward the Franciscan and Junian. Cahill's work in bioethics and medical ethics, for example, attended to the concerns of women living in poverty, "realigning Catholic priorities" toward the option for the poor in a global context.[31] Her contributions are aimed at the kind of cultural and structural change needed to make a measure of health possible for all people and communities. Her pathbreaking contributions to the conversations on just war, pacifism, and peacebuilding are attuned to the reality of human sinfulness that leads to violence and the devastation left in its wake, particularly for poor communities of color where women are often unrecognized agents of change.[32]

Similarly, her work in the ethics of sex and gender navigates tensions around cultural differences in the social construction of gender and gender roles, while insisting that common humanity (across intersecting axes of sex, gender, sexual orientation, race, class, culture, etc.) anchors the potential for differences to exist in creative tension. When considering moral decisions about sexual activity in various contexts, Cahill raises the crucial question about whether choices that optimize personal health and social relationships are even available to many persons, especially

---

[29]Thank you to my colleague James Corkery, SJ, for this phrase.
[30]Cahill, "Catholic Feminists and Traditions," 41.
[31]Lisa Sowle Cahill, "Realigning Catholic Priorities: Bioethics and the Common Good," *America* 191, no. 6 (2004): 11–13, at 11.
[32]In this volume, see the chapters of Kate Jackson-Meyer and Angela Senander.

to women and girls.[33] And if they are not, she asks, what social sins and forms of institutionalized violence need to be challenged and transformed according to the norms of justice and equity? How can local and grassroots efforts at gender and sexual justice be honored and supported by mediating institutions and forms of international organization? How can persons living in diverse forms of sexual and marital relationship be both challenged and supported so that these relationships are more adequately connected to the needs of the vulnerable and the common good at large?

Catholic feminist ethics of sex and gender also has its growing edges. One to highlight is the need for greater inclusion of LGBTQ+ voices and experiences. Because Cahill's approach to any ethical issue is marked by her attention to new experience and the best evidence available, her work can be a point of departure for queer theological ethics, and her students are well poised to make critical contributions for the future of the discipline with regard to sexual relationships and bioethical concerns regarding, for example, gender alignment and other aspects of transgender medicine.[34] In *Sex, Gender, and Christian Ethics* she writes, "Ethicists, Christian and humanistic, may need to acknowledge ambiguity and a certain 'incoherence' to human life as embodied. Tension among the constitutive components of our nature gives morality and culture the character of a *project of integration*, rather than a *call to authenticity* to our 'real' or 'true' nature."[35] How might this view inform a conversation with *all persons* who seek integration of their sexual and gendered (or neither) selves? How might the Church be enriched when the voices of those who have had to discern this quite explicitly are allowed to rise?[36]

While applying concepts like "LGBTQ+" back onto other historical contexts is fraught with dangers, we can with confidence claim that LGBTQ+ persons have *always* been making scholarly and pastoral contributions to the life of the Church. The moment when they might make these contributions *as LGBTQ+ theologians and pastors* to speak about sex, gender, and all aspects of life in the risen Christ is upon us and long overdue.

---

[33]Lisa Sowle Cahill, "AIDS, Justice, and the Common Good," in *Catholic Ethicists on HIV/AIDS Prevention*, ed. James F. Keenan, SJ, with Jon D. Fuller, SJ, MD, Lisa Sowle Cahill, and Kevin Kelly (New York: Continuum, 2000), 282–93.

[34]See, for example, Craig A. Ford Jr., "Transgender Bodies, Catholic Schools, and a Queer Natural Law Theology of Exploration," *Journal of Moral Theology* 7, no. 1 (2018): 70–98.

[35]Cahill, *Sex, Gender, and Christian Ethics*, 97 (emphasis in the original).

[36]See Mary M. Doyle Roche, "Inclusive Church for the 21st Century: Dreaming beyond the Binary with LGBTQ Youth," in *American Catholicism in the 21st Century: Crossroads, Crisis, or Renewal?*, ed. Benjamin T. Peters and Nicholas K. Rademacher, Catholic Theology Society 63, (Maryknoll, NY: Orbis Books, 2018), 114–25.

Junia: Mistaken Identity and a Call to Mystery

Cahill's tour through models of Catholic feminist thought from Augustinian, through neo-Thomistic and Franciscan, toward Junian, lays the foundation for a bridge to the next "growing edge" for Catholic feminist ethics. As Cahill herself looks to the future of Catholic feminist ethics, she looks first to the Scriptures and finds Junia. We encounter Junia in Paul's letter to the Romans. In her SCE plenary address, Cahill makes several observations about Junia and why she chose her as the patron saint of scholars at the forefront of feminist theological ethics today. Junia, together with Andronicus, whom we take to be her spouse, is called "apostle" by Paul. Cahill notes that Junia "belongs to the local church in Rome, but she is united to Christian communities around the Mediterranean by a common baptism, Eucharist, and what Paul calls 'the good news that I proclaimed to you' and 'handed on.'" Junia "exercised existential apostleship in a gender-unequal church" along with other women from diverse communities and cultures.[37]

A focus on Romans 16 is itself a feminist move. Indeed, as Scripture scholar Beverly Roberts Gaventa has noted, there is a tendency to pass over this ending of Romans, in favor of more deliberate attention to the theological claims the letter makes. As she writes, "The conventional wisdom that Romans was a summary of Christian theology caused attention to fall heavily on the doctrine unpacked in the letter, with little attention left over for the people the letter addressed."[38] Attention to the potential for Paul's greeting to reach us today highlights the ways in which "Catholic women are united internationally in action that hands on this message in practical ways through Catholic infrastructures such as women's religious congregations, Catholic universities, associations of scholars, networks of activists, and Catholic nongovernmental organizations."[39] These women and their partners in ministry invite all Catholics into deeper relationship with the Church local and universal. It is this multivalent ecclesial setting in which theory and practice are always in dynamic interaction with one another that is at the heart of what Cahill has drawn from the Junians. Their contributions "rework and reinvent" tradition in light of the "six defining commitments" of Catholic ethics: difference in unity, moral realism, social meliorism, human equality, preferential option for the poor, and interreligious dialogue.[40]

---

[37] Cahill, "Catholic Feminists and Traditions," 39.
[38] Beverly Roberts Gaventa, "Foreword," in Eldon Jay Epp, *Junia: The First Woman Apostle* (Minneapolis: Fortress Press, 2005), ix–xiv, at ix.
[39] Cahill, "Catholic Feminists and Traditions," 39.
[40] Ibid., 41.

Junia is a fascinating figure, and her story, as well as the story of scholarship about her, can offer additional lessons for Catholic feminist ethics and suggest future directions for the enterprise. The eventual resolution of a debate about Junia's gender helps to shore up claims about women's roles in the early Church and provides ground to imagine new possibilities for women's leadership in the present and future. It also may be a call to look beyond a gender binary and more intentionally toward the mystery we are to ourselves and one another.

Biblical scholar Michael Peppard has written about women in the early Church who are not "household names" today, women like Junia, Prisca, and Phoebe. Of Junia in particular he writes, "Junia was a victim of the Bible's manuscript tradition, in which she was erased from existence by her transition to a man named 'Junias.'" Translated as Junia for centuries, and understood to be a woman, "The masculine 'Junias' was introduced at a later date by copyists, if not intentionally then perhaps unintentionally due to a subconscious bias that someone called an 'apostle' would also be a man."[41] Early references to Junia by the likes of Origen, Jerome, Peter Abelard, Peter Lombard, and John Chrysostom offer her praise, apparently not bothered (though perhaps surprised) by the notion that a woman was called apostle in the early Church. The evidence from Chrysostom reads, "Even to be an apostle is great, but also to be prominent among them—consider how wonderful a song of honor that is. For they were prominent because of their works, because of their successes. Glory be! How great the wisdom of this woman that she was even deemed worthy of the apostle's title."[42] According to Peppard, "None of the church offices, including those ascribed to men, were clearly established and defined by the mid-first century. (In any case, the most important term of authority at that time was not bishop, presbyter, or deacon, but 'apostle,' the title for which Paul fought so hard—and the one which he presumed everyone in Rome knew Junia already had.)"[43]

It is much later that the "impossibility" that a woman could have been an apostle, or rather, could be now in the line of the apostles, dictated that the name in the manuscript be retranslated to a masculine form, Junias (though research indicates that Junias was not a name in use). Bernadette Brooten makes the point quite bluntly: "What reasons have commentators given for this change? The answer is simple: a woman could not

---

[41] Michael Peppard, "Household Names: Junia, Phoebe, and Prisca in Early Christian Rome," *Commonweal* 145, no. 10 (2018): 11–14, at 11.

[42] Bernadette Brooten, "'Junia . . . Outstanding among the Apostles' (Romans 16:7)," in *Women Priests: A Catholic Commentary on the Vatican Declaration*, ed. Leonard Swidler and Arlene Swidler (New York: Paulist Press, 1977), 141–44, at 141.

[43] Peppard, "Household Names," 12. See also Epp, *Junia*, 70.

have been an apostle. Because a woman could not have been an apostle, the woman who is here called apostle could not have been a woman."[44] In that moment, Junia, female apostle, was lost in a case of what might generously be called a case of mistaken identity, only to be found again after some careful scriptural sleuthing decades later.[45]

Even when the error in translation was corrected, the debate continued. Exploring interpretations of the words "distinguished among the apostles," Epp writes, "Over time, however, this phrase, in spite of its clarity in the early centuries of the Church, has become a major factor in the debate about whether Junia was, in fact, an apostle, or, alternatively, whether 'apostle' really means 'Apostle.'"[46] As Epp notes, Junia, a female, returns but is "cut down," demoted from "apostle" herself, to someone merely known and admired by the *real* apostles.[47]

Junia's role as a female apostle, one who was "in Christ" before Paul, is "pivotal for determining women's roles in early Christianity" and so too in grounding claims to present and future ecclesial leadership.[48] The evidence is in, and it is compelling,[49] yet this may not fully capture what this episode in mistranslation (at best) or erasure (at worst) might teach us with respect to sex and gender in Catholic feminist thought. There is much we do not know about Junia, or for that matter, about any of the apostles, disciples, saints, or prophets through the ages. Where there is uncertainty, there is possibility, and ambiguity presents both challenges and gifts. Perhaps one lesson is that we ought to hold on to gender and gender identity lightly; to explore and interrogate cisgendered and heteronormative assumptions and imaginations. If Catholic communities can do that with the figures in their history, we might be able to realize greater solidarity in the present.

To the Church at Rome, All the Churches of Christ Greet You. . . .

In appreciating Cahill's legacy, it is tempting to focus exclusively on the work of the scholars who have written dissertations under her direction, some included in this volume, and have gone on to make innovative scholarly and pedagogical contributions to the field of theological eth-

---

[44] Brooten, "'Junia . . . Outstanding among the Apostles,'" 142.
[45] Thank you to my colleague, Scripture scholar Caroline Johnson Hodge, for sharing her enthusiasm for Junia and this case of "mistaken identity."
[46] Epp, *Junia*, 69.
[47] Ibid., 72.
[48] Ibid., 21.
[49] Ibid., 79–80.

ics. Many, many others who have been influenced by her have gone on to pastoral and social justice work. This may be the heart of the matter. One highly visible example is James Martin, SJ, who has long garnered attention as a gifted communicator about Ignatian spirituality. He has of late become a more prominent ally of LGBTQ+ persons, and his recently revised *Building a Bridge* (reviewed by Cahill in *Theological Studies*) proceeds with appreciation, suspicion, and attention to praxis.[50] Many readers of this volume will surely be able to name others. I offer one additional illustration from my personal experience.

The campus where I teach has had to confront the tragedies of sexual harassment, misconduct, assault, homophobia, and forms of gender-based discrimination and violence against LGBTQ+ persons. We are far from alone. In response, a small group of women who teach and minister on campus gathered to share our outrage and grief, and to sustain one another in our faith, if not always in the Church. Several of us share some of the "BC/Cahill DNA," as we like to call it. We have formed an open community for weekly prayer and preaching led by women and inspired by women's experiences—appreciation, suspicion, and praxis. The readings focus on women in the Scriptures and traditions of the early Church. On my first day to preach, I was given Romans 16. *What*, I thought, *will I do with this laundry list of people whose names are unfamiliar, and reminds me of an awards speech that goes on just a bit too long?* I decided to try some Ignatian contemplation.

I invite you now, dear reader, to pause here, visit Romans 16, and contemplate these greetings from Paul. Taking a cue from Ignatian spirituality, which animates Lisa's longtime academic home, set the scene and place yourself there. Give your imagination some license. Christians are gathered to hear the word from Paul. The letter has been long and complicated. Perhaps you are nodding off or lost in thought. Do you perk up a bit as you hear names being called toward the end? Perhaps you imagine yourself as Phoebe, the one who has journeyed to bring the letter. After listening to the long epistle, this package that you have taken such great risk and care to deliver, are you caught unawares to hear your name read aloud? Do you blush when you hear yourself counted among the saints who are worthy of help and resources for your important work? Perhaps you are Junia or Andronicus. Perhaps you have been given the honor of reading the letter. If your name is called, does the swell of pride

---

[50] James Martin, SJ, *Building a Bridge: How the Catholic Church and the LGBTQ Community Can Enter into a Relationship of Respect, Compassion, and Sensitivity* (New York: Harper One, 2018). Cahill's review of the first edition is in *Theological Studies* 79, no. 1 (2018): 212–14.

also raise suspicion? Are you prompted to look around and ask about who has been left out or deliberately silenced, who is waiting in the wings of this stage? Or perhaps you wait and wait, straining to hear, but your name is not mentioned.

Is the Church at Rome in your imagination a small base-community of sorts? What challenges and consolations do you hear? Or is it the Rome we might imagine today, a site of power and privilege for the Church? Perhaps many, many names are being called by the Spirit and many ministries are being commended, but these saints, apostles, and prophets of the good news—even perhaps the esteemed Lisa Sowle Cahill—have not been invited to be among this elite group gathered to hear such weighty matters. I invite you to hear your name, the name you know in your heart to be yours. *All the churches of Christ greet you.*

Method and the Use of Scripture

Sarah M. Moses

At the outset, it is important to historically locate the trajectory of Lisa Sowle Cahill's work within a dynamic and fruitful time of interaction between the scholarly fields of Christian ethics and biblical studies.[1] Cahill's own mentor, James Gustafson, was a major figure who helped initiate this time of scholarly inquiry with essays in which he urged ethicists to more systematically reflect upon the use of Scripture in Christian ethics.[2] At that time, Gustafson lamented a "paucity of material" relating the fields of biblical studies and ethics "in a scholarly way."[3] He also emphasized the need for ethicists to draw upon biblical studies and, concomitantly, for biblical scholars to provide studies that ethicists could draw on when incorporating the Bible into their method. In the decades that followed, a whole body of scholarly literature arose in which ethicists sought to respond to questions arising out of modern biblical studies, especially from historical-critical methods: Does the historical particularity of biblical texts undermine their relevance for contemporary communities? Does the internal diversity (and contradiction) found within the biblical canon invalidate Scripture as a source for shaping a coherent Christian ethic? Do texts that promote practices repugnant to contemporary moral sensibilities undercut the Bible's authority for the Church? Cahill's work thus offers both important analysis of and extensive contributions to that

---

[1] For further insight into the development of this scholarly discussion, see Bruce Birch and Larry Rasmussen, *Bible and Ethics in the Christian Life* (Minneapolis: Augsburg Publishing House, 1976), 11–78; Allen Verhey, *The Great Reversal: Ethics and the New Testament* (Grand Rapids: William B. Eerdmans, 1984), 153–69.

[2] James M. Gustafson, "Christian Ethics," in *Religion*, ed. Paul Ramsey (Englewood Cliffs, NJ: Prentice-Hall, 1965), 285–354; James M. Gustafson, "The Place of Scripture in Christian Ethics," *Interpretation* 24, no. 4 (1970): 430–55. Cahill refers to Gustafson's 1970 piece as a "magisterial article on Scripture and ethics that was to become a standard point of departure for discussions of the topic, at least in the United States" (Lisa Sowle Cahill, "The New Testament and Ethics," *Interpretation* 44, no. 4 [October 1990]: 383–95, at 383).

[3] Gustafson, "Christian Ethics," 337.

scholarly discussion as it continues in twenty-first-century Christian ethics.

The approach of this chapter is to analyze Cahill's methodological approach to Scripture in order to better understand the state of the question and the terms of debate within our discipline today. My analysis contains three major sections: analysis of Cahill's method, an example of how she applies her method to a contemporary moral issue, and the implications of her method for the larger scholarly debate. In this analysis I argue that the guiding principle of Cahill's method is what I call a "hermeneutic of transformation": that within the diversity of biblical voices, there emerge *patterns* of moral practice aimed at *transformation* of wider cultural values and norms. By way of *analogy*, Cahill proposes, Scripture can then function as one *authoritative* source for contemporary Christian ethics in shaping communal moral praxis toward transformation in its own historical-cultural context. In laying out this hermeneutic of transformation, we will see that Cahill's approach reveals defining questions and debates within Christian ethics at the end of the twentieth century and the beginning of the twenty-first, and indicates important directions for the future.

The Hermeneutic of Transformation

One of the most significant ways in which Cahill's method has contributed to the disciplinary discussion of the use of Scripture in ethics is in her engagement with and constructive use of biblical studies scholarship. Cahill argues that the explosion of social-scientific and historical approaches to the Bible should be welcomed as "new energy" by Christian ethicists, and as providing ways of answering long-debated questions concerning how scholars can and should relate ancient texts to contemporary circumstances.[4] For Cahill, the most important contribution of historical and sociological biblical scholarship to ethics is in revealing how early Christian practices shaped the early Church's relationship to the wider culture.

From biblical studies, Cahill focuses primarily on historical methods, and within that large umbrella, she draws on sociocultural studies of the New Testament world that emphasize the social history of early Christianity.[5] Cahill sees "the use of social history and sociology" as particularly

---

[4]Lisa Sowle Cahill, "Kingdom and Cross: Christian Moral Community and the Problem of Suffering," *Interpretation* 50, no. 2 (April 1996): 156–68, at 156.

[5]Here I would point out that Cahill's method draws heavily on the New Testament and much less on the Hebrew Bible. Thus, her primary sources within biblical studies come from New Testament and early Christianity scholars. See Lisa Sowle Cahill, "The Bible and

relevant to ethics because this method of biblical criticism illuminates "the communities that produced the Bible" and the "social stance" that their patterns of life would have created in their original settings.[6] Together with modern biblical studies, Cahill is profoundly interested in the "historical circumstances of Christian origins," and thus her appropriation of Scripture is attentive to the Jewish background of the New Testament and influences from Greco-Roman culture, including the dominant political and economic structures.[7] For Cahill, these methods are important not primarily because they provide an accurate analysis of the *past* meanings of texts, but rather because of what they reveal to us about the *communities* producing and being shaped by biblical texts. She writes, "Both the first Christian communities and latter-day ones are transformations and 'resocializations' that sometimes challenge, sometimes reorder, but also sometimes incorporate the values and structures in which their members participate; the shape and reality of life in Christian community is constantly responsive to its actual circumstances."[8] For Cahill, it is these actual circumstances that sociohistorical methods reveal to us, and, for ethics, she thinks it is particularly important to notice the ways in which early Christian communities "are responding to and challenging highly stratified social relationships."[9]

A second defining feature of Cahill's methodology is that she is not interested in specific texts or rules found within Scripture but rather the overall pattern of life of the community that Scripture and sociohistorical analysis reveals. In other words, Scripture is not important for ethics because it provides a rulebook or a systematic ethical theory, but rather because it shows us *communities* of moral praxis. Cahill's writings have various ways of describing this. In an analysis of Paul's New Testament

---

Christian Moral Practices," in *Christian Ethics: Problems and Prospects*, ed. Lisa Sowle Cahill and James F. Childress (Cleveland: Pilgrim Press, 1996), 3–17, at 6; Lisa Sowle Cahill, "The Ethical Implications of the Sermon on the Mount," *Interpretation* 41, no. 2 (April 1987): 144–58, at 147. Cahill also acknowledges the importance of historical-critical methods for feminist biblical interpretation in North America upon which she depends. See Lisa Sowle Cahill, "Bible, Ethics, and the Global Church," in *The Bible and Catholic Theological Ethics*, Catholic Theological Ethics in the World Church, ed. Yiu Sing Lúcás Chan, James F. Keenan, SJ, and Ronaldo Zacharias (Maryknoll, NY: Orbis Books, 2017), 55–79, at 57.

[6] Cahill, "The Bible and Christian Moral Practices," 5.

[7] Lisa Sowle Cahill, "Gender and Strategies of Goodness: The New Testament and Ethics," *Journal of Religion* 80, no. 3 (July 2000): 442–60, at 444; Lisa Sowle Cahill, "Sex and Gender Ethics as New Testament Ethics," in *The Bible in Ethics: The Second Sheffield Colloquium*, ed. John W. Rogerson, Mark Daniel Carroll Jr., and Margaret Davies (Sheffield, UK: Sheffield Academic Press, 1995), 272–95, at 273.

[8] Cahill, "The New Testament and Ethics," 389.

[9] Cahill, "Sex and Gender Ethics," 273.

writings, she speaks of the "new moral pattern" of the early Christian communities and the "mode of life" Paul sought to encourage.[10] She argues that the task of Christian ethics is to discern in Scripture a "pattern of faith and life" of the historic religious community.[11] In fact, Cahill's hermeneutic is profoundly shaped by the lens of community: she argues that "communal identity is essential to Christian ethics."[12] This emphasis on the communal reality of Christian moral practice is evident when Cahill writes, "Community inaugurating the basilea of God is the source and criterion of authentic biblical interpretation."[13] Cahill insists that "no one biblical text" can be taken as revelatory or authoritative on its own but rather must be seen within the whole of biblical literature and "the dynamic communal history."[14] From this perspective, contemporary Christian ethics need not defend all "specific moral stances" found within Scripture but rather look for normative moral guidance from Scripture taken as a whole.[15]

These methodological commitments lead to Cahill's fundamental hermeneutical principle and the central argument running throughout her writings: taken as a whole and understood within the sociohistorical setting, the moral praxis and ethical values of early Christian communities recorded in Scripture represent a "transforming impetus" in relation to the surrounding culture and a "reversal" of cultural values.[16] Nowhere is this hermeneutic principle more clear than when Cahill argues that "Scripture guides ethics by revealing ways in which Jesus and early Christianity transformed standard cultural patterns of moral relationships, making them less hierarchical and status-oriented and more inclusive and compassionate."[17] Referencing the importance of sociohistorical biblical analysis, Cahill writes, "As sociology and social history demonstrate, early Christian community and moral behavior tended to undermine institutions and relationships that permitted powerful elites, both religious and political, to exploit the large majority of people."[18] For Cahill this "transforming"

---

[10] Cahill, "The Bible and Christian Moral Practices," 12, 14.

[11] Cahill, "Gender and Strategies of Goodness," 445, 449.

[12] Ibid., 449. On this point Cahill identifies her overlap with Gustafson's emphasis on "communities of moral discourse" and Stanley Hauerwas's language of "communities of character." In fact, Cahill explicitly positions herself within the scholarly trajectory that seeks to "relate the Bible to ethics primarily as communal praxis" (Cahill, "The New Testament and Ethics," 384).

[13] Cahill, "Bible, Ethics, and the Global Church," 66.

[14] Cahill, "Gender and Strategies of Goodness," 458; Cahill, "Sex and Gender Ethics," 274.

[15] Cahill, "Sex and Gender Ethics," 294.

[16] Cahill, "Gender and Strategies of Goodness," 458.

[17] Cahill, "Kingdom and Cross," 156.

[18] Cahill, "The Bible and Christian Moral Practices," 14.

impulse begins with the traditions about Jesus found in the gospels, which "entailed a reversal of worldly values" and a "breaking down of social barriers."[19] New Testament writings about the early Church also provide Christian ethics "specific ways in which the first Christians embodied a transformed way of life."[20] Thus, while "specific rules" for behavior in the New Testament may not be "directly applicable today," they are still instructive because they may "represent challenges to the social order and its standard ways of structuring human relationships according to status hierarchies and dominance."[21]

Given her emphasis on a pattern of transformation (rather than specific rules and values), it is not surprising that Cahill is most sympathetic to the paradigm of "analogy" for thinking about the relationship between biblical texts and contemporary theological ethics.[22] Studying the patterns of transformation in the New Testament sets the "task" for contemporary Christian ethics: "to define patterns that will have analogous effect in subsequent eras."[23] To address the question of how ancient Scripture can be related to the contemporary world, Cahill argues that it is "analogy" of "effect" that enables Christian ethicists to "move from biblical narrative to moral formation and judgment."[24] Thus, the task of Christian ethics is to identify "types of status differentiation" in the contemporary period to which one can "critically and analogically" appropriate the transformative stance.[25] In other words, what should be analogous for contemporary Christian ethics is the "function" that New Testament moral instruction had in its context.[26] She argues, "Christian ethics seeks contemporary practices whose function is *analogous* to the destabilizing effect of early Christianity on patterns of social relationship."[27]

Cahill's focus on the pattern of social transformation revealed by

---

[19]Ibid., 8. See also Cahill, "Gender and Strategies of Goodness," 446–47. Cahill explicitly cites Elisabeth Schüssler Fiorenza for this sociohistorical analysis of the Jesus traditions. See Cahill, "Sex and Gender Ethics," 277. For an overview of feminist approaches to biblical interpretation, see Elisabeth Schüssler Fiorenza, *But She Said: Feminist Practices of Biblical Interpretation* (Boston: Beacon Press, 1992), 20–50.

[20]Cahill, "The Bible and Christian Moral Practices," 5.

[21]Ibid. In "Kingdom and Cross," Cahill argues that rather than focusing on the specific rules themselves, ethicists should be looking for the "basic moral stance" they reveal vis-à-vis the wider culture (157). See also Cahill, "Sex and Gender Ethics," 293, 295.

[22]Cahill, "Kingdom and Cross," 157; Cahill, "The New Testament and Ethics," 389; Cahill, "The Bible and Christian Moral Practices," 3; Cahill, "Gender and Strategies of Goodness," 458.

[23]Cahill, "Kingdom and Cross," 156.

[24]Ibid., 157.

[25]Cahill, "Gender and Strategies of Goodness," 450.

[26]Cahill, "Sex and Gender Ethics," 274, 280.

[27]Cahill, "The Bible and Christian Moral Practices," 5.

Scripture is also the key to understanding her response to questions concerning the authority of the Bible for the contemporary church, for her understanding of what the Bible provides the contemporary ethicist defines how Scripture exercises authority: it is not specific rules within the Bible that are authoritative for Christians in all times and places, but rather the transformative "social stance" Scripture reveals.[28] Here Cahill is responding directly to the argument that ethical norms and rules found in the Bible that are repugnant to contemporary thought diminish the authority of the Bible for Christian ethics today. To this argument Cahill responds, "To see the New Testament as a historical 'prototype' of faith in action, rather than as a set of moral rules, frees us from the need to justify all its specific moral stances—as well as from the need to reject its moral authority entirely because of undeniable errors. What remains authoritative is a process of social transformation. . . ."[29] In an essay on gender in the New Testament, Cahill uses the phrase "strategies of goodness" to move away from specific rules to "a fluid, socially responsive, even pragmatic approach to moral behavior."[30] For Cahill this also implies that as later Christian communities gain status and power in societies, "their obligation to seek social change grows proportionately."[31] While acknowledging the internal complexity of the biblical record, Cahill still insists on a form of biblical authority for the Church today: "We are challenged to discover or create moral practices and patterns of life that are not substantively identical to those reflected in the biblical narratives, but that enable the Church to have the same transformative cultural effect it had in the first century—however incipiently, incompletely, and sometimes retrogressively."[32] In that regard, ethicists must exercise a "creative and analogical imagination" in identifying a communal moral praxis that embodies the transformative pattern of the New Testament.[33]

The Hermeneutic of Transformation Applied

Having sketched the basic contours of Cahill's methodological approach to Scripture, it is helpful to see that method in practice. One of Cahill's other major contributions to Christian ethics is a vast record of

---

[28]Ibid.
[29]Cahill, "Sex and Gender Ethics," 294.
[30]Cahill, "Gender and Strategies of Goodness," 442.
[31]Cahill, "Bible, Ethics, and the Global Church," 60.
[32]Cahill, "Kingdom and Cross," 158; see also Cahill, "The Bible and Christian Moral Practices," 5.
[33]Cahill, "Gender and Strategies of Goodness," 460.

engaging with contemporary moral issues such as bioethics and peacemaking with Scripture as a primary source for her ethical analysis. To illustrate Cahill's method applied to a particular issue in contemporary Christian ethics, I use an example from her book *Family: A Christian Social Perspective* (2000).[34] In this work Cahill devotes an entire chapter to "New Testament Sources," and thus it provides a very clear, substantive example of her method of drawing on Scripture as a source for Christian ethics.[35] In addition, Cahill's engagement with sociohistorical biblical studies is prominent in her approach to New Testament texts regarding the family. Based on what I have argued about Cahill's method, it is notable that she begins the chapter *not* with specific Scripture texts but rather by describing the family and society within the larger first-century Mediterranean world, including Greco-Roman and Jewish values and practices.[36] She draws upon scholarship in the classics and in biblical studies to explain the economic, legal, and social structure of families at this time, with the assumption that Christian families exist in a "cross-cultural situation" in which their identity and practices are shaped by Greco-Roman and Jewish cultures.[37] Reflecting her commitment to feminist methodology, Cahill also draws on this historical and sociocultural material to highlight the roles of women within the domestic sphere and religious cults at this time.[38]

When turning to the New Testament record itself, Cahill affirms a basic tenet of modern biblical studies that insists upon the plurality found within the canon itself: "Both the Gospels and the letters present us with varied rather than univocal reactions to the family."[39] With this in mind, Cahill engages the New Testament material "as a whole," and avoids taking any single text or section in isolation; for instance, she analyzes both the "anti-family" sayings of Jesus and the household codes found in the

---

[34]In this volume, for a full analysis of Cahill's ethics of sex, gender, and family, see the chapters written by Mary M. Doyle Roche and Matthew Sherman.

[35]Likewise, Cahill provides an entire chapter called "The Bible and Ethics" in Lisa Sowle Cahill, *Between the Sexes: Foundations for a Christian Ethics of Sexuality* (Philadelphia: Fortress Press, 1985), 15–44. See also Cahill's use of the New Testament in relation to the concept of the kingdom of God in Jesus's teachings and how that relates to treatment of the poor and to gender equality in Lisa Sowle Cahill, *Global Justice, Christology, and Christian Ethics*, New Studies in Christian Ethics, ed. Robin Gill (New York: Cambridge University Press, 2013), 94–109. In the present volume, see Marianne Tierney FitzGerald's chapter, "Christology and Christian Ethics," for Cahill's use of the New Testament in relation to Christology and ethics.

[36]Lisa Sowle Cahill, *Family: A Christian Social Perspective* (Minneapolis: Fortress Press, 2000), 19–28.

[37]Cahill, *Family*, 19. In another essay on gender in the New Testament, Cahill also explicitly draws on historical scholarship on the Greco-Roman world for her analysis of biblical texts; see Cahill, "Gender and Strategies of Goodness," 454.

[38]Cahill, *Family*, 21.

[39]Ibid., 45.

deutero-Pauline letters. For Cahill, these diverse reactions to family are all significant for the contemporary ethicist, but not as isolated, universally binding rules; rather, each represents a "strategy" or "pattern" in which the community sought to live in faithful response to God in particular circumstances. Thus, Cahill's appropriation of New Testament sources for an ethics of the family today reflects the hermeneutic of transformation outlined in our previous section. She argues that, understood within the particular sociohistorical context, the New Testament record as a whole presents "a prototype of the socially transformative family" that both overlaps with and negotiates against Greco-Roman and Jewish understandings of family.[40]

For example, Cahill's interpretation of the antidivorce sayings of Jesus focuses on their critique and rejection of a family structure in which divorce was a way men exercised arbitrary power over women and protected "male interests in patriarchal marriage."[41] Rather than approaching Jesus's sayings as yielding timeless moral rules to be applied identically in all circumstances, Cahill focuses on the way Jesus's teachings had "subversive social meaning" and represent a form of resistance to "controlling social hierarchies."[42] Likewise, Cahill's treatment of the household codes focuses on their interaction with the wider cultural values and practices of the time. As Cahill notes, given the centrality of the household within the Greco-Roman and Jewish worlds, it is not surprising that households served an important role in the spread of the Christian movement.[43] Consistent with recognition of the diversity of voices in the New Testament, Cahill's analysis explicitly discusses historical changes within the early Church reflected in differences we see between the record of house churches and the household codes found in later material. Her treatment of these later texts seeks to demonstrate both the ways in which Christian praxis around family pushed against surrounding cultural norms and incorporated the structure of the patriarchal household.[44] Cahill concludes her analysis of New Testament material regarding the family by acknowledging "tensions and contradictions between Christian identity and cultural forms of family life."[45] Rather than deny the patriarchy and inequality found in the household codes, she treats such texts as evidence of an ongoing process of negotiation with cultural norms. But what Cahill argues is normative for contemporary Christian ethics is an overall pattern from

---
[40] Ibid., 19.
[41] Ibid., 32.
[42] Ibid.
[43] Ibid., 34.
[44] Ibid., 41.
[45] Ibid., 44.

New Testament material in which families and household-based communities "transfigure human relationships" and resocialize members into "an ethos of mutuality, equality, and solidarity."[46]

The Hermeneutic of Transformation: Contributions and Questions

In an introductory essay regarding the history of Scripture's relationship to Christian moral thought and practice, Charles Cosgrove observed, "By the close of the twentieth century, the role of the Bible in Christian ethics had become a highly complex theological and intellectual problem. Except in fundamentalist circles, one could no longer simply equate biblical ethics with Christian ethics."[47] In the final section of this chapter, I want to draw out some of the important implications of Cahill's method for how Christian ethics is done, including ongoing questions that those working in the field must address. When surveying the vast breadth of Cahill's work, certainly it is accurate to say that she has substantively and consistently engaged this methodological debate throughout her career, and thus her work has broad ecumenical relevance within contemporary Christian ethics as regards the use of Scripture in ethical reasoning. Within the more specific world of Roman Catholic moral theology, Cahill is an illustrative figure whose work represents what Cosgrove describes as a post–Vatican II shift in which "there was greater interest in a renewal of moral theology nourished by study of Scripture."[48] It is also important to note that among North American Christian feminist ethicists, Cahill's work contributes much to cross-cultural engagement with ethicists from outside Europe and North America for whom the Bible remains an essential source for Christian life and thought.[49] For the scholar and student of Christian ethics, study of Cahill's work offers illuminating exposure to the defining trajectories and questions that arose in the latter half of

---

[46]Ibid., 47. With this move Cahill shows her strong alignment with feminist biblical scholars like Elisabeth Schüssler Fiorenza, whose work highlights the countercultural and antipatriarchal traditions present within Scripture; see ibid., 33.

[47]Charles H. Cosgrove, "Scripture in Ethics: A History," in *Dictionary of Scripture in Ethics*, ed. Joel B. Green (Grand Rapids: Baker Publishing Group, 2011), 13–25, at 24.

[48]Ibid., 23. Already in his 1965 essay, James Gustafson noted evidence for this growing shift to which Cahill will contribute: "If a study of more recent Roman Catholic ethics leaves a correct impression, it is clear that the Bible is coming to play a far more significant role and have a more central location in Catholic literature" (Gustafson, "Christian Ethics," 323).

[49]For a global view of the contemporary Catholic moral tradition's engagement with Scripture, see the variety of essays included in *The Bible and Catholic Theological Ethics*, ed. Yiu Sing Lúcás Chan, James F. Keenan, SJ, and Ronaldo Zacharias, Catholic Theological Ethics in the World Church (Maryknoll, NY: Orbis Books, 2017).

the twentieth century among scholars grappling with the intellectually complex question of Scripture's relationship to ethics.

The first set of implications relates to how Christian ethics conceptualizes its relationship to biblical studies, and here I think Cahill offers a model of collaborative though critical engagement. In this sense, she has done much to address the "paucity" of interaction between biblical studies and ethics that her own mentor, James Gustafson, identified in his landmark 1965 essay. The argument inherent in Cahill's hermeneutic of transformation is that ethicists *need* sociohistorical biblical studies scholarship in order to use Scripture as a source for contemporary Christian ethics.[50] Cahill's writings demonstrate extensive knowledge of past and current biblical studies scholars, and thus her method forces any of us working in Christian ethics to examine the rigor of our own use of the insights coming from biblical studies. Furthermore, Cahill reminds us that the importance of sociohistorical methods *for ethics* is not primarily about determining the meaning of texts in the past, but rather about seeing patterns of communal life that have relevance for today's communities of moral praxis. For Cahill, the impetus to transformation is revealed not in the texts themselves but rather in understanding how the text, and the community of praxis it represents, functioned in its particular context. It is the "basic social stance" that Scripture presents that interests Cahill, not discrete rules.[51]

However, Cahill's approach to biblical studies also urges a critical distance between ethics and biblical studies, or what I would describe as scholarly independence appropriate to the ethical task. And here Cahill's method has implications for how we think about the authority of Scripture and about the relationship between the descriptive and the normative tasks. In some ways Cahill's embrace of sociohistorical methods makes her approach open to arguments that modern biblical criticism undercuts Scripture's function as an authoritative source for Christian ethics. As Cahill herself acknowledges, some biblical studies scholars have in fact "used historicity precisely to discount authority."[52] In contrast, Cahill is clear in her position: Scripture still carries author-

---

[50]Here it should be noted that ethicists could use other contemporary methods of biblical criticism, such as the narrative approach to the Bible; see Mark Allan Powell, *What Is Narrative Criticism?*, Guides to Biblical Scholarship: New Testament, ed. Dan O. Via Jr. (Minneapolis: Fortress Press, 1990). For example, in my own work on ethics and contemporary aging, I draw on the narrative method to integrate Scripture as a source for a Christian ethic of long-term care; see Sarah M. Moses, *Ethics and the Elderly: The Challenge of Long-Term Care* (Maryknoll, NY: Orbis Books, 2015), 82–110.

[51]Cahill, "The Bible and Christian Moral Practices," 5.

[52]Cahill, *Between the Sexes*, 31.

ity, "though not sole authority."[53] In the hermeneutic of transformation, historical and sociocultural methods of analysis, far from relativizing New Testament norms, provide the necessary particularizing of a text needed to reveal the transformative *pattern* that is authoritative for the Church today. Her method thus stands in contrast to scholars who hold that "historical and cultural studies of early Christianity relativize any moral content the Bible might offer and threaten its normativity for contemporary readers."[54] With regard to the idea of shared authority, Cahill argues for a complex, dynamic process in which authoritative insight may come from "philosophy, science, and individual and cultural experience."[55] Such a model helps ethicists articulate the authority of Scripture, but not an exclusive authority, and to allow for "sensitive and nuanced incorporation of insights from philosophy, the sciences, other religious traditions, and common human experience."[56] Furthermore, the Catholic tradition insists that particular interpretations of the Bible must be considered together with the authority of tradition—that is, the "general parameters" set by "the universal community of the Church over time."[57]

As with the topic of authority, Cahill offers ethicists a way to respond to questions about the descriptive and normative tasks in a manner appreciative of modern biblical studies but also critical of some methodological conclusions. In her own use of sociohistorical research on the Bible, Cahill rejects an absolute theoretical wall between the descriptive (historical/sociological) and the normative (constructive). While methods such as social history and sociology have the *descriptive* task of understanding the communities that created the Bible and of explaining what texts might have meant in their original settings, she argues that "descriptions of the first Christians can contribute to normative ethics by allowing us to see what their interpretation of discipleship in light of the gospel meant in practice."[58] In making this argument, Cahill is quite aware of the tension with biblical studies: "Flying, perhaps, against prevailing winds in biblical scholarship, I will adopt a forthrightly normative and theological approach to the relevance of the Bible to ethics."[59] The relation of the descriptive and normative tasks is a question that anyone working in Christian ethics must continue to engage, particularly for normative claims that depend upon certain descriptions of the early communities forming and being

---

[53]Cahill, "Gender and Strategies of Goodness," 444.
[54]Ibid.
[55]Ibid., 460.
[56]Cahill, "The Bible and Christian Moral Practices," 3.
[57]Cahill, "Bible, Ethics, and the Global Church," 57.
[58]Cahill, "The Bible and Christian Moral Practices," 5.
[59]Cahill, "Sex and Gender Ethics," 272.

formed by Scripture. Cahill's work represents a clear argument that sociohistorical investigation serves normative ethics: "Historical research thus becomes a necessary first step in the constructive ethical task, and the concrete social strategies of biblical narratives become components of their 'normative' status."[60] Ethicists need to consider this kind of question in the interpretative process, and Cahill's approach suggests the possibility of affirming the biblical studies scholar's commitment to accurate, nonideological description of the sociohistorical world of the Bible, while retaining the Christian ethicist's use of Scripture for constructive purposes for communities today.[61]

A second set of implications flowing from Cahill's method relates to how the ethicist thinks about the Church as a moral community, particularly with regard to global diversity within the Church and engagement with those outside the Church. On the challenge of global diversity I think Cahill's approach validates a significant range of difference in how communities embody the norm of transformation. Much more than a rule-based approach to Scripture, Cahill's focus on a general pattern or stance discernible in Scripture allows local communities a legitimate freedom in shaping their moral praxis. Here Cahill's approach to the diversity within early Christianity informs how we might view diversity within the Church today around questions of moral praxis: the presence of plurality does not negate coherence. Commenting directly on scholarship that reveals the plurality and internal contradiction found within the New Testament, Cahill states, "But it simply goes too far to say that there are no consistent New Testament bases for the moral life."[62] For Cahill, sociohistorical methods, which have revealed the internal diversity of the Scriptures, simply confirm what we know about the Church as a human moral community: that it is constantly involved in an ongoing, fluid process of discernment and revision regarding its moral values and praxis as it responds to and exists within specific social and cultural realities.[63] Just as we can see radical contextuality in Scripture in terms

---

[60] Cahill, "The New Testament and Ethics," 383.

[61] In a 1985 presidential address to the annual meeting of the Society of Biblical Literature, New Testament scholar Wayne A. Meeks began his remarks by insisting upon a clear separation between historical description and normative argument; see Wayne A. Meeks, "Understanding Early Christian Ethics," *Journal of Biblical Literature* 105, no. 1 (March 1986): 3–11, at 3.

[62] Cahill, "Gender and Strategies of Goodness," 453. In "Sex and Gender Ethics," she identifies what she considers a "consistency" in the moral ethos presented in the gospels about Jesus: the kingdom of God, inclusive behavior, compassion, active solidarity, and inclusion of the marginal (273).

[63] Cahill writes, "All human experiences, beliefs, and expressions take shape in some context and will reflect that process of interaction" (Cahill, "Gender and Strategies of

of the variety of ways early communities sought to embody moral bases such as solidarity, inclusive community, and mutual regard, so too will there be radical contextuality today as local communities negotiate with the political, economic, and social structures within which they exist. Cahill's method suggests that specific rules or practices may legitimately differ between Christian communities globally as long as they embody a shared pattern of transformation.

On the topic of engagement with those outside the Church, I would argue that while Cahill's approach to ethics is decidedly communal, it is not narrowly communitarian in its vision of how the Church interacts with the wider society as a community of moral praxis. While Cahill acknowledges that it is "within the Church as faith community that the Scriptures assume authority," this does not mean Christians live in isolation from other identities and multiple belongings.[64] Cahill explicitly notes her disagreement with more communitarian approaches: "perhaps against Hauerwas I believe the New Testament itself models transformative engagement of disciples with the world in a process of mutual influence that has positive as well as negative effects on Christian identity."[65] We see here also Cahill's use of sociocultural studies of the Bible that make clear the ways in which the values and beliefs of early Christian communities were formed in interaction with wider cultural influences, and "not in communitarian insulation from non-Christian values."[66] Cahill draws on the work of New Testament scholar Wayne Meeks in describing early Christians as "resocialized" into a new communal reality defined by discipleship to Christ, and yet still existing within "the world of the Roman empire and its subcultures—Jewish and gentile, village and urban—as the environments in which adherents to the Christian movement lived and thought."[67] Just as in the early Christian communities, Cahill views Christians today as having "a number of overlapping identities (cultural, political, familial), providing multiple understandings of themselves and

---

Goodness," 444).

[64]Cahill, "The New Testament and Ethics," 384.

[65]Cahill, "Gender and Strategies of Goodness," 444. Cahill provides an excellent overview of what she calls the "turn to community" in theological ethics, including figures like Stanley Hauerwas and John Howard Yoder. See Cahill, "The New Testament and Ethics," 385–88.

[66]Cahill, "The Bible and Christian Moral Practices," 3.

[67]Cahill, "Gender and Strategies of Goodness," 449. In this essay Cahill has an entire section where she presents scholarship showing the overlap between New Testament values and ideas and Greco-Roman and Jewish traditions, such as the parallel between Jesus's life and the asceticism of Cynic philosophers. For the concept of "resocialization," see Wayne A. Meeks, *The Origins of Christian Morality: The First Two Centuries* (New Haven, CT: Yale University Press, 1993), 1–36.

their world."[68] Given the porous nature of Christian community and identity, Cahill considers it an ongoing imperative for ethicists appropriating the Bible as an authoritative source to consider how the Christian moral tradition can "permit cross-traditional conversations about morality."[69] Thus, Cahill's method is a helpful model for ethicists seeking to shape a Christian ethic that can engage the public square while still being informed by traditional Christian sources.

Conclusion

Having discussed some of the key contributions and implications of Cahill's method, I would like to close with a few questions intended to continue scholarly engagement with the important issue of how Scripture functions as a source for Christian ethics. For ethicists who wish to draw heavily on sociohistorical research of the Bible, how does one pursue constructive purposes without distorting historical complexity and accuracy? For instance, does the normative emphasis on a pattern of transformation obscure the instances of oppression evident in the biblical text? Second, for ethicists who want to emphasize normative *patterns* or *stances* within Scripture taken as a whole (as contrasted with an emphasis on principles or rules), is a concept like "transformation" too vague to inform a contemporary ethic if it does not include *some* specific rules or practices (and likewise excludes some others)? Third, while the emphasis on pattern and sociohistorical context allows for legitimate diversity of moral praxis, it is also open to challenge where differences in praxis seem to be in direct contradiction to one another. For instance, on the issue of sexuality, how does a more progressive ethical approach respond to conservative Christian communities who argue precisely that their more traditional views of sexuality are meant to transform more liberal views of sexuality dominant in the United States today? That Cahill's method points scholars working today to such important questions evidences the enduring value of her work for the field of Christian ethics.

---

[68]Cahill, "The Bible and Christian Moral Practices," 4; see also Cahill, "Kingdom and Cross," 157; Lisa Sowle Cahill, "Canon, Authority, and Norms? Recent Studies in Biblical Ethics," *Interpretation* 40, no. 4 (October 1986): 414–17, at 417.
[69]Cahill, "The New Testament and Ethics," 394.

PART II

Christian Social Ethics

Throughout her career Lisa Sowle Cahill has engaged with an impressive breadth of issues within the field of social ethics. Furthermore, she addressed these pressing moral concerns with an ecumenical approach, while remaining grounded in the Roman Catholic moral tradition, especially Catholic social teaching. Thus, her moral reflection has shaped the development of both Catholic and Protestant social ethics in the twentieth century and provides resources for the twenty-first century as moral theologians, the Church, and societies continue to grapple with social ethics issues.

In this part, the contributors analyze some of the most prominent ethical challenges that Cahill's work addresses: just war, peacemaking, family, bioethics, healthcare, and the environment. In each chapter the authors seek to outline the major themes and sources found in Cahill's approach to ethical reflection, while also identifying ongoing challenges and future directions for engagement with these topics. Because of the depth and range of Cahill's writings in social ethics, these chapters expose the reader to the history of Christian social ethics, to prominent Roman Catholic and Protestant thinkers, and to awareness of wider societal, legal, and political viewpoints.

Catholic Social Teaching

Insights for a Fragmented U.S. Church

Raymond E. Ward

Writing in anticipation of the 2016 election, Catholic ethicist Michael Baxter pointed out a deep rift that had emerged in the last fifty years, cutting the American Catholic electorate in two: "The schism is between those Catholics in the United States who identify with liberal politics and those who identify with conservative politics in the secular sphere. The division is pervasive and deep, and it is tearing the U.S. Catholic community apart."[1] That such division exists is no surprise to anyone who has been paying attention to the Catholic Church's involvement in public life in the United States, and even less so to those familiar with the internal strife over ecclesial, liturgical, and ethical issues within the Church.

For many participants in this struggle, Catholic social teaching (CST) is at the center of the conflict. Historically, CST emerged during trenchant debates about Catholicism's response to modernity during the nineteenth century in Europe, and in many ways the current U.S. fragmentation is a continuation of those debates.[2] Catholic immigrants who came to the United States during this period benefitted from CST's support of poor urban industrial workers. Catholic immigrants tended to align with the Democratic Party, attracted in the twentieth century by a pro-labor platform and leaders like Al Smith and Franklin Roosevelt, an allegiance capped off by 78 percent of Catholics supporting John F. Kennedy for

---

[1] Michael Baxter, "Murray's Mistake: The Political Divisions a Theologian Failed to Foresee," *America* 209, no. 7 (September 23, 2013): 13–18, at 13.

[2] Julian Bourg, "The Enduring Tensions between Catholicism and Modernity," *Integritas* 6, no. 1 (Fall 2015): 1–22. It is worth noting that Pope Pius X's responses to these developments inspired some of the most trenchant traditionalist, if not *sede vacante*, Catholic groups in the United States today. See Chad J. Glendinning, "The Priestly Society of Saint Pius X: The Past, Present, and Possibilities for the Future," *Studia Canonica* 48, no. 2 (2014): 331–72.

president in 1960.[3] However, since then the Church in the United States has been riven over domestic debates on race, war, and abortion, dividing loyalties between different social agendas and political parties.[4] Today, Twitter and other social media exacerbate these trends, where Pope Francis's exhortations on the environment, immigration, and the economy are met with polarized responses at a time when Catholics "struggle with their coreligionists to define what is central and peripheral to the faith."[5]

Given the fact of this division among Catholics in the United States, and the role that CST has in these debates, we turn to the work of Lisa Sowle Cahill for insights into overcoming fragmentation for the common good. Cahill is known for "speaking across divides" and being a "bridge builder," a scholar whose work is "critical yet not divisive . . . [inviting] dialogue and debate in constructive ways."[6] Cahill's work in Christian ethics has consistently lived in the space between extremes, carefully forging together the links of Catholic thought and action to extend the Church's long tradition of love and justice. The result is a body of work that is exemplary not only in its ability to engage amid polarization on particular issues but to address the problem of division itself, as her work on peacebuilding is particularly demonstrative.

In this chapter I draw on Cahill's work to present three CST-based strategies that respond to current polarization and division: finding common ground, advocating for structural change, and undertaking shared action. While on their own each of these presents a viable strategy for addressing fragmentation among American Catholics, I argue that the third is particularly needed in our current context. Moreover, if joined together, these three approaches present a cohesive strategy of social

---

[3]John T. McGreevy, "Shifting Allegiances: Catholics, Democrats & the GOP," *Commonweal* 133, no. 16 (September 22, 2007): 14–19, at 14. For a sample of the ideological divide brewing beneath the election results for Kennedy, see William F. Buckley Jr., "The Catholic in the Modern World: A Conservative View," *Commonweal* 73, no. 10 (December 16, 1960): 307–10; William Clancy, "The Catholic in the Modern World: A Liberal View," *Commonweal* 73, no. 10 (December 16, 1960): 310–13.

[4]Massimo Faggioli, "A View from Abroad: The Shrinking Common Ground in the American Church," *America* 210, no. 6 (February 24, 2014): 20–23.

[5]Maureen K. Day, "From Consensus to Division: Tracing the Ideological Divide among American Catholic Women, 1950–1980," *Journal of Media and Religion* 16, no. 4 (2017): 129–40, at 129. See also Andrew Brown, "The War against Pope Francis," *The Guardian*, October 27, 2017. Also: Christopher Lamb, "Francis Agrees with His Critics: A Pope Can Be Wrong," *National Catholic Reporter* (April 19, 2018). For a broader assessment, see Mary Ellen Konieczny, Charles C. Camosy, and Tricia C. Bruce, eds., *Polarization in the U.S. Catholic Church: Naming the Wounds, Beginning to Heal* (Collegeville, MN: Liturgical Press, 2016).

[6]Michelle Gonzalez, "Lisa Sowle Cahill: Speaking across Divides," *National Catholic Reporter* (October 11–24, 2013): 3. See also William Bole, "No Labels, Please: Lisa Sowle Cahill's Middle Way," *Commonweal* 138, no. 1 (January 14, 2011): 9–15.

engagement, inspired by Catholic scholars and practitioners striving for justice and peace across the world, which is sorely needed for living the gospel today in the U.S. Catholic Church.

Strategy 1: CST as Dialogue—Seeking Common Ground

From the outset, Catholic social teaching has often found itself occupying a space between opposing poles of pressing social arguments. Pope Leo XIII's 1891 encyclical *Rerum novarum*, the first of the papal letters forming the main body of CST, addressed changing economic realities in a rapidly industrializing and politically tumultuous Europe. Released in the midst of ongoing debates over Catholicism's relation to modernity, Pope Leo's measured defense of workers' rights and private property charted a middle way between the interests of capitalists and socialists of the day. As ethicist Thomas Shannon observed, "No group, apparently, was satisfied with the positions of the encyclical. All [liberals, moderates, socialists, ultraconservatives, revolutionaries, etc.] thought it was lacking in critical issues and that it surrendered too much to 'the other side,' whoever that might be."[7]

This is a prime example of CST staking out middle ground between disparate positions in a diplomatic tone. Many of the early encyclicals and papal addresses adopted this stance toward the political conflicts of their day, perhaps due to Popes Pius XI and Pius XII having to negotiate the tenuous political circumstances of the Vatican within Italy and Europe at large until after the Second World War.[8] There is also an underlying commitment running throughout modern papal teaching to resist the kinds of rapid social transformation that can erode the humanizing communities that are needed for the care of persons in society, resulting in a culturally conservative starting point in papal writings on social concerns.

A third and vital reason for this moderate stance is the place of natural law in Catholic social teaching. Championed by Pope Leo XIII and established as authoritative in the 1917 Code of Canon Law, the phi-

---

[7]Thomas A. Shannon, "Commentary on *Rerum Novarum* (*The Condition of Labor*)," in *Modern Catholic Social Teaching: Commentaries and Interpretations*, ed. Kenneth R. Himes, OFM, with associate eds. Lisa Sowle Cahill, Charles E. Curran, David Hollenbach, SJ, and Thomas A. Shannon, 2nd ed. (Washington, DC: Georgetown University Press, 2018), 133–57, at 152–53.

[8]Christine Firer Hinze, "Commentary on *Quadragesimo anno* (*On Reconstruction of the Social Order*)," in Himes et al., *Modern Catholic Social Teaching*, 158–82, and John P. Langan, SJ, "The Christmas Message of Pius XII (1939–1945): Catholic Social Teaching in a Time of Extreme Crisis," in Himes et al., *Modern Catholic Social Teaching*, 183–98.

losophy and theology of Thomas Aquinas use a natural law framework for addressing questions of morality.[9] According to natural law thinking, rational creatures are able to discern God's eternal precepts about right action through a reasoned assessment of the created natural world, with Christians having the added benefit of supernatural guidance from Scripture and the Church. Taken up methodologically in CST, moral norms for society are, therefore, likewise grounded in human reason's participation in the divine law, meaning that "all people in principle can discern the basic requirements of justice."[10] Following Aristotle, Aquinas identified human virtue and right action as a mean between extremes,[11] and the function of practical reason and prudence is seeking out this mean.[12] Part of the philosophical makeup of CST, therefore, is to approach social concerns with a disposition toward moderating extreme positions and finding middle ground.

As a result, many of the principles that are used to sum up some of the core tenets of Catholic social teaching have this character of a middle way, presenting a Catholic "both-and" answer to vexing social challenges. Discussions of the common good in CST, for example, balance utilitarian-sounding concerns about the good of all with a simultaneous insistence on the good of each as well.[13] Likewise, the view within later CST that positive rights entail corresponding personal responsibilities binds together poles of political debates around property ownership and what is owed to one's neighbors.[14] Working in this way, CST has sustained a "big tent" with regard to social questions, allowing a wide range of views to find some proximity to Church teachings, while excluding the most extreme.

This open, conciliatory approach has defined much of Cahill's work as a Christian ethicist. She has taken up the commitment to speaking out of the Catholic tradition in the language of universally accessible and contextually responsible claims about justice for Catholic and non-Catholic audiences.[15] This commitment inflects her work on feminist ethics, for

---

[9]Stephen J. Pope, "Natural Law in Catholic Social Teachings," in Himes et al., *Modern Catholic Social Teaching*, 43–74.

[10]Lisa Sowle Cahill, "Catholic Social Teaching," in *The Cambridge Companion to Christian Political Theology*, ed. Craig Hovey and Elizabeth Phillips, Cambridge Companions to Religion (Cambridge: Cambridge University Press, 2015), 67–87, at 69.

[11]Thomas Aquinas, *Summa Theologiae* (hereafter, *ST*), trans. Fathers of the English Dominican Province (New York: Benzinger Brothers, 1947), I-II, q. 64, a. 1.

[12]*ST* II-II, q. 47, a. 7.

[13]David Hollenbach, SJ, *The Common Good and Christian Ethics*, New Studies in Christian Ethics 22, ed. Robin Gill (Cambridge: Cambridge University Press, 2002).

[14]Thomas Massaro, SJ, *Living Justice: Catholic Social Teaching in Action*, 2nd classroom ed. (Lanham, MD: Rowman and Littlefield, 2012), 92–95.

[15]For example, consider the closely argued discussion of Augustine and procreation with Gilbert Meilaender in Lisa Sowle Cahill, "Using Augustine in Contemporary Sexual Ethics:

example, finding common ground in gender equality across a wide range of traditions, as well as her efforts in bioethics to build consensus around access to healthcare for the poor.[16] Her research on the ethics of war and peace likewise negotiates between just war theory and pacifist positions, and on the topic of global ethics, Cahill has long sought to maintain an inclusive and coherent conversation about shared moral truths across cultures.[17]

Perhaps most exemplary of this kind of effort is Cahill's work on abortion. In addressing one of the thorniest moral and political issues that Catholics face, Cahill has focused on reducing the frequency of abortions by highlighting the Church's call to address the underlying causes of social problems. She writes, "Catholic discussions of abortion, sex, and gender should take their keynote from our great tradition of social encyclicals, with their optimistic confidence that reasonable public discourse is possible and can lead to greater consensus and social cooperation on justice issues."[18] In taking this approach, Cahill refuses to view social concerns narrowly in terms of a single issue or political goal, seeking instead to build consensus around a broadly shared set of values articulated by Cardinal Joseph L. Bernardin's consistent ethic of life.[19] This has meant that Cahill sometimes occupies a somewhat marginal place in partisan discussions, viewed as conservative by progressives and vice versa, but her appeal to reasonableness and optimism remains as relevant today as it was when she first made it over twenty-five years ago.[20]

A Response to Gilbert Meilaender," *Journal of Religious Ethics* 29, no. 1 (2001): 25–33.

[16]Lisa Sowle Cahill, "Catholic Feminists and Tradition: Renewal, Reinvention, Replacement," *Journal of the Society of Christian Ethics* 34, no. 2 (Winter 2014): 27–51, and Lisa Sowle Cahill, "Bioethics, the Gospel, and Political Engagement," *Christian Bioethics* 21, no. 3 (December 2015): 247–61.

[17]Lisa Sowle Cahill "Toward Global Ethics," *Theological Studies* 63, no. 2 (2002): 324–44.

[18]Lisa Sowle Cahill, "Abortion, Sex and Gender: The Church's Public Voice," *America* 168, no. 18 (May 22, 1993): 6–11, at 6. This article is an adaptation of her John Courtney Murray Forum lecture at Fordham Law School.

[19]Joseph L. Bernardin, "A Consistent Ethic of Life: Continuing the Dialogue," William Wade Lecture (Saint Louis University, March 11, 1984), cited in Kevin J. V. Mannara, CSB, "Bernardin and Bergoglio: What the Cardinal's Legacy Offers to a Church Led by Pope Francis," *New Theology Review* 28, no. 2 (March 2016): 38–46, at 41.

[20]Cahill has also been an active board member of the Catholic Common Ground Initiative's steering committee since 1998. The initiative, founded by the late Joseph Cardinal Bernardin of Chicago in 1996 at a time of worsening political division among Catholics in the United States, is built around a method for holding respectful dialogue across differences within the Catholic Church. See Joseph Bernardin, *Called to Be Church in a Time of Peril*, 1996, http://catholiccommonground.org/called-to-be-catholic-church-in-a-time-of-peril/. For a brief history and comparison to other historical moments of polarization, see Martin Zielinski, "The Common Ground Initiative: A Historical Perspective," *Chicago Studies* 45, no. 3 (2006): 280–97.

Strategy 2: CST as Advocacy—Fighting for Structural Change

Following the 2008 election, it seemed that there might be an opening for the kind of common-ground work Cahill sought. A legislative package was introduced in Congress, with support from pro-life and pro-choice members, offering a comprehensive approach to reducing the number of abortions sought by women. However, the opportunity for collaborative efforts to reduce abortion was lost in the intense partisan battles over the Affordable Care Act.[21] The culture-war debates that ensued also brought out incisive critiques from within the Church of this sort of common-ground approach, including criticism from some of the Church hierarchy.

In this fractious political and ecclesiastical climate, dialogue and consensus building can seem better suited to developing principles and visions than achieving tangible results for the common good.[22] There is an aspect of CST, however, that embraces the oppositional nature of politics by picking sides in a given struggle and rallying support for social change on that issue. Whereas CST as common ground is typified by a "both-and" approach to social conflict, this approach more clearly articulates a no response to unjust circumstances, and in turn is more able to move forward with a yes on specific policy issues. This is CST as advocacy.

Pope John XXIII's *Pacem in terris* (1963) is the first and perhaps boldest example of this approach. Written in the midst of nuclear tensions between the United States and the Soviet Union, the letter denounced war and posed an almost utopian vision for peace on earth.[23] Pope Paul VI's *Populorum progressio* (1967) inaugurated a series of encyclicals addressing international development, including Pope John Paul II's *Sollicitudo rei socialis* (1987) and Benedict XVI's *Caritas in veritate* (2009).[24] This recasting of economic concerns in terms of the development of the Global South effectively shifted modern CST away from *Rerum novarum* as the

---

[21]John Gehring, "Farther Than Ever from Common Ground? Absolutism and Abortion Politics," *Commonweal* (May 23, 2019), https://www.commonwealmagazine.org/farther-ever-common-ground.

[22]Cf. Charles Camosy, writing about a renewed consistent life ethic, choosing to "avoid making arguments for particular policies [since] doing so would distract us from the opportunity of the present moment ... [for developing] a new moral and political vision" (Charles C. Camosy, *Resisting Throwaway Culture: How a Consistent Life Ethic Can Unite a Fractured People* [Hyde Park, NY: New City Press, 2019], 23).

[23]Drew Christiansen, SJ, "Commentary on *Pacem in terris* (*Peace on Earth*)," in Himes et al., *Modern Catholic Social Teaching*, 226–52.

[24]Cahill, "Catholic Social Teaching," 79. She refers to Allan Figueroa Deck, SJ, "Commentary on *Populorum progressio* (*On the Development of Peoples*)," in Himes et al., *Modern Catholic Social Teaching*, 302–25.

touchstone encyclical for discussions of economic justice. In a similar way, the most recent addition to the CST canon, Pope Francis's *Laudato si'* (2015), builds on many of these themes and concerns with a focus on environmental aspects, development, and global disparity.[25] Starting with *Pacem in terris*, and characteristic of this CST-as-advocacy approach, these encyclicals are each addressed to people of goodwill, offer a strong critique of a human-made crisis, and use rights-based discussions to respond to the signs of the times.

Several factors supported this turn to more direct advocacy in CST. For one, John XXIII pursued a policy of political disengagement in Italian politics and supported religious liberty abroad following World War II, freeing the papacy to act as a moral rather than a political leader.[26] Developments in neo-Scholastic philosophy and theology also allowed more creative explorations of human flourishing in the context of domestic pluralism and global diversity.[27] But a turn to the world by the Second Vatican Council truly validated this activist approach in CST, opening the way for more explicit taking of sides in social conflict around the world. This is also clear in the CST principles that have been more fully developed since the Council. The preferential option for the poor and vulnerable, solidarity, and care for creation deny easy, middle-way approaches to social problems.[28]

The application of these and other CST principles, however, has largely been left to others, and Cahill belongs to the first generation of Catholic ethicists to take up the task since Vatican II. With regard to economic and development questions, for example, Pope John Paul II deferred to others for specific prescriptions, arguing that the Church does not have the expertise to offer "technical" solutions to these problems.[29] Instead,

---

[25] Christiana Zenner Peppard, "Commentary on *Laudato si'* (*On Care for Our Common Home*)," in Himes et al., *Modern Catholic Social Teaching*, 515–50. Also, Barrett Turner, "*Pacis Progressio*: How Francis' Four New Principles Develop Catholic Social Teaching into Catholic Social Praxis," *Journal of Moral Theology* 6, no. 1 (2017): 112–29.

[26] J. Bryan Hehir, "Papal Foreign Policy," *Foreign Policy*, no. 78 (1990): 26–48.

[27] Pope, "Natural Law in Catholic Social Teachings," 53. Also David Hollenbach, SJ, "*Pacem in Terris* and Human Rights," *Journal of Catholic Social Thought* 10, no. 1 (Winter 2013): 5–15.

[28] Stephen J. Pope, "Proper and Improper Partiality and the Preferential Option for the Poor," *Theological Studies* 54, no. 2 (June 1993): 242–71; Meghan J. Clark, "Pope Francis and the Christological Dimensions of Solidarity in Catholic Social Teaching," *Theological Studies* 80, no. 1 (March 2019): 102–22; Pablo A. Blanco González, "*Laudato Si'*: Care for Creation at the Center of a New Social Issue," *Journal of Religious Ethics* 46, no. 3 (September 2018): 425–40.

[29] John Paul II, Encyclical Letter on the Social Concern of the Church, *Sollicitudo rei socialis* (1987), no. 41, www.vatican.va. See also Charles E. Curran, Kenneth R. Himes, OFM, and Thomas A. Shannon, "Commentary on *Sollicitudo rei socialis* (*On Social Concern*)," in Himes et al., *Modern Catholic Social Teaching*, 429–49. There is variation in

scholars, activists, and others are called to join the authors of official CST to expound on the Catholic worldview and its implications for social life. Together, they formed another, broader sense of "unofficial" CST: Catholic social *thought*.[30] As a lay American woman, Cahill joined a male and predominantly European set of popes, bishops, and priests in deliberating about Catholic social justice following the Council. Her work with Catholic and non-Catholic peers of the day also helped set the tone for ecumenism and interdisciplinarity in contemporary Catholic ethics.[31]

While we have already seen how Cahill favors a common-ground approach on a wide range of concerns, she has nonetheless taken up advocacy positions on a number of issues. Though her positions may seem moderate today, her early work on feminist ethics was groundbreaking at a time when the Catholic hierarchy viewed it as radical, as was her leadership on the issue of healthcare access within the context of U.S. politics. She also clearly took sides in the clergy sexual abuse crisis, indicting the institutional bureaucracy that fostered and hid that abuse in Boston and beyond.[32] Perhaps more significant, though, are Cahill's contributions to theological method in Catholic social ethics, which have supported a more radical expansion of the activist vein in CST. First, following Vatican Council II, a widening division emerged between the deductive natural law method used for Catholic personal ethics, and the more inductive "see-judge-act" approach used in Catholic social ethics.[33] By extending the methodology of CST into family ethics, sexual ethics, and bioethics, Cahill sought to find common ground in these areas but also set the table for a conflict over a bifurcation of method.[34] Second, Cahill has explored the ways in which personal experience necessarily and rightly informs moral decisions.[35] In this research she helped open the

---

this tendency as, for example, Benedict offers some concrete discussion of labor unions, finance, consumer associations, social media, and biotechnology in *Caritas in veritate*; and Francis critiques carbon credits in *Laudato si'*, no. 171. See also Celia Deane-Drummond, "*Laudato Si'* and the Natural Sciences: An Assessment of Possibilities and Limits," *Theological Studies* 77, no. 2 (2016): 392–415, at 396.

[30] John A. Coleman, SJ, "The Future of Catholic Social Thought," in Himes et al., *Modern Catholic Social Teaching*, 610–36, at 611.

[31] Lisa Sowle Cahill, "James M. Gustafson and Catholic Theological Ethics," *Journal of Moral Theology* 1, no. 1 (2012): 92–115.

[32] Lisa Sowle Cahill, "A Crisis of Clergy, Not of Faith," *New York Times*, March 6, 2002, A21.

[33] Bob Pennington, "The Cardijn Canon: A Method of Theological Praxis in Contemporary Catholic Social Teaching," *Praxis: An Interdisciplinary Journal of Faith and Justice* 1, no. 2 (2018): 85–103.

[34] Lisa Sowle Cahill, "Commentary on *Familiaris consortio* (Apostolic Exhortation on the Family)," in Himes et al., *Modern Catholic Social Teaching*, 377–402.

[35] Susan L. Secker, "Human Experience and Women's Experience: Resources for Catholic Ethics," *Annual of the Society of Christian Ethics* 11 (1991): 133–50.

way for including previously marginalized voices in CST, and Catholic ethicists today are advocating for social change out of a wide range of human experiences, as black Catholics, for example, or as people with disabilities or transgendered persons.[36] Thanks in part to these methodological developments, an advocacy-oriented approach is flourishing in U.S. Catholic social ethics today.

Strategy 3: CST as Shared Action—Building Community for Justice

What are we to make of these two strategies for responding to a fractured Catholic Church in the U.S.? On the one hand, those committed to finding common ground seem to have had some success in creating dialogue among Catholics, though less so in achieving meaningful social change. On the other hand, while Catholic advocacy has been more effective in obtaining results, its tendency to focus on single issues can exacerbate fragmentation as it seeks not to bind up old wounds but to press forward to a better future.

Given these seemingly disparate options, Cahill's recent work offers a third strategy, embodied in the important role that shared communal activity can have in the transformative work of peacebuilding.[37] Looking to the personal change needed for reconciliation, she writes, "Profound changes in worldview and attitudes do not occur unless there is the kind of practical validation of social trust that occurs when people share in activities together around shared goals."[38] Cahill's work has long taken social practice into account, largely as a way to contextualize moral judgments, framing both individual agency and values, appreciating the way they empower or limit action, and shape evaluation.[39] In her peacebuilding work, though, she highlights the potential for developing new social practices that can have a transformative impact on society.

Social practice and collective action have never been far from the heart

---

[36]See, for example, Bryan N. Massingale, *Racial Justice and the Catholic Church* (Maryknoll, NY: Orbis Books, 2010); Mary Jo Iozzio, "Radical Dependence and the *Imago Dei*: Bioethical Implications of Access to Healthcare for People with Disabilities," *Christian Bioethics* 23, no. 3 (December 2017): 234–60; Craig A. Ford Jr., "Transgender Bodies, Catholic Schools, and a Queer Natural Law Theology of Exploration," *Journal of Moral Theology* 7, no. 1 (2018): 70–98.

[37]For more extensive treatment of this topic in this volume, see the chapters by Kate Ann Jackson-Meyer and Angela Senander.

[38]Lisa Sowle Cahill, *Blessed Are the Peacemakers: Pacifism, Just War, and Peacebuilding* (Minneapolis: Fortress Press, 2019), 340.

[39]Lisa Sowle Cahill, "'Abortion Pill' RU 486: Ethics, Rhetoric, and Social Practice," *Hastings Center Report* 17, no. 5 (1987): 5–8.

of CST. It rests, in large part, on the long tradition of Catholic charitable work stretching back past the work of early modern saints, past medieval religious orders and lay confraternities, to the welcoming Christian communities of New Testament times.[40] When addressing a new set of modern social concerns, *Rerum novarum* inspired waves of local social engagement under the umbrella name of Catholic Action.[41] These initiatives took a wide variety of forms throughout the Catholic world and influenced the writing of successive CST, not least through the formation of a youth named Giovanni Battista Montini, known later as Pope Paul VI. Other forms of Catholic social engagement—from the Catholic Worker movement to innumerable Catholic nonprofits doing work in education, healthcare, and international development—are all types of Catholic social practice.[42] In these we find a third version of CST: beside both official Catholic social *teaching* and the wider collection of Catholic social *thought*, the Catholic social *tradition* includes all these charitable efforts and social initiatives of Catholics, lay and religious, around the world.[43] Some rightly raise concerns about a too-easy embrace of service that neglects systemic and structural concerns. Instead, service must be tethered to advocacy, with both rooted in and striving for solidarity and building a community for justice.[44]

The types of action Cahill presents are often purposeful communal efforts at healing, but sometimes the focus is as much on shared interests or values as it is on direct dialogue or reconciliation. In the same vein, Eboo Patel, founder of the Interfaith Youth Core (IFYC), writes about a 2015 garbage collection campaign in Beirut that brought together disparate religious groups following Lebanon's civil war.[45] IFYC works with colleges to foster greater mutual appreciation across diverse faith backgrounds. One major component of their strategy is to delay interfaith *dialogue* in favor of interfaith *cooperation*. They argue that dialogue is most fruitful after some degree of familiarity, trust, and mutual respect is developed by undertaking "compelling projects that highlight shared values and create

---

[40] James F. Keenan, SJ, *The Works of Mercy: The Heart of Catholicism*, 3rd ed. (Lanham, MD: Rowman & Littlefield, 2017).

[41] John Pollard, "Pius XI's Promotion of the Italian Model of Catholic Action in the World-Wide Church," *Journal of Ecclesiastical History* 63, no. 4 (October 2012): 758–84.

[42] Kevin J. Ahern, *Structures of Grace: Catholic Organizations Serving the Global Common Good* (Maryknoll, NY: Orbis Books, 2015).

[43] Erin M. Brigham, *See, Judge, Act: Catholic Social Teaching and Service Learning* (Winona, MN: Anselm Academic Press, 2013).

[44] Fred Kammer, SJ, *Doing Faithjustice: An Introduction to Catholic Social Thought* (Mahwah, NJ: Paulist Press, 2004), and Suzanne C. Toton, *Justice Education: From Service to Solidarity* (Milwaukee: Marquette University Press, 2006).

[45] Eboo Patel, *Interfaith Leadership: A Primer* (Boston: Beacon Press, 2016), 97.

the space for powerful sharing, storytelling, and relationship building."[46] Applying these insights to divisions within the Church, U.S. Catholics should engage in service together with other Catholics with whom they disagree. This is nothing new: Catholic schools and confirmation classes do it, and it reinforces the Church's shared values, builds bonds of community among the participants, and sets the table for deeper engagement together in the future.[47]

This kind of shared action opens possibilities for relationship across difference among the "participants," but this is ultimately secondary to the work that is being done in and through them. Service guided by contemporary CST draws Catholics of all backgrounds into new settings to engage with global challenges, inviting them to cooperate across racial, ethnic, and religious divides as well as political ones. And in those experiences of service, Pope Francis asks us to look for moments of encounter, not only of one another across divisions, but of "Jesus who serves, who helps ... who is compassionate with all those in need ... including ourselves."[48] In a culture of *encuentro*, the divide between servant and served is subverted as well.

Conclusion: CST as Communal Praxis

Taking inspiration from the work of Cahill and from CST (in all three senses of the term: Catholic social teaching, thought, and tradition), this chapter has proposed three strategies for responding to political and ecclesial fragmentation in the U.S. Catholic Church: finding common ground, advocating for structural change, and undertaking shared action. These strategies may seem at odds with one another, particularly since the common-ground approach aims for consensus, while the advocacy-oriented approach can lead to even greater polarization. The shared action approach takes from both, working toward establishing trust by advancing communal activity based on simple, shared values and interests.

Based on my own work with interfaith cooperation and community organizing, these three approaches seem less like separate strategies and more like moments in what is called the "organizing cycle." The setting of a common-ground agenda through dialogue is crucial for solidifying one's coalition, and pushing for tangible victories through activism and

---

[46]Ibid., 143.

[47]Andrew Herr and Jason King, "Does Service and Volunteering Affect Catholic Identity?," *Praxis: An Interdisciplinary Journal of Faith and Justice* 1, no. 2 (Fall 2018): 104–22.

[48]Pope Francis, "Morning Meditation in the Chapel of the *Domus Sanctae Marthae*: For a Culture of Encounter" (September 23, 2016), www.vatican.va.

advocacy is how structural change is realized. These are what Faith in Action's Gordon Whitman calls the "Base" and "Power" conversations in the cycle. Missing, though, are the initial "Purpose," "Story," and "Team" conversations in which organizers find their own footing for the journey ahead.[49] Experiences of shared service and encounter are needed to clarify the deeper purpose and identity out of which we act together for change. In the view of Stephen J. Pope, "Community organizing . . . provides the most effective practical venue for Catholic communities that want to take seriously the Church's commitment to social justice."[50] Taken together, the approaches of shared action, dialogue, and advocacy offer a complete community organizing tool kit. They offer to U.S. Catholics, in the midst of deep divisions, a form of communal praxis that is grounded in and can contribute to the ongoing work of CST.[51]

Perhaps more importantly, though, this renewed praxis might be able to draw U.S. Catholics out of a deadening parochialism and into encounter with a much wider range of experiences in the world. So much of the fragmented Catholic conversation in the United States takes place within a narrow view that does not often leave one's own (increasingly homogenous) neighborhood. Baxter, among others, calls for deeper engagement in "experiments in face-to-face community where democracy is not an empty slogan: unions, buying cooperatives, houses of hospitality, credit unions and so on."[52] And yet, even beyond this, Cahill's work demonstrates for U.S. Catholics the kind of engagement for global justice that has been championed by CST since John XXIII. This call for Catholics to engage across parishes and dioceses, across racial and ethnic lines, across religious lines and national borders, is what has sustained Cahill's ability to work for greater unity in the Church and greater justice in the world, and is the future of CST.

---

[49] Whitman devotes a chapter to each of these five concepts in his book. See Gordon Whitman, *Stand Up! How to Get Involved, Speak Out, and Win in a World on Fire* (Oakland, CA: Berrett-Koehler Publishers, 2018).

[50] Stephen J. Pope, "Integral Human Development: From Paternalism to Accompaniment," *Theological Studies* 80, no. 1 (2019): 123–47, at 147.

[51] I.e., a form of reflective action that seeks social change by discerning and acting upon a theory-laden social environment. Cf.: "A revolution is achieved with neither verbalism nor activism, but rather with praxis, that is, *reflection* and *action* directed at the structures to be transformed" (Paulo Freire, *Pedagogy of the Oppressed*, trans. Myra Bergman Ramos [New York: Continuum, 1970], 126).

[52] Michael Baxter and William T. Cavanaugh, "More Deeply into the World: Michael Baxter and William T. Cavanaugh Respond to 'A View from Abroad,' by Massimo Faggioli (2/24)," *America* 210, no. 14 (April 21, 2014): 8.

Just War, Peace, and Peacemaking

Moral Dilemmas

Kate Ann Jackson-Meyer

War is the paradigmatic moral dilemma. In a moral dilemma, an agent ought to do actions A and B, yet is unable to fulfill both obligations.[1] When lives are at stake and war is considered, killing and refusing to kill are both failures to uphold Jesus's commands to refrain from violence and to protect the vulnerable. However, war is rarely regarded as a moral dilemma in Christian theological ethics, which tends to deny the possibility for dilemmas. Rather, pacifism and the just war tradition dominate discussions about the ethics of war and peace. For Christian pacifists, the gospels' demands for nonviolence are nonnegotiable, while Christian just war theorists make space for compromise in an effort to combat sin.

Lisa Sowle Cahill comes to regard pacifism as the most genuine expression of the gospels, yet she defends the usefulness of the just war tradition in light of our fallen world, and her later work focuses on peacebuilding. These might seem like disparate positions to take, but these surprising views encapsulate Cahill's most significant contributions to the ethics of war and peace. To the extent that over the course of her career she defends just war, Cahill offers a necessary and important version that is as slow to employ violence as it is deeply informed by Cahill's appreciation for pacifism. Over her career, Cahill has become increasingly concerned about the moral ambiguity of killing and refusing to kill, and as a result she eventually comes to critique both just war theory and pacifism for ignoring "'irreducible moral dilemmas.'"[2] This

---

[1] For an excellent overview, see Christopher Gowans, "The Debate on Moral Dilemmas," in *Moral Dilemmas*, ed. Christopher W. Gowans (New York: Oxford University Press, 1987), 3–33.

[2] Lisa Sowle Cahill, *Blessed Are the Peacemakers: Pacifism, Just War, and Peacemaking* (Minneapolis: Fortress Press, 2019), viii.

explains her turn to peacebuilding. In peacebuilding, Christians work to bring about social transformation.

Moral Dilemmas

Moral dilemmas grapple with hard cases.[3] Traditional Roman Catholic moral theology vis-à-vis Thomas Aquinas denies dilemmas and instead relies on strategies such as the principle of double effect (PDE) and the hierarchy of goods to deal with difficult ethical situations. But these approaches fall short of resolving all hard cases. Cahill develops her own concepts—"sinning bravely" and "adverse virtues"—before later accepting the possibility for moral dilemmas.[4]

Strategies to Solve Hard Cases

The PDE is often invoked to justify killing in war. Rooted in Aquinas's reflection on murder and culpability, the PDE follows Aquinas's claim that one action may have multiple effects—the intended and the unintended effects.[5] The PDE, as used today, asserts that a moral act is permissible so long as the action is good or neutral, the evil is not directly intended, the good is not achieved through the evil effect, and the evil caused is proportionate to the good effect(s).[6] According to the PDE, a small number of civilian deaths caused by bombing a military target is permissible because the civilian deaths are unintended and proportionate consequences.

The PDE has been criticized for being overly permissive, especially in war when considering noncombatant deaths.[7] The major problem, in my view, is that it is impossible to identify consequences that are foreseen, yet unintended. Is it not the case that when determining certain deaths as likely and foreseeable outcomes of a bombing that those deaths are,

---

[3] For in-depth analyses of moral dilemmas, moral dilemmas in relation to Aquinas, Christian moral imperatives, and a proposal for tragic dilemmas within Christian virtue ethics, see Katherine Jackson-Meyer, *Tragic Dilemmas and Virtue: A Christian Feminist View* (PhD diss., Boston College, 2018).

[4] Lisa Sowle Cahill, *Between the Sexes: Foundations for a Christian Ethics of Sexuality* (Philadelphia: Fortress Press, 1985), 149; Lisa Sowle Cahill, *Theological Bioethics: Participation, Justice, and Change*, Moral Traditions, ed. James F. Keenan, SJ (Washington, DC: Georgetown University Press, 2005), 118–20.

[5] Thomas Aquinas, *Summa Theologiae* (hereafter, *ST*), trans. Fathers of the English Dominican Province (New York: Benzinger Brothers, 1947), II-II, q. 64, a. 7.

[6] John C. Ford, "The Morality of Obliteration Bombing," *Theological Studies* 5, no. 3 (September 1, 1944): 261–309, at 289.

[7] Ibid., 289–309.

in fact, intended? Furthermore, elsewhere Aquinas offers a distinction between foreseen consequences and unforeseen consequences, suggesting that this may have been operating as a distinction when discussing the case of murder.[8] This raises doubt about insisting on a category of actions that are somehow foreseeable, yet unintended.

The hierarchy of goods is another Thomistic strategy to adjudicate hard cases. It claims that all goods are ordered toward God in a hierarchy and that practical reason is needed to discern the highest good when goods conflict.[9] But the hierarchy of goods falls short when goods of equal value are at odds—for instance, when deciding which child hostages to save.

Early in her career, Cahill developed her own approaches to dealing with hard cases. In her work on sexual ethics, Cahill explains that "sinning bravely" describes those times when the best course of action is also considered a sin. She defines *sinning bravely* as "causing some evil for what is perceived as an *obligatory* good."[10] She writes, "I am not willing to disallow in principle the possibility of moral conflicts so radical that the agents caught in them cannot be absolved by refraining from the 'direct' causation of material evil, by taking as an absolute the principle 'Do no harm,' or by refusing to decide."[11] In this way, Cahill draws out how difficult situations sometimes call for wrongdoing.

Later, Cahill introduced "adverse virtues." Unlike sinning bravely, these virtues do not involve moral transgressions. The concept arises out of Cahill's discomfort over a bioethics case from the Philippines that relies on the PDE.[12] When a mother is reluctant to remove the respirator of her seventeen-year-old son who is being kept alive at a financial cost the family cannot endure, the mother (and readers) are "'reassured'" that PDE ensures that the right decision is being made.[13] Cahill laments that this analysis ignores the structural issues that render finances burdensome. She harshly criticizes the PDE used in this way as "not only futile but inhumane" and a "self-deceiving abdication of responsibility for the larger factors of unjust resource distribution that forced her [the mother's] choice."[14] Cahill worries that the PDE can obscure societal injustices that place agents in difficult

---

[8]*ST*, I-II, q. 20, a. 5. See also Rosemary B. Kellison, "Impure Agency and the Just War: A Feminist Reading of Right Intention," *Journal of Religious Ethics* 43, no. 2 (2015): 317–41, at 328.

[9]*ST*, I-II, q. 94, a. 2. See also Daniel J. McInerny, *The Difficult Good: A Thomistic Approach to Moral Conflict and Human Happiness* (New York: Fordham University Press, 2006).

[10]Cahill, *Between the Sexes*, 149.

[11]Ibid.

[12]Cahill, *Theological Bioethics*, 118–20.

[13]Ibid., 118.

[14]Ibid., 119.

situations. A possible implication of this critique is that the PDE may perpetuate injustices because society does not have to confront problems when individual agents are given a "way out" of hard cases.

Cahill offers "adverse virtues" as an alternative approach. These occur "when choices represent human attempts to act with integrity in the midst of unavoidable conflict and adversity."[15] Adverse virtues are enacted when there are no virtuous means and when right actions seem to fall short of flourishing. The force of this concept is twofold: it names and indicts unjust social structures that compel agents to act in difficult situations, and it underscores that right action is still possible.

But adverse virtues are incomplete. As ethicist Charlie Curran critiques, this concept needs further specification.[16] And in my view, Cahill is unclear about how adverse virtues and the PDE interact. Do they replace the need for the PDE, or are they used with the PDE? Also, the concept is vague. Sometimes Cahill uses adverse virtues to refer to cases that would be better described as (what she would later recognize as) irreducible moral dilemmas.[17] Other times she uses adverse virtues to highlight unfortunate and unanticipated consequences of bioethical decisions.[18]

Sinning bravely and adverse virtues both represent Cahill's early attempts to wrestle with hard choices in difficult circumstances. Later, she turns to the concept of irreducible moral dilemmas. While moral dilemmas do not encompass all the cases she covers with the earlier ideas, it does combine the most significant issues that the earlier concepts raise—arduous circumstances that are the result of structural injustices, agents courageously performing moral transgressions, and agents doing the right action during great hardship.

Understanding Moral Dilemmas

Moral dilemmas occur when agents cannot fulfill competing obligations. Within the philosophical literature on moral dilemmas, some theorists affirm a distinction between dilemmas with equally impermissible options and dilemmas with one impermissible action that can be justified over the other impermissible choice(s).[19] Theology has tended to resist

---

[15]Ibid.

[16]Charles E. Curran, *Diverse Voices in Modern US Moral Theology*, Moral Traditions, ed. David Cloutier, Kristin Heyer, and Andrea Vicini, SJ (Washington, DC: Georgetown University Press, 2018), 158.

[17]Cahill, *Theological Bioethics*, 190.

[18]Ibid., 162, 149, 167.

[19]Rosalind Hursthouse, *On Virtue Ethics* (New York: Oxford University Press, 2001), 43–87.

the possibility of dilemmas (using the strategies described above) because only a seemingly unjust God would place humans in impossible moral situations. However, this position ignores the reality that many moral dilemmas occur for the same reason many ethical issues arise—sinful human action. War is a prime example. Theology has also tended to follow traditional philosophy in rejecting moral dilemmas because they are nonsensical. How can an agent be obligated to fulfill a requirement that is impossible to fulfill? This view in great part relies on the logic concept "'ought' implies 'can,'" which claims that agents are only morally required to fulfill obligations that are able to be fulfilled.[20] So, in the situations of perceived moral dilemmas, if doing A makes it impossible to then also do B, the obligation to do B falls away.

But for philosopher Bernard Williams, the unmet obligation is not necessarily eliminated.[21] Williams identifies feelings of regret following moral events that he claims are indicative of enduring obligations. As theorists since Williams have argued, this "remainder" may occur because some moral obligations are, essentially, moral absolutes.[22] As such, these obligations do not disappear when they are not acted on even when they are impossible to fulfill. What this means for Christian ethics remains unclear, as Williams argues from a secular, relativist standpoint. In my view, nonnegotiable Christian obligations arise from relationships and the needs of others. These obligations occur and persist because others' needs do not dissolve even when we are physically or logically unable to meet them.

Cahill contributes to theological ethics by arguing for the possibility of moral dilemmas within a theological framework. She focuses on "irreducible moral dilemmas," defined as "situations in which there is no available course of action that does not somehow involve the agent in wrongdoing, *even though* the action on the whole may be justified."[23] In an irreducible moral dilemma an agent performs a moral transgression even when doing the best action because the situation is such that it is impossible to avoid wrongdoing, yet exactly what this means remains vague.

Cahill identifies the Christian commands of nonviolence and protect-

---

[20]Explained well in Terrance McConnell, "Moral Dilemmas," in *The Stanford Encyclopedia of Philosophy*, ed. Edward N. Zalta (Stanford, CA: Metaphysics Research Lab, Stanford University, 2014), https://plato.stanford.edu/archives/fall2014/entries/moral-dilemmas/.

[21]Bernard Williams, "Ethical Consistency," in *Problems of the Self: Philosophical Papers 1956–1972* (New York: Cambridge University Press, 1973), 166–86.

[22]Lisa Tessman, *Moral Failure: On the Impossible Demands of Morality* (New York: Oxford University Press, 2015).

[23]Cahill, *Blessed Are the Peacemakers*, viii.

ing the vulnerable as nonnegotiable moral obligations, but does little to define or elucidate the demand to protect the vulnerable.[24] Despite Cahill's position, the Christian tradition has not unequivocally supported either as moral absolutes. As the next part of this chapter shows, there is much debate regarding how to live out Jesus's example—and, as seen earlier with the PDE, killing can be justified under certain conditions.

Cahill argues that the existence of irreducible moral dilemmas is supported by the inherent ambivalences and tensions within the thought of just war thinkers and pacifists. This innovative approach is also discussed in the next part of this chapter. However, her line of argumentation leaves open some theoretical issues, particularly culpability. Proponents of moral dilemmas share no consensus on whether or to what extent agents are morally culpable when acting amid a moral dilemma. Cahill proposes that agents ought to accept "some degree of moral culpability," but the conditions and limits of this are vague.[25] She distinguishes between complicity that involves agent "cooperation" and dilemmas that involve direct perpetration.[26] Moral responsibility occurs in moral dilemmas because agents directly perpetrate an action. She also differentiates between moral dilemmas that individuals face and "dirty hands" that describe the dilemmas faced by those involved in politics.[27] She acknowledges that agents and groups should participate in some kind of reconciliation after a moral dilemma, but she does not specify what that is, how it works, or how it relates to culpability.[28] Following philosopher Rosalind Hursthouse, Cahill asserts that participation in a moral dilemma can "mar" an agent.[29] This occurs because agents have participated in actions that "undermine the self's sense of moral integrity," but Cahill does not say much on how this comes about.[30]

If moral dilemmas are plausible, then they can encompass a range of actions—from conflicting social plans to dire situations. This gamut is cited by the detractors of the concept of moral dilemmas who worry about the efficacy of ethics if so many moral events can be considered dilemmatic. Cahill handles this in two ways—by limiting her discussion to irreducible moral dilemmas and by focusing on extreme cases marked by the demands to protect life and the vulnerable. In my view, she is dis-

---

[24]Ibid., 161–62.
[25]Ibid., 162.
[26]Ibid., 124.
[27]Ibid., 125.
[28]Ibid., 128–32.
[29]Hursthouse, *On Virtue Ethics,* 74–87. Referred to in Cahill, *Blessed Are the Peacemakers,* 126, 163.
[30]Cahill, *Blessed Are the Peacemakers,* 163.

cussing a particular kind of moral dilemma—the kind that include great loss, and so are properly called "tragic dilemmas."[31] This adds a specificity and pointedness to Cahill's project.

Just War and Pacifism

Christian just war theorists and Christian pacifists regard themselves as honoring Jesus's example. Pacifism deems violence as anathema to the gospels, while just war makes space for the possibility that violence is unfortunately necessary in a world marred by sin. Cahill offers fresh insights into Augustine, Aquinas, Dietrich Bonhoeffer, and Dorothy Day by using tensions in their work to defend the possibility for irreducible moral dilemmas. She proposes an unconventional vision of just war that is appreciative of pacifist ideals and that constrains violence.

Jesus and the Kingdom

Jesus's commitment to nonviolence is clear throughout the gospels, especially in the Sermon on the Mount and the Lord's Prayer.[32] Jesus preached to love enemies, to turn the other cheek, and to follow the example of the Good Samaritan. Importantly, and instructively, he resisted violence when the authorities apprehended him. The early Christians followed a pacifist lifestyle, but this became less tenable, or at least more complicated, after Christians garnered more responsibilities and political power beginning with the reign of Constantine.

Jesus's kingdom is both "already" and "not yet" present.[33] Emphasizing the "not yet" aspect highlights the difficulty of totally cohering with Christian expectations in this world, rendering war and violence as sometimes permissible. But overemphasizing this incompleteness can eliminate the need for restraint. Alternatively, some pacifists with a "not yet" emphasis see the political realm as unlikely to change and thus conclude that nonviolent ideals must be lived out in the Church only. On the other hand, many pacifists regard nonviolence as possible precisely because God's kingdom is near.

---

[31]Hursthouse, *On Virtue Ethics*, 71–87; see also Jackson-Meyer, *Tragic Dilemmas and Virtue*.

[32]Mt 5 and 6. See Cahill, *Blessed Are the Peacemakers*, 55–70; see also Lisa Sowle Cahill, *Love Your Enemies: Discipleship, Pacifism, and Just War Theory* (Minneapolis: Fortress, 1994), 26–41.

[33]Cahill, *Blessed Are the Peacemakers*, 21–26, 42–55; see also Cahill, *Love Your Enemies*, 15–26.

Pacifism

Pacifism takes different forms and is further complicated by Cahill's attention to how difficult it is to live out. Influential contemporary forms of pacifism come from the works of John Howard Yoder and Stanley Hauerwas, who preach the inviolability of Jesus's example of nonviolence.[34] For them, the Church and world are at odds. From this standpoint, pacifism has merit not only because it is the most authentic expression of the gospel, but also because it shows the world what it means to be church. Thus, pacifism is efficacious not when it eliminates violence, but when it stands in opposition to violent ways of living. Other pacifists see themselves as integrated in society. Cahill describes this type of pacifism as "empathetic or compassionate," and it can be seen in activists like Walter Rauschenbusch, Dorothy Day, and Thomas Merton.[35] For instance, Day lived out her pacifist commitments by creating Catholic Worker houses where she lived in solidarity with the poor and marginalized.[36]

The strength of pacifism is its fidelity to the gospels. Even though she is not a pacifist, Cahill believes that pacifism comes out of the experience of conversion and is aligned with Jesus's message. She asserts that, unlike the just war tradition, pacifist approaches share the belief that nonviolence is not an "extrinsic duty," but rather a mode of being, "a living out of that which has *already* transpired."[37] And despite being criticized for aligning Christian pacifism with discipleship, Cahill defends her view that pacifism is a better way of adhering to the gospels. In her later work Cahill writes, "I remain unconvinced that just war embodies the gospel as well as pacifism."[38]

Despite this praise, Cahill makes a major contribution to pacifist studies by arguing that pacifism is unfeasible at times. She uses this assumption to illustrate that it is morally problematic to subscribe to nonviolence when inaction leads to loss of life. For instance, she reflects on Bonhoeffer, who was a pacifist, but who was part of a movement to assassinate

---

[34]Key writings include Stanley Hauerwas, *The Peaceable Kingdom: A Primer in Christian Ethics* (Notre Dame, IN: University of Notre Dame Press, 1991); John Howard Yoder, *The Politics of Jesus*, 2nd ed. (Grand Rapids: Eerdmans, 1994). Yoder's contributions are undercut by his egregious acts of sexual abuse. See Karen V. Guth, "Doing Justice to the Complex Legacy of John Howard Yoder: Restorative Justice Resources in Witness and Feminist Ethics," *Journal of the Society of Christian Ethics* 35, no. 2 (2015): 119–39.

[35]Lisa Sowle Cahill, "Theological Contexts of Just War Theory and Pacifism: A Response to J. Bryan Hehir," *Journal of Religious Ethics* 20, no. 2 (Fall 1992): 259–65, at 262.

[36]Dorothy Day, *The Long Loneliness* (New York: HarperOne, 1997).

[37]Cahill, "Theological Contexts of Just War Theory and Pacifism," 262.

[38]Cahill, *Blessed Are the Peacemakers*, x.

Hitler.[39] Despite his belief that nonviolence is critical to following Jesus, Bonhoeffer was compelled to act violently to protect the lives of many. The principle of nonviolence did not trump his moral duty to take care of the vulnerable, and when these were at odds he reluctantly resorted to violence. Cahill also explains that Day viewed pacifism as the best way of living out gospel values in her concrete reality, with the apparent caveat that this could look differently in other situations.[40] This is why Day supported the Cuban revolution, to the dismay of many. Cahill makes a case for the existence of irreducible moral dilemmas by showing that the lived reality of pacifism is complex.

Just War

Augustine and Aquinas are famous early promulgators of just war theory, and Cahill offers new insights about their uncertainty toward war. The just war tradition has been critiqued for being overly permissive, but Cahill uses it as a tool to limit war. Contemporary just war theory analyzes three stages of war: *jus ad bellum* (justice of going to war), *jus in bello* (justice in war), and *jus post bellum* (justice after war).[41] Augustine and Aquinas are concerned with *jus ad bellum*, asserting that it is just to go to war if war is determined by legitimate authority, right intention, and just cause, with slight variations in their interpretations of these conditions. Today, *jus ad bellum* ethics also includes the criteria of proportionality, reasonable success, and last resort.

Cahill analyzes Augustine's approach to war, highlighting his two inconsistent arguments to justify killing.[42] In some places, Augustine claims that killing in the case of war can be an appropriate punishment, and thus an act of love and a fulfillment of the Sermon on the Mount.[43] Cahill is critical of this claim and calls it Augustine's "oxymoronic conclusion," for how can killing be loving?[44] In other places, Augustine argues that the Sermon on the Mount requires "not a bodily action, but an inward

---

[39]Ibid., 297–305.

[40]Ibid., 305–12.

[41]National Conference of Catholic Bishops of the United States, *The Challenge of Peace: God's Promise and Our Response: A Pastoral Letter on War and Peace by the National Conference of Catholic Bishops* (May 3, 1983), nos. 84–110, http://www.usccb.org.

[42]Cahill, *Blessed Are the Peacemakers*, 91–138; see also Cahill, *Love Your Enemies*, 55–80.

[43]Augustine, "Letter 138, to Marcellinus," 46, http://www.newadvent.org/fathers/1102138.htm; Augustine, "On the Sermon on the Mount," 1.1.20.63, http://www.newadvent.org/fathers/16011.htm. See also R. A. Markus, *Saeculum*, 2nd ed. (Cambridge: Cambridge University Press, 1989).

[44]Cahill, *Blessed Are the Peacemakers*, 111.

disposition."[45] In this view, the command of nonviolence is relegated to intention only. As Cahill points out, this raises questions about what actions are permissible and how action and intention are separated.[46] Augustine's second position seems unnecessary if violence can be justified as an act of love. Cahill successfully questions the coherence of Augustine's approach by focusing on these tensions. Augustine's unwieldy views suggest that he circles around an issue that he does not fully grasp: moral dilemmas.

Cahill argues that Augustine's miserable judge also makes way for the possibility of irreducible moral dilemmas, because even though virtue and happiness are aligned in Augustine's thought, Augustine asserts that the judge who makes a choice to torture for the good of society is "guiltless" yet unhappy.[47] For Cahill, the lack of guilt points to the fact that, as with an irreducible moral dilemma, the judge acts rightly. And the unhappiness highlights that, as with an irreducible moral dilemma, he commits a transgression. However, unlike Cahill, I think the miserable judge shows that Augustine is aware that sometimes right action is hard and can lead to unhappiness, but this does not necessarily mean a sin is involved.

Aquinas presents another influential defense of war and justifies it in terms of the common good. He addresses war under the question of charity, asking if it is "always sinful," thus indicating that it is usually sinful.[48] While Aquinas's views have been interpreted in various ways,[49] Cahill contributes to just war and Thomistic studies when she argues that Aquinas is "ambivalent about the morality of war," particularly the moral status of killing and the extent to which war fulfills the demands of charity.[50] She uses this as evidence for war as an irreducible moral dilemma. Although Aquinas discusses war under the question of charity, he does not endorse war as charitable but defends it on the basis of the common good, justice, and peace.[51] Aquinas's distinction between clerics who should not participate in violence and the rest of Christians who can participate in war in the right circumstances seems odd if war fulfills the

---

[45] Augustine, "Contra Faustum," 22.76, http://www.newadvent.org/fathers/140622.htm.
[46] Cahill, *Blessed Are the Peacemakers*, 114–15.
[47] Augustine, "The City of God," 19.6, http://www.newadvent.org/fathers/120119.htm; referenced in Cahill, *Blessed Are the Peacemakers*, 102–3, 124–26.
[48] *ST*, II-II, q. 40; see also Cahill, *Blessed Are the Peacemakers*, 146.
[49] For a sample of texts on this, see Nigel Biggar, *In Defence of War* (Oxford: Oxford University Press, 2013), 106–10; James Bernard Murphy, "Suarez, Aquinas and the Just War: Self-Defense or Punishment?," in *From Just War to Modern Peace Ethics*, ed. Heinz-Gerhard Justenhoven and William A. Barbieri Jr. (Boston: Walter de Gruyter GmbH & Co., 2012), 175–96; Gregory M. Reichberg, *Thomas Aquinas on War and Peace* (Cambridge: Cambridge University Press, 2016).
[50] Cahill, *Blessed Are the Peacemakers*, 139–72, at 158.
[51] *ST*, II-II, q. 40.

demands of charity.[52] Cahill points out that elsewhere Aquinas challenges this idea when he explains that all Christians are bound by charity and soldiers can fulfill the love command.[53] Cahill shows that Aquinas's views on killing are equivocal when he makes an uneasy distinction between political agents who are permitted to kill intentionally for the common good and individuals who are allowed to kill only if the death is unintended. All this suggests to Cahill that Aquinas is dealing with a moral dilemma where war can satisfy charity and justice *and* killing is wrong.

What Cahill identifies as Aquinas's "ambivalence" can also be interpreted positively as Aquinas's appreciation for how circumstances and intentions inform moral acts. That the moral status of war and violence changes in different settings illustrates how Aquinas does not hold "not killing" as a moral absolute. I think the more pressing issue is why this is the case when Aquinas accepts other moral absolutes, such as that lying is always wrong.[54] Nevertheless, Cahill problematizes whether Aquinas's just war theory adequately handles the problem of killing.

Cahill relies on Augustine, Aquinas, and other thinkers to contextualize different just war perspectives. She argues that Augustine develops a "paradoxical and dialectical" approach to justify war and killing that later thinkers such as Paul Ramsey and Reinhold Niebuhr follow.[55] Aquinas, on the other hand, develops a defense of war in light of the common good, which church leaders such as John Paul II follow.[56]

Unfortunately, just war theory has been used to easily justify war.[57] Cahill's views after the tragedies of September 11, 2001, showcase her distinctive approach that does not wholly reject violence, but profoundly resists it.[58] She explains that just war theory should operate with a presumption against war and should restrain violence by interrogating intentions, proportionality, chances of successes, and whether war is a last resort. She specifically questions whether bombings in Afghanistan violate "non-combatant immunity." She suggests alternatives to violence, such as police intervention and international courts. These challenges seem inspired by pacifist resistance to violence.

---

[52] *ST*, II-II, q. 40, a. 2.

[53] *ST*, II-II, q. 188, a. 3.

[54] *ST*, II-II, q. 110. This raises the issue of intrinsic evil, which is beyond this chapter's scope.

[55] Cahill, "Theological Contexts of Just War Theory and Pacifism," 262–66.

[56] Ibid., 263–64.

[57] Tobias Winright, "Introduction," in *Can War Be Just in the 21st Century?*, ed. Tobias Winright and Laurie Johnston (Maryknoll, NY: Orbis Books, 2015), xiii–xxvii.

[58] Lisa Sowle Cahill and Michael Baxter, CSC, "Is This Just War?," December 2001, *US Catholic*, https://www.uscatholic.org/culture/war-and-peace/2011/09/just-war-two-catholic-perspectives-war-afghanistan.

Peacebuilding

In light of these difficulties within pacifism and just war theory, Cahill makes the case that the Church must turn to peacebuilding.[59] Peacebuilding will likely involve dilemmas and so does not escape the problem of irreducible moral dilemmas, but it shifts the focus from just war and pacifism to how Christians can make a practical difference. Cahill writes, "Christian peacebuilding is a way of yoking gospel nonviolence to effective action for change, despite the existentially and morally ambiguous circumstances in which its mission must be embodied."[60] Peacebuilding aims to transform societies by creating just structures that put an end to conflict, while affirming human dignity and finding ways to heal from war. It is about forming just relationships, creating opportunities for forgiveness, and bringing about change from within. Peacebuilding is an act of hope in a world wounded by sin. Cahill believes the inbreaking of God's kingdom can result in real social change now, even though the completion of God's reign will happen at the end of times. The "already" nature of the kingdom inspires Cahill's hope in the possibility for social transformation, while the "not yet" aspect ensures that Cahill keeps her eye on what is realistically achievable.

Peacebuilding requires the cooperation of many groups—Christians and non-Christians, secular and religious. Cahill accommodates this by retrieving Thomistic thought, affirming that humans share some fundamental inclinations and basic goods.[61] This retrieval serves as the basis for how different constituents can work together to bring about shared goals. But peacebuilding is not a monolithic worldview, as it can be taken up by people with varying attitudes on what is realistically possible in this world and how much force is permissible in the pursuit of change.

Cahill defends peacebuilding by showcasing the efficacy of nonviolent efforts, especially the often-ignored work of women.[62] For instance, she highlights Christian and Muslim women during the Second Liberian Civil War who used protests and a "sex strike" to affect politics.[63] Cahill stresses

---

[59] Lisa Sowle Cahill, "A Church for Peace? Why Just War Theory Isn't Enough," *Commonweal* 143, no. 14 (September 9, 2016): 9–11; and see Cahill, *Blessed Are the Peacemakers*.

[60] Cahill, *Blessed Are the Peacemakers*, 21.

[61] Cahill's early views on this are clearly articulated in Lisa Sowle Cahill, "The Catholic Tradition: Religion, Morality, and the Common Good," *Journal of Law and Religion* 5, no. 1 (1987): 75–94.

[62] Cahill, *Blessed Are the Peacemakers*, 325–63.

[63] Ibid., 328–29.

that peacebuilding is especially necessary in the United States, where racism has taken the lives of innocent black Americans.[64] She identifies Black Lives Matter as a nonviolent movement working for change.[65]

Conclusion

While Cahill urges that the Church focus on peacebuilding, she does not propose to eliminate just war and pacifist ideas.[66] She explains that pacifism reminds us of Jesus's message and has become increasingly important in Roman Catholic teachings on war, while just war theory gives a framework for how to live in a world bombarded with sin. Cahill argues that the existence of both pacifism and the just war tradition reveals that the Church is dealing with a moral dilemma.[67] As this chapter has contended, war is a case where nonviolence and love of neighbor conflict. More research must be done to define moral dilemmas and to investigate their implications for theology.

In her work, Cahill emphasizes that peacebuilding relies on the contributions of diverse and multiple social players. The challenge moving forward will be uniting partners amid an increasingly divisive and polarized political environment. The Roman Catholic Church may also have difficulty encouraging collaborations and motivating local and global action given that the Church's integrity as a moral leader has been severely undermined by the horrific sex abuse scandals. Thankfully, the fine work of theologians such as Cahill inspires us.

---

[64]Ibid., 345–60.
[65]Ibid., 358.
[66]Cahill, "A Church for Peace?"
[67]Cahill, *Blessed Are the Peacemakers*, 323.

Lisa Sowle Cahill's Family Ethics

Matthew Sherman

As I finalize this essay, I am in my office, "playing hooky" from my family. This is not what I want, but it is where I find myself. I will miss our family dinnertime, my bedtime story with my daughter, and final "play time" with my very young son on his dinosaur mat. The only comfort in all of this is the fact that my wife and my in-laws saw that I needed a late night in the office and drew together to cover for me. My in-laws changed their plans, cared for the kids and the yard alongside my wife, and told me that it was a privilege to do so. My wife, also a theologian, packed me extra provisions and said, "Let us help you." I was deeply moved by their generosity, and I also remembered why I study marriage and family. Family life is where God's grace finds us in our need, our vulnerability, and our imperfection: through relationships of solidarity and compassion, we are sent out to do our work.

Over four decades Lisa Sowle Cahill has worked to connect an ecclesiology of justice to the realities that face Christian families, particularly in the United States. She began her work on family ethics early in her career, because she knew that her perspective was relatively unprecedented. She was a theologically educated, married, Roman Catholic laywoman. Furthermore, her education at the University of Chicago introduced her to a variety of critical tools that allowed her to evaluate family ethics with a postmodern and feminist lens that was not limited to Catholic principles and politics. As such, her family ethics is marked by a deep concern to align the biblical and Christian social traditions with the experiences and needs of Catholic family life. Across her works, her guiding thesis is that families are not ideal forms that exist apart from the forces of society, economics, or nature, but rather, it is imperfect families that create more just communities out of the socioeconomic realities confronting them.

Cahill's major works in this area are *Between the Sexes* (1985), *Sex, Gender, and Christian Ethics* (1996), and *Family: A Christian Social Perspective* (2000). It is important to note, at the outset of this discussion, that Cahill's works do not easily distinguish between marriage and family. As will be seen below, in the light of the gospel and on-the-ground observations, Cahill's writing asserts (1) that Christian families, regardless of constitution, are defined by the moral values that "humanize" all relationships and that are communicated by the gospel, namely, reciprocity and inclusion.[1] Rather than privileging the family's Christian origins—in creation, in baptism, or in marriage—Cahill focuses on the family's Christian destiny, that is, its discipleship lived out through the creation of social and ecclesial systems marked by inclusion and justice. Moreover, Cahill resists defining the family along only nuptial or heteronormative lines.[2] Therefore, (2) not all marriages exhibit Christian ethics and not all ethical families involve marriage. For this reason, this chapter largely treats the Christian family, with the assumption that Christian family includes, but is not limited to, sacramental marriage. In this chapter, I examine Cahill's contribution to family ethics in terms of (1) her method and central theological ideas, (2) current trends in marriage and family theology, in which her influence can be felt, and (3) the tools that scholarship can provide for the future development of family ethics, using Pope Francis's *Amoris Laetitia* as a catalyst for exploration.[3]

Hermeneutics and Major Themes

Bearing Cahill's overarching convictions in mind, I explore four hermeneutical keys that can explain her approach to the study of family in the Christian tradition. These keys are feminist biblical exegesis, shared human experiences, liberative historical trajectories in Christian ethics, and Catholic social teaching. From these four hermeneutical keys, two theological concepts—the domestic church and middle axioms—provide a foundation for Cahill's work.

First, informed by a feminist hermeneutic, Cahill believes that revelation privileges inclusive networks of belonging and the resistance to kinship affiliations that are nationalistic or exclusionary. Cahill sorts through a wide array of biblical studies in order to ground her work in early Christian practices, and she pays close attention to the texts and contexts of Scripture. Cahill believes that the gospel's call to prioritize the

---

[1] Lisa Sowle Cahill, *Sex, Gender, and Christian Ethics*, New Studies in Christian Ethics, ed. Robin Gill (New York: Cambridge University Press, 1996), 215.
[2] Ibid., 101, 215.
[3] Pope Francis, Post-Synodal Apostolic Exhortation *Amoris Laetitia* (2016), www.vatican.va.

poor, women, and children is the most normative aspect of its teaching.[4] For instance, she draws upon Paul's willingness to utter, "I say (and not the Lord)" in 1 Corinthians 7:12–16 as a kind of "communal criterion."[5] Paul accepts Christ's prohibition of divorce because it is good for the Christian community; however, when divorce between a convert and an intransigent unbeliever is best for the community, it is permissible.[6] This allows Paul, and any authentic interpreter of his writing, to extend or limit some of Christ's injunctions on the basis of whether they will build up or tear down oneself and one's neighbors. The communal priority of Christians does not mean that they will look completely different from their surrounding cultural expectations. Rather, Cahill observes that early Christians lived within traditionally structured Roman families in ways that were nevertheless marked by surprising mutuality and equity for women, children, and slaves.[7]

Second, Cahill's family ethics relies on shared experiences of body, relationship, and reason that serve to express human flourishing cross-culturally. Here, she draws upon the capability theory of philosopher Martha Nussbaum, which she is happy to embrace from a Catholic feminist perspective. As Cahill explains, "The assumption that human embodiedness and sociality provide a common platform from which to dismantle dehumanizing oppressions is quite pronounced in feminist theology," especially from a "Thomistic heritage."[8] Under capability thinking, family wellness is determined by the realization of social and biological agency afforded by basic health and shelter, in addition to a measure of political, economic, and religious agency. While not often a Western assumption, this kind of human agency is not necessarily expressed in individual rights, and Cahill leaves open the possibility that both parenthood and community-building are capabilities that families and individuals need to thrive.[9] Furthermore, Cahill draws upon the sociobiological claims of Sydney Callahan to affirm that our rational and social nature allows that "the 'successful' family does not ensure only its own welfare, or even that of the clan, but is able to extend altruistic identification with, and

---

[4] Lisa Sowle Cahill, "Feminist Theology, Catholicism, and the Family," in *Full of Hope: Critical Social Perspectives on Theology*, ed. Magdala Thompson (Mahwah, NJ: Paulist Press, 2002), 94–111, at 96.

[5] Lisa Sowle Cahill, *Between the Sexes: Foundations for a Christian Ethics of Sexuality* (Philadelphia: Fortress Press, 1985), 73.

[6] Ibid.

[7] Ibid., 62.

[8] Cahill, *Sex, Gender, and Christian Ethics*, 62.

[9] Don Browning, "Feminism, Family, and Women's Rights: A Hermeneutic Realist Perspective," *Zygon* 38, no. 2 (2003): 317–32, at 327; Cahill, *Between the Sexes*, 62.

sacrifice for, kin to include neighbors, more distant community members, and even strangers."[10]

Cahill's third hermeneutical key is the importance of listening to the liberative moral trajectories developed throughout the Christian tradition. She has confidence that, when theological ideas find continued valence across generations, such ideas must speak authentically to Christian experiences. In order to flesh out themes of family formation, reciprocity, and shared economic responsibility across Christian epochs, Cahill draws widely upon figures such as John Chrysostom, Augustine of Hippo, Thomas Aquinas, Martin Luther, and Jonathan Edwards. For instance, Cahill appreciates Aquinas's resistance, in the *Summa Contra Gentiles*, to making marriage a "servile relationship."[11] In another instance, Cahill argues that Martin Luther's *Commentary on Genesis* is compelling because of his "frank" appreciation for "relationships in which responsibilities in many realms are shared."[12] As with her biblical analysis, Cahill draws upon the Christian tradition's two-millennia-long trajectory of being open to just relationships, the joy of friendship and partnership, and communal commitment.

Fourth, Cahill's family ethics privileges the Christian social tradition, particularly regarding practices of solidarity and inclusion. She believes that some of the most tradition-backed claims of Christianity involve resistance to behaviors that exclude or limit kinship networks without reference to the kinship of God's Kingdom, and points to the rich tradition of Catholic social teaching to affirm this. For example, referring to John Paul II's labor encyclical, *Sollicitudo rei socialis*, Cahill notes that "the materialism and consumerism that often propel market relations undermine the 'authentic liberation' of all peoples."[13] Likewise, Cahill underlines the significance of the U.S. Bishops' call to protect the role of the family within society, particularly drawing on the pastoral letter *Economic Justice for All*. The document affirms that families and family members, as economic and political agents with rights, deserve policies that combat discrimination and provide equal opportunity for adequate

---

[10]Cahill, *Sex, Gender, and Christian Ethics*, 107.

[11]Cahill, *Between the Sexes*, 113; see also Thomas Aquinas, *Summa contra Gentiles: Book Three, Part II: Providence*, trans. Vernon J. Bourke (Notre Dame, IN: University of Notre Dame Press, 1975), 3/II.124.

[12]Cahill, *Between the Sexes*, 129–30; see also Martin Luther, "Commentary on Genesis," in *Luther's Works*, vol. I: *Lectures on Genesis: Chapters 1–5*, ed. Jaroslav Pelikan (St. Louis, MO: Concordia, 1961), 1:161.

[13]Lisa Sowle Cahill, *Family: A Christian Social Perspective* (Minneapolis: Augsburg Fortress Press, 2000), 89; see also John Paul II, *Sollicitudo rei socialis* (1987), no. 46, www.vatican.va.

work and compensation.[14] In concert with Catholic social teaching, Cahill believes that families are called to be "transformative agents" in the world, not only receiving, but advocating for, rights such as a just wage that eliminates family poverty, access to education, and racial and gender-based justice in all aspects of American family life.[15]

Even so, Cahill is also critical of Catholic magisterial teaching with regard to two kinds of romanticism. With John Paul II, Cahill is concerned that his use of a romanticized male-female complementarity locks the family's meaning and purpose into biological origins, rather than its social destiny.[16] And, regarding the U.S. Bishops, Cahill is concerned that they are perhaps "too idealistic" about the social reforms and solidarity that can be achieved in the U.S. market economy.[17] Too-high ideals and firm role prescriptions can (1) exclude the vocational work of Christian families that fall outside dyadic, heteronormative, and sacramental bounds and (2) preclude Christian families from the gospel call to be committed to other persons and communities, especially the marginalized.[18]

Out of these four interpretive keys, Cahill makes two significant theological claims about the nature of the family. First, the family is a domestic church; while this image can have a sacramental dimension, Cahill most often invokes its social dimensions. True to her method, she gives weight to this social understanding of the domestic church because of its preponderance in the tradition of the Church going back to John Chrysostom; Cahill understands Chrysostom as giving the family "a positive function in Christian formation," including the upbuilding of the poor in their communities.[19] Drawing largely upon John Paul II's *Familiaris consortio*, Cahill notes that families "participate in, contribute to, and benefit from the common good."[20] The family serves as a microcosm of the global Church and is an arena for formation in which Christians practice being a just and inclusive Church, oriented toward social transformation for the "least well off."[21] To be a unit of transformation, a family does not need to have great privilege or ideal circumstances. In fact, as Cahill suggests,

---

[14]Cahill, *Family*, 105; see also National Conference of Catholic Bishops, *Economic Justice for All: Pastoral Letter on Catholic Social Teaching and the U.S. Economy* (Washington, DC: United States Catholic Conference), no. 196.

[15]Cahill, "Feminist Theology, Catholicism, and the Family," 95; Cahill, *Family*, 104; see also National Conference of Catholic Bishops, *Economic Justice for All*, nos. 19, 178, 193.

[16]Cahill, *Family*, 91.

[17]Ibid., 129.

[18]Ibid.

[19]Ibid., 52; see also 54.

[20]Ibid., 90; see also John Paul II, *Familiaris consortio* (1981), nos. 17, 42, 46, www.vatican.va.

[21]Lisa Sowle Cahill, "Families Offer Way to Transform Society," *National Catholic Reporter* (March 8, 1996): 12.

"Families under duress can often imitate the inclusive generosity of the reign of God more faithfully than privileged families."[22]

Second, Cahill generally employs the tradition of middle axioms in her family-based thinking. As she defines the tradition, middle axioms grew up in Reformed reflection during the twentieth-century interwar period. They represent an attempt to aspire to Christian ideals in an imperfect and political world, where the promotion of Christian values can be best achieved through compromise and common causes. Cahill understands middle axioms as a way of articulating the aims of (1) the virtue tradition, in negotiating the mean between the extremes to make Christian ethics practicable, and (2) Catholic casuistry, the tradition of applying Catholic wisdom to concrete cases that demand clarity in the midst of moral complexity.[23] This middle-axiom approach allows Cahill to advocate for balanced pro-family policy. Cahill is suspicious of capitalistic reforms that only advance "market elites," yet she also states that militant socialism is not the answer to family empowerment.[24] It is "questionable" simply to eliminate capitalism because, under any political-economic system, human relationships are capable of being "perverted" by self-interest.[25]

Current Conversation

In the years following the publication of Cahill's major works on the subject, the conversation on marriage and family has been trending in roughly four directions, all of which find precedent in Cahill's work of linking the family's ecclesial vocation to social ethics and in advancing practicable concepts that respond to family needs. First, Cahill's feminist concern about recognizing the potential for marginalization even within the family has inspired other scholars to work in the areas of parental and children's agency within the family.[26] Bonnie Miller-McLemore is one such entrant into this conversation. Drawing upon both social history and the theological tradition, Miller-McLemore demonstrates that the task of the Christian family is to raise children to participate in Christian community while avoiding the conscription of children's agency through psychological projection or market commodification.[27]

---

[22]Cahill, *Family*, 129.
[23]Lisa Sowle Cahill, *Theological Bioethics: Participation, Justice, and Change* (Washington, DC: Georgetown University Press, 2005), 44–46.
[24]Cahill, *Family*, 106–7.
[25]Ibid., 107.
[26]Ted Peters, "Feminist and Catholic: The Family Ethics of Lisa Sowle Cahill," *Dialog* 35, no. 4 (Fall 1996): 269–77.
[27]Bonnie Miller-McLemore, *Let the Children Come: Reimagining Childhood from a*

Mary M. Doyle Roche also explores the Christian duty to raise children within a more just and agential community. Doyle Roche's particular concern is to resist consumeristic and depersonalizing influences that confront children in contemporary culture. In line with Cahill, she notes that the Christian social tradition privileges the role of family as a unit of solidarity that moves outward: "Members of a family that first learned to care for one another, learn then to care for others, especially the poor."[28] This is in contrast to the objectification and distractions of a modern economy, pointing toward the common good, rather than acquisition and domination.[29]

In another example, Jacob Kohlhaas turns his attention to parenthood more broadly, inclusive of maternity and paternity; here he follows a Cahill-like method of examining common threads in the teaching documents of the Roman Catholic Church over the past century. He offers the critique that Catholic teaching, and Catholic theology more broadly, is often reactive to sociocultural pressures instead of being proactive. Whereas much of Catholic theology argues about what parents can or cannot do on the basis of gender or sexual function, Kohlhaas notes that it rarely turns to the more constructive task of showing what parenthood is or has the potential to be.[30]

Another dimension of marriage and family theology focuses on the domestic church and/or an ecclesiology of virtue, particularly an ecclesiology of friendship, hospitality, and justice. These authors generally take up Cahill's concern to elevate the domestic church as a viable concept for family social ethics, and proceed to examine how, in day-to-day family life, the family can live out its social vocation through life-giving practices. Some authors, like David Matzko McCarthy, focus on the economic and political side of the family's Christian practice—adopting a lifestyle that resists atomism, objectification, and consumerism.[31] The ideal for McCarthy is a matter of having what he calls an "open home," one that is deliberately vulnerable to its neighbors; such a home is immersed in practices like the passing on of hand-me-down clothes, and helping neighbors with snow removal.[32] For McCarthy, Catholic social virtues of

---

Christian Perspective (San Francisco: Jossey-Bass, 2003), 164–70.

[28] Mary M. Doyle Roche, *Schools of Solidarity: Families and Catholic Social Teaching* (Collegeville, MN: Liturgical Press, 2015), 37.

[29] Ibid., 32, 40.

[30] Jacob Kohlhaas, "Constructing Parenthood: Catholic Teaching 1880 to the Present," *Theological Studies* 79, no. 3 (2018): 631–32.

[31] David Matzko McCarthy, *Sex and Love in the Home: A Theology of the Household*, 2nd ed. (London: SCM Press, 2004), 114, 172.

[32] Ibid., 107, 111, 195; see also Lisa Sowle Cahill, "Marriage: Developments in Catholic Theology and Ethics," *Theological Studies* 64, no. 1 (March 2003): 78–105, at 100–101.

subsidiarity and solidarity are not only macro-level concepts for economic policy, but micro-level concepts to be employed in daily household life.

Other authors stress the role of the domestic church in creating a community of Christian hospitality—through responsible care of resources, outreach in the community, the care of illness, family meal-sharing, and forgiveness—which allows the family to learn gospel practices and to radiate them into the world. These authors show how family practices are really an expression of Christian virtue. For example, Julie Hanlon Rubio argues that self-gift, self-love, mercy, and social transformation happen within the context of faithful sexual expression within marriage, through inclusive table fellowship, service in the community and parish, and regular practices of family prayer.[33]

Paralleling Cahill's reliance on shared human experiences that ground Christian ethics, other authors explore family practices through direct observation and conversation with Christian couples. Bridget Burke Ravizza and Julie Donovan Massey, drawing on interviews with married Catholics, ground their Christian vision in the human need for communion and in finding God through our relationships; they then explain that "married partners *become* sacrament to the world insofar as they live out the virtues and 'bring more God into the world.'"[34] Emily Reimer-Barry, responding in part to interviews with Catholic family members affected by HIV and AIDS, extends the family's moral purview not only to hospitality and service but also to promoting the practices of self-care and the acceptance of love in the midst of illness and suffering.[35] In all, practice-oriented authors focus on how to live out familial friendship, marital fidelity, and child-rearing in a climate where all families must grapple faithfully with loneliness, serious illness, and economic and political pressures toward social ostracism.[36] This approach is faithful to the

---

[33]Julie Hanlon Rubio, *Family Ethics: Practices for Christians*, Moral Traditions, ed. James F. Keenan, SJ (Washington, DC: Georgetown University Press, 2010), 111, 118, 129, 165, 209, 234, 242–44.

[34]Bridget Burke Ravizza and Julie Donovan Massey, *Project Holiness: Marriage as a Workshop for Everyday Saints* (Collegeville, MN: Liturgical Press, 2015), 66–67.

[35]Emily Reimer-Barry, *Catholic Theology of Marriage in the Era of HIV and AIDS: Marriage for Life* (Lanham, MD: Lexington Books, 2015), 88–93.

[36]While it is beyond the scope of this essay, some authors explore both singleness and dating as extensions of an adequate theology of marriage and family. For instance, Jana Marguerite Bennett's *Water Is Thicker than Blood: An Augustinian Theology of Marriage and Singleness* (New York: Oxford University Press, 2008) uses the content and context of Augustinian theology to construct a theology of both the single and married vocations as coexisting within the Household of God. See also Jason King's *Faith with Benefits: Hookup Culture on Catholic Campuses* (New York: Oxford University Press, 2017), which explores the complexity of hookup culture and the need for an adequate theology of relationships in Catholic college life.

tradition of middle axioms and the real-world struggle and compromise that mark the Catholic social tradition.

The focus on Christian practices that arise within families also aligns with liturgical and sacramental formation. Therefore, it is sensible that a final area of development in family theology concerns connections between liturgy, the sacraments, and family life. For instance, Florence Caffrey Bourg, drawing on Cahill's preference for historical retrieval, develops a sacramental and social understanding of the domestic church from the early Church to the present. She argues that the family is a domestic church because, founded in both baptism and marriage, it is an expression of the sacramentality of all life.[37] This life includes ecstatic moments of sublime peace and unity, but also broken and messy moments of paschal "dying and rising."[38] Likewise, Julie Hanlon Rubio sees that Christian marriage is liturgically and morally distinct from secular marriage, in that it does not simply form a contractual union, but rather a Christian and sacramental communion with Christ.[39] For this reason, these authors are especially comfortable acknowledging that sacramentally infused charity is central to family solidarity and the practice of mercy and justice in the world.[40]

Thus, we see an emphasis, in a number of current reflections, on the distinctiveness of Christian families, which are rooted in faith-informed conceptions of solidarity, virtue, and sacrament; this emphasis differs from Cahill's concern to root family ethics in common human needs and capacities. While different in some areas of content, I would argue that much of contemporary family scholarship is actually quite aligned with Cahill in terms of method. Such scholarship tends to be grounded in Scripture, draws upon authoritative voices and images from the Christian tradition, and is applicable to human experience and need. This general structure of using Scripture and tradition to dialogue with the world is not only a point of consonance between Cahill and those who are influenced by her work, but also between many contemporary theologians of the family and the hopes of the Second Vatican Council. Perhaps this is why Pope Francis's Post-Synodal Apostolic Exhortation *Amoris Laetitia* seems to align well with the pursuits of contemporary academic reflections on the family.

---

[37] Florence Caffrey Bourg, *Where Two or Three Are Gathered: Christian Families as Domestic Churches* (Notre Dame, IN: University of Notre Dame Press, 2004), 104–06.

[38] Ibid., 79–80.

[39] Ibid., 30.

[40] Ibid., 127; Florence Caffrey Bourg, "The Family Home as the Place of Religious Formation," *Concilium: The Religious Education of Boys and Girls*, ed. Werner C. Jeanrod and Lisa Sowle Cahill, 4 (2002): 9–16, at 10; see also Matthew Sherman, "Before the Eucharist, a Familial Morality Arises," *Journal of Moral Theology* 6, no. 2 (2017): 22–31.

Amoris Laetitia and the Task of Family Ethics

By way of summary and conclusion, the remainder of this chapter focuses on a brief analysis of *Amoris Laetitia*'s family theology. In particular, it will note Pope Francis's advocacy for the family's role as a community of solidarity, an agent of virtue, and a sacramental reality—all of which align with the concerns of academic scholarship. Drawing upon Thomas Knieps-Port Le Roi and Roger Burggraeve's helpful analysis of the Exhortation, it will suggest that *Amoris Laetitia*'s strengths and weaknesses are instructive for future developments in family ethics and theology.

First, to highlight one of *Amoris Laetitia*'s accomplishments: it strikes a new tone of hope for conscientious social action as the vocation of the Catholic family; it is a tone not of perfection and idealism but of hope for growth and mercy.[41] In contrast to John Paul II's heightened sense of marriage as an eschatological sign, Pope Francis speaks of marriage in terms of Thomistic virtue, as the gradual deepening of friendship, which becomes sacramentalized.[42] Marriage is thus an "imperfect sign" of the love between Christ and the Church.[43] As imperfect but real units of paschal friendship, families also have social responsibilities, including care of the family unit, conscience formation, and social outreach.[44] The family ought to "reflect the covenant which God sealed with mankind in the cross" through the sharing of the "eucharistic love which makes us one body."[45] *Amoris Laetitia* begins to launch a new ecclesial project that sees persons and families as marked by growth and the need for mercy, recognizing that greater malleability in family and gender roles might even provide for greater family equity.[46]

Here is what the document does not accomplish: despite its openness toward a vocation of growth and change, *Amoris Laetitia* concurrently affirms static claims about reproduction and male-female complementar-

---

[41]Thomas Knieps-Port Le Roi and Roger Burggraeve, "New Wine in New Wineskins: *Amoris Laetitia* and the Church's Teaching on Marriage and Family," *Louvain Studies* 39, no. 3 (2015): 284–302, at 285–87. See also Kevin Schemenauer, "The Works of Mercy: Francis and the Family," *Journal of Moral Theology* 6, no. 2 (2017): 32–47, at 40.

[42]Knieps-Port Le Roi and Burggraeve, "New Wine in New Wineskins," 291, 295; see also Francis, *Amoris Laetitia*, no. 127.

[43]Knieps-Port Le Roi and Burggraeve, "New Wine in New Wineskins," 293; see also Francis, *Amoris Laetitia*, no. 72.

[44]Knieps-Port Le Roi and Burggraeve, "New Wine in New Wineskins," 291, 295–97; see also Francis, *Amoris Laetitia*, nos. 146, 295, 305; Michael G. Lawler and Todd A. Salzman, "*Amoris Laetiti*a a Turning Point: Cohabitation Revisited," *Irish Theological Quarterly* 84, no. 3 (2019): 268–86, at 275, and Francis, *Amoris Laetitia*, nos. 37 and 303.

[45]Francis, *Amoris Laetitia*, nos. 318, 186.

[46]Kohlhaas, "Constructing Parenthood," 631, and Francis, *Amoris Laetitia*, no. 286.

ity; these claims seem to limit the growth and discernment that marks the rest of the document.[47] The concern here is reminiscent of Cahill's critique of John Paul II: it is difficult to define the family by its social destiny of paschal solidarity—using the cross and Resurrection to share in the pain and healing of our communities—and, at the same time, to confine the family's definition to its biological and prescribed origins. The former aim focuses on a reality that sinners can achieve; the latter aim focuses on a perfection that no one has achieved since creation. Why would Christians want to grow and discover their vocation if their roles were already scripted from the beginning of time? Likewise, for divorced, remarried, and LGBT+ Christians, who are on the margins of Catholic teaching on marriage and family, do they have any hope of growing in the Christian life?

So what are we to make of *Amoris Laetitia*, and what is the future of family ethics and theology? Both questions can be answered with contributions from recent trends in family scholarship and from Cahill's own method. First of all, many entrants into the conversation about Christian marriage and family prefer, with Cahill, to define the family by its vocational destiny of social transformation, and not by its physical or biological constitution. Christian families are not distinguished by anatomy but rather by their social agency and sacramentality. This is why the most compelling parts of *Amoris Laetitia* surround powerful ideas of sacramental growth, charitable friendship, and evangelical mercy. These ideas are, as Cahill would note, faithful to the gospel, backed by the tradition, and oriented toward social transformation. The most potent parts of the Exhortation are those that speak both with and for the tradition.

Likewise, *Amoris Laetitia* is less successful in its reprisal of reproductive ethics and gender complementarity precisely because it casts Christian family vocation in terms of Greco-Roman natural law and not gospel-backed understandings of radical Christian community, mercy for the transgressor, and inclusion for the marginalized who are *imago Christi*. Such reliance on natural law also tends to supplant the more nuanced insights into the human person, which social science and psychology afford. As Kohlhaas notes, future marriage and family theology will need to engage in a discussion of mothers, fathers, and children not with reference to sexuality and reproduction, but with real attention to a Christian anthropology.

Here, it is worth reprising David Cloutier's claim, in a 2004 article, that family ethics can and should be assessed on the efficacy of its theology—one

---

[47]Knieps-Port Le Roi and Burggraeve, "New Wine in New Wineskins," 301, and Francis, *Amoris Laetitia*, nos. 80, 251; Kohlhaas, "Constructing Parenthood," 631, and Francis, *Amoris Laetitia*, nos. 172–75, 197.

that reflects the contours of the paschal mystery.[48] To present a vision of community without a sense of radical discipleship and apostolicity, mercy without the Passion, and strength without the Resurrection is to ignore the eschatological, and perhaps most real, aspects of the Christian narrative. Moreover, in Cloutier's understanding, "concepts ... such as 'solidarity' and 'communion,' must be given flesh and bones so that this language can function forcefully...."[49] He addresses his critique not only to Cahill's work directly but also to the future of Christian thought on marriage.

I would contend, along with Kohlhaas, that Cloutier's challenge remains at least partially unanswered. Without being overly consumed by debates about sexual identity and expression, how can Christian family theology address the role of the Incarnation in the family, and the deep experience of body-care that comes with domestic life? Throughout the life cycle, how does the Passion inform care for children and for spouses? What, then, is it to experience childhood and parenthood in the shadow of the cross? In the light of the Resurrection? We all find ourselves in the midst of family life as imperfect companions and sinful caregivers, but we are sustained by a grace and vocation that keeps us on the path of Christian growth. As Cahill eloquently notes at the conclusion of *Family: A Christian Social Perspective*:

> The Christian family is not the perfect family but one in which fidelity, compassion, forgiveness, and concern for others, even strangers, are known. In striving to embody these virtues, however imperfect its success, a family lives in the presence of God and begins to transform its surroundings. A Christian family is such a family.[50]

As recent authors have exemplified, through the process of creating distance from sexual function and reproduction, family ethics may arrive at some of the Christological, eschatological, and ecclesiological conclusions that will renew the assertion that families are really subordinate to Christ and the gospel call to transform community. Moreover, with some theological distance from debates about sex and gender, it may be that family ethics will be better able to return to issues of human sexual identity with renewed creativity.

---

[48]David Cloutier, "Composing Love Songs for the Kingdom of God? Creation and Eschatology in Catholic Sexual Ethics," *Journal of the Society of Christian Ethics* 24, no. 2 (2004): 71–88, at 82.
[49]Ibid., 84.
[50]Cahill, *Family*, 137.

Theological Bioethics and Bridge Building

Virginia M. Ryan

The culture wars have been a part of U.S. presidential politics for the last several decades, and the Catholic Church has been one of the participants, at times using the Eucharist as the weapon of choice. In 2004 Cardinal Raymond Burke, then archbishop of St. Louis, threatened to refuse communion to Democratic presidential nominee John Kerry. More recently, a priest in South Carolina refused communion to Democratic presidential candidate Joseph Biden. For his decision, he received support from a number of prelates. Cathleen Kaveny notes that the rhetorical style of the "culture warrior" adopted by the United States Conference of Catholic Bishops (USCCB) has often been focused on one issue, abortion.[1] Some applaud the American Bishops for their prophetic witness and for continuing to stand on a perceived moral high ground, but at what cost and for what end? In a world that is increasingly pluralistic, complex, and fragmented, is there a better way to communicate the essential values and commitments of the Catholic Church as regards bioethical issues?

It would be difficult to imagine a Roman Catholic ethicist who has had more influence on the field of bioethics than Lisa Sowle Cahill. For more than forty years Cahill has conversed with the work of the greatest minds in Christian bioethics about some of the most pressing issues in scientific research, clinical practice, and national and international health policy. She has absorbed and advanced insights and perspectives from a myriad of disciplines and fields, all the while anticipating future issues and broader contexts. While it is impossible to offer an adequate summary of the ways in which Cahill has deepened and broadened our understanding of bioethics, we can discern essential themes in her thought and work. In

---

[1] Cathleen Kaveny, "Bridge Burners: What the Culture Warriors Get Wrong," *Commonweal* 146, no. 17 (December 2019): 9.

this chapter, I focus on what I consider one of the most significant themes of Cahill's work: building bridges among diverse academic and nonacademic constituencies. In many ways, Cahill's lifelong efforts have been to "call in" rather than "call out," to use the terms of those engaged in social justice work. While the prophetic work of "calling out" those believed to be acting wrongly is sometimes necessary in urgent situations, as a style of moral leadership it often leads to the burning of bridges and a position of irrelevance and isolation. Calling in is a request for deeper exploration, understanding, and response rather than reaction. In this way, Cahill has persistently and consistently attempted to repair the breaches that have kept disciplines, institutions, and communities from deeply listening to the shared wisdom they can only possess together.[2]

A good place to begin is with Cahill's response to the question "What is Christian about Christian bioethics?,"[3] in the 2015 volume of *Christian Bioethics: Non-Ecumenical Studies in Medical Ethics*, since her answer reflects her methodological and intellectual commitment to finding common ground in her work as a Roman Catholic ethicist. She wrote,

> I am an ecumenical Roman Catholic social ethicist who believes that the gospel provides a "common denominator" of Christian ethics at a depth level, not a superficial one. I view the biblical literature, read in light of critical historical and theological interpretation, to be essential to Christian theology and ethics. To engage the gospel with political life, I draw not only on Aquinas and Catholic social teaching, but also on theologians more central to Protestant Christianity, such as Augustine and Luther. I also consult recent and contemporary Protestant thinkers, such as Reinhold Niebuhr and Jürgen Moltmann. In addition, new feminist theologies and global theologies of liberation, as well as the work of philosophers and scholars of the human and natural sciences, provide valuable insights for twenty-first-century Christian social ethics. At the practical political and social levels, Christians share moral spaces and endeavors with members of other traditions, both religious and nonreligious.

---

[2] "You shall be called the repairer of the breach, the restorer of streets to live in" (Is 58:12). This promise comes after a rebuke about the practices of personal piety and purity as not the fasting that pleases God. The entire passage, Is 58:1–12, is a call for Israel to become a radically inclusive people, a community that is built on just and generous relationships and a universal circle of compassion. Unless noted otherwise, all biblical quotes in this chapter are from *The Holy Bible: New Revised Standard Version* (Nashville: Thomas Nelson, 1989).

[3] Lisa Sowle Cahill, "Bioethics, the Gospel, and Political Engagement," *Christian Bioethics: Non-Ecumenical Studies in Medical Morality* 21, no. 3 (July 2015): 247–61.

To better realize Christian values in medical practice, law or policy usually if not always requires interreligious cooperation and cooperation with "secular" counterparts.[4]

Unlike those who burn bridges for the sake of principles thought to be evident without any context or interpretation, the metaphor of one who builds bridges, who restores breaches, closely aligns with Cahill's dedication to finding common ground, which is a means for various communities to find each other across divides that have set them apart. In this chapter I work with the image of bridge builder as a way of understanding the breadth and depth of Cahill's contribution. She remains a builder of bridges, much like Isaiah's image, "the repairer of the breach, the restorer of streets to live in" (Is 58:12).

Bridge Builder among Theological Ethicists

Cahill's contributions to bioethics began with her dissertation, "Euthanasia: A Protestant and a Catholic Perspective," under the direction of James Gustafson in 1976. In it she sought to find connections between the Protestant and Catholic traditions, and just as importantly, she highlighted the ways in which they could correct and expand one another and bring about a richer context for considering the issue of euthanasia. Gustafson's emphasis on prophetic and narrative modes of discourse,[5] Paul Ramsey's ethic of covenantal fidelity,[6] and Richard McCormick's proportionalism[7] were some of the sources for Cahill's perspective. She continues to incorporate Protestant and Catholic themes and insights in bioethics and advance the ethical deliberations of the generation of Christian bioethicists who preceded her, appreciating their work to bring Christian insights to the forefront of bioethical deliberations at a national level.

In addition, Cahill may be best known in the field of bioethics for moving its center away from the academic and policy-making areas toward broader areas of concern. For instance, in her book *Theological Bioethics*,

---

[4]Cahill, "Bioethics, the Gospel, and Political Engagement," 247–48.
[5]Lisa Sowle Cahill, *Theological Bioethics: Participation, Justice, and Change*, Moral Traditions, ed. James F. Keenan, SJ (Washington, DC: Georgetown University Press, 2005), 38.
[6]Lisa Sowle Cahill, "Paul Ramsey: Covenant Fidelity in Medical Ethics," *Journal of Religion* 55, no. 4 (1975): 470–76.
[7]For an overall survey of the proportionalist movement, see Bernard Hoose, *Proportionalism: The American Debate and Its European Roots* (Washington, DC: Georgetown University Press, 1987).

she added a fifth mode of moral discourse, the participatory, to Gustafson's four types: ethical, policy, narrative, and prophetic.[8] This was in many ways a natural outgrowth of Gustafson's schema and at the same time one of the central principles of Catholic social teaching, which views the principle of participation as the "right and duty of all to participate in the common good by enlarging and enhancing it as well as by benefiting from it."[9] Similarly, Cahill furthered the work of twentieth-century Roman Catholic moral theologians such as Richard A. McCormick, SJ, and Charles E. Curran, who moved Roman Catholic moral theology away from the manualist (and often physicalist) tradition of the 1940s and 1950s toward a moral analysis, sometimes referred to as *proportionalism*, that included the insights from Vatican II. Cahill brought proportionalism,[10] or post–Vatican II moral theology, to a natural next step, that is, a more thoroughgoing focus on the social dimensions of healthcare.

Of course, the Catholic emphasis on the natural sociality of the person was always an aspect of moral deliberations, but Cahill expanded and grounded this emphasis in lived experience. She states, "Bioethics in the twenty-first century must in every case be social ethics, not just as theory but as engagement."[11] On the one hand, she maintains a commitment to the Vatican II emphasis on the "integral and adequate" understanding of the person as a moral agent.[12] There is a palpable aspect of respect in her own work for that of earlier contemporaries in theological bioethics. Additionally, she builds upon the depth and breadth of centuries of moral reflection, from Thomas Aquinas, Francisco de Vitoria, OP, and John de Lugo to Gerald Kelly in the mid-twentieth century. These and the post–Vatican II moral theologians were and continue to be her interlocutors, together with contemporary voices from the various continents. On the other hand, Cahill includes a variety of sources from the social sciences as well as the burgeoning reflection stemming from Vatican II on Catholic social teaching.

---

[8] Cahill, *Theological Bioethics*, 38.

[9] Lisa Sowle Cahill, "Bioethics, Theology, and Social Change," *Journal of Religious Ethics* 31, no. 3 (Winter 2003): 363–98, at 380.

[10] The term *proportionalism* refers to a particular method of analysis within Roman Catholic moral theology that places an emphasis on the importance of proportionate or commensurate reasoning in determining the moral licitness of an act. See Hoose, *Proportionalism*, and Aline H. Kalbian, "Where Have All the Proportionalists Gone?," *Journal of Religious Ethics* 30, no. 1 (2002): 3–22.

[11] Cahill, *Theological Bioethics*, 2.

[12] Lisa Sowle Cahill, "Reframing Catholic Ethics: Is the Person an Integral and Adequate Starting Point?," *Religions* 8, no. 10 (2017): 215, doi:10.3390/rel8100215.

Bridge Builder among Secular and Theological Bioethics

In a 2003 article titled "Bioethics, Theology, and Social Change," Cahill argued that the common perception that American bioethics was "thin" was incorrect. While the emphasis on the four principles of medical ethics—respect for autonomy, beneficence, nonmaleficence, and justice—might be considered "thin" or primarily procedural and meant to consider the individual in abstraction, the underlying framework of secular bioethics is indeed thickly populated by the largely unexamined symbols, myths, and beliefs of modern science and market capitalism.[13] The preeminence of autonomy and choice in mainstream secular bioethics is perhaps an illusion or, more cynically, a useful tactic for market-driven entities to insert themselves into all aspects of healthcare. In other words, secular and religious bioethics both appeal to descriptive and evaluative "thick" ethical traditions that rely on competing understandings of the "good." Rather than withdrawing from public bioethical discussions and setting a flag of protest upon the hill of religious arguments, Cahill suggests that religious and theological voices have a responsibility to present a challenge in the public square, offering an alternative view of the good society that supports advocacy for healthcare as a basic human right, as well as a critique of the for-profit influence in clinical medicine, medical research, and biotechnology.

While the theological bioethics Cahill envisions contributes to secular academic journals, conferences, and government boards, perhaps more importantly it offers theological support for the work of healthcare activists and nonprofit networks of care in the United States and throughout the globe. The major themes of Cahill's *Theological Bioethics*—participation, justice, and change—reflect the direction Catholic bioethics ought to take if it is to have a significant impact on the field and, more importantly, on the lives of marginalized individuals and communities. Strikingly, Cahill's penchant for the middle way, for the Protestant "middle axioms,"[14] and the Catholic social teaching principle of subsidiarity is actually subversive in reference to the lived experiences of people, particularly those living on the edges of healthcare and environmental security. She writes,

> While some recommend a return to a more distinctive community witness against cultural trends, others try to reinvigorate community

---

[13]Cahill, "Bioethics, Theology, and Social Change." Cahill notes that "the real conflict is not between 'thin' and 'thick' moral languages and views of the good, but between competing 'thick' worldviews and visions of ultimacy, complete with concepts of sin and salvation, good and evil, saints and sinners, liturgies and moral practices" (ibid., 364).

[14]Cahill, *Theological Bioethics*, 46–47, 145, 152, 167, 189, 193, 234, 253.

commitment to what is still ultimately an engagement with legislators and policymakers on their own terms. Yet neither of these alternatives fully appreciates the potential of religious communities to engage with others for the common good, while voicing rather than repressing their own identities.[15]

Kaveny's essay "Bridge Burners" brings to the forefront the dangers of the self-congratulatory and self-righteous prophetic stance for those who stand on the island of moral principlism.[16] They may find themselves isolated and irrelevant. The difficult work of authentically listening to the perspectives of other people and communities brings with it a strengthened commitment to the common good and a hope that is based on the trust that divine goodness runs deep within creation.

Bridge Builder between the Personal, Political, and Communal

Cahill began her work in theological bioethics at a time when Catholic ethicists in the decades following Vatican II had moved away from the manualists' approach of the 1940s and 1950s toward proportionalism. Proportionalism is a perspective that embraces the more general movement of personalism, which regards the category of "person" as a more adequate basis than "nature" from which to describe and evaluate a person's relationship to society.[17] David F. Kelly has suggested that personalism "represents an important reaction against and criticism of the physicalism and ecclesiastical positivist methods used in pre–Vatican II Catholic medical ethics."[18] The personalist emphasis in Catholic theological bioethics allowed for a less physicalist, more nuanced approach to the role of the natural law in medical ethics, but it remained tied to an

---

[15] Ibid., 5.

[16] Kaveny, "Bridge Burners." The theory of "principlism" is primarily associated with bioethicists Thomas Beauchamp and James Childress, who developed this bioethical theory on the basis of four fundamental moral principles: respect for autonomy, beneficence, nonmaleficence, and justice. See Tom L. Beauchamp and James F. Childress, *Principles of Biomedical Ethics*, 8th ed. (New York: Oxford University Press, 2019).

[17] *Personalism* is a philosophical orientation that includes various types such as realism or idealism. In its application in Christian ethics, it emphasizes elements such as solidarity and the value and dignity of each person. Brief summaries of philosophical and theological personalism can be found in James F. Childress and John Macquarrie, eds., *The Westminster Dictionary of Christian Ethics*, 2nd ed. (Philadelphia: Westminster Press, 1986), 469–70, and Richard P. McBrien, ed., *The Harper Collins Encyclopedia of Catholicism* (San Francisco: HarperCollins, 1989), 988.

[18] David F. Kelly, *The Emergence of Roman Catholic Medical Ethics in America* (New York: Edwin Mellen Press, 1979), 233.

essentially act-centered moral analysis. Cahill offered a response to the question "Is the Person an Integral and Adequate Starting Point?" that clearly departed from the lingering focus on the moral act, even when the lived experiences of the person performing the act were considered. She notes that

> person is not an "integral" starting point because of the ongoing social constitution not only of the person, but also of moral knowledge, intention, and action. Similarly, the person is not an "adequate" starting point because the communities and social relations that shape personal identity and agency are also essential. In addition to the person, we need to consider traditions and communities "integrally and adequately."[19]

A full appreciation of the importance of the person *in relationship*, living within culturally bound families, communities, and institutions, has been the direction of Cahill's work throughout the decades. Whether in reference to the "middle axioms" or to the principle of subsidiarity, Cahill has sought out the middle way, not as a form of indecisiveness or for the sake of compromise, but as a matter of conviction that the lived experiences and actions of individuals will always be mediated through family, religious institutions, neighborhoods, and so on. She also sees in this middle space the possibility of creative and transformative responses to the moral questions that have arisen in an increasingly complex set of bioethical issues.

Bridge Builder between Eurocentric Clinical Bioethics and Global Health Ethics

By recognizing the familial, cultural, and communal contexts in which individuals live their lives as moral beings, Cahill opened the door for a collaboration and dialogue among non-Eurocentric and American and European bioethicists regarding healthcare in clinical, research, and policy settings. Yet she wonders if the Catholic Church is open to this more expansive, global conversation. The Church's tendency to speak in broad ideals, its hierarchical approach to social justice concerns, and its naïveté in regard to global realities may prevent the Church from being "a catalyst for accessible and affordable care for all in a just and compas-

---

[19] Cahill, "Reframing Catholic Ethics," 4.

sionate healthcare system."[20] Over the past decades, Cahill has developed a theological bioethics that is based on an inverted pyramid where the people of God are the source of moral resources and discernment.[21] The image of the inverted pyramid leads to a profound theology of reversal, where those without a place at the table, without access to the most basic form of healthcare are the leaders, the voices that cry out in the wilderness. The central challenge of the great reversal in the gospels runs throughout Catholic social teaching and certainly in Cahill's theological bioethics, but it is in contrast to the Church's pyramidical structure.

Cahill's earlier work in bioethics dealt with particular issues arising in the highly technological, research-based clinical medicine practiced in the United States and other parts of the resource-rich world. However, in more recent decades, she has challenged the deeper assumptions and influences that inform a market-driven system of medical practice: "Theological bioethics as participatory must explicitly link religion and theology to practices and movements in civil society that can have a subversive or revolutionary impact on liberalism, science, and the market."[22] This is a different direction than the USCCB's resolute focus on "pro-life" issues such as reproductive technologies, abortion, and physician-assisted suicide, as well as its tendency to rely on the rhetorical style of the prophet who convicts and condemns rather than calls to repentance and reconciliation. As a result, issues arising at the beginning and end of life have taken up much of the American Bishops' attention—and most people, Catholics and non-Catholics alike, know very little about the Church's stance regarding CHIP (Children's Health Insurance Program), the Affordable Care Act, or any number of issues related to a just and compassionate healthcare system. For example, in the "Introductory Letter" published in November 2019 to accompany *Forming Consciences for Faithful Citizenship*, a document that is intended to prepare Catholics for the 2020 presidential election, the bishops write, "The threat of abortion remains our preeminent priority because it directly attacks life itself, because it takes place within the sanctuary of the family, and because of the num-

---

[20] Lisa Sowle Cahill, "Good News and Bad," *Health Progress* 80, no. 4 (July–August 1999): 18–23, at 18.

[21] Pope Francis referred to the image of an inverted pyramid in his address during the "Ceremony Commemorating the 50th Anniversary of the Institution of the Synod of Bishops" (October 17, 2015), www.vatican.va. He stated that "Jesus founded the Church by setting at its head the Apostolic College, in which the apostle Peter is the 'rock' (cf. Mt 16:18), the one who must confirm his brethren in the faith (cf. Lk 22:32). But in this church, as in an inverted pyramid, the top is located beneath the base. Consequently, those who exercise authority are called 'ministers,' because, in the original meaning of the word, they are the least of all."

[22] Cahill, *Theological Bioethics*, 39.

ber of lives destroyed."[23] In contrast, shortly after Terri Schiavo's death, Cahill warned that there is a danger in thinking that all bioethical issues are situated in the technologically advanced medical facilities of major cities throughout the United States:

> We're forgetting the 45 million people in this country with no health insurance; we're forgetting people in other parts of the world who don't have even basic medical care; we're forgetting about our national obligation, which we've not met, to the global fund to fight AIDS, malaria, and tuberculosis. What is the bigger picture for health resources and humane care? The dangers as we focus on end-of-life issues are not necessarily the ones that we immediately perceive.[24]

Committed to a global perspective, Cahill incorporates principles of Catholic social teaching into her work with an eye toward their application in particular circumstances. In an article in *Theological Studies*, Cahill noted that a global ethics of the common good for the twenty-first century will have to be revised "in light of a much more pluralistic and decentralized philosophical, theological, and ecclesial situation" than was the case when Leo XIII published *Rerum Novarum*.[25] Cahill noted that, "If postmodern, deconstructive philosophy and politics have worked as strategies of liberation for the oppressed, now common good theories can become strategies of accountability for the oppressors."[26] As an abstraction, the principle of human dignity can be used to shore up privileged choices, actions, and lifestyles. The common good may support entitlement rather than sacrifice. For Cahill, the option for the poor is the principle that holds the other principles in right relation to one another. Cahill has dedicated much of her writing to bringing voices from the South and the East together with those from the North and West, giving preference to those of the South and East. This stems from her abiding commitment

---

[23] United States Conference of Catholic Bishops, "Forming Consciences for Faithful Citizenship: Introductory Letter" (November 11, 2019), 2, www.usccb.org/about/leadership/usccb-general-assembly/upload/usccb-forming-consciences-faithful-citizenship-introductory-letter-20191112.pdf. See also United States Conference of Catholic Bishops, *Forming Consciences for Faithful Citizenship: A Call to Political Responsibility from the Catholic Bishops of the United States with Introductory Note* (Washington, DC: United States Conference of Catholic Bishops, 2015), http://www.usccb.org/issues-and-action/faithful-citizenship/upload/forming-consciences-for-faithful-citizenship.pdf.

[24] Lisa Sowle Cahill, "Judgment Call," *Boston College Magazine* (Spring 2005), http://bcm.bc.edu/issues/spring_2005/ft_endoflife.html.

[25] Lisa Sowle Cahill, "Toward Global Ethics," *Theological Studies* 63, no. 2 (2002): 324–44, at 330.

[26] Ibid.

to the ways in which Catholic social thought can offer a blueprint for an ever-expanding circle of compassion. One outgrowth of Cahill's expansive and inclusive approach to theological bioethics are the many younger Catholic ethicists, many of whom are her students, who are working on collaborative projects. They have joined global academic and activist communities and associations such as Catholic Theological Ethics in the World Church and the Community of Sant'Egidio, while writing, speaking, and acting for greater participation, justice, and change for a more robust common good, intentional subsidiarity, and authentic solidarity.

A Vision for Bridge Builders of the Future

I would like to close by considering how Cahill's work and vision can support future bridge building, particularly among a new generation of healthcare professionals and policy makers. For as we have seen, Cahill's theological bioethics is ultimately about advancing human dignity, solidarity, and the common good through a participatory, dialogical, and inclusive methodology.

Over the past seven years I have taught a first-year undergraduate seminar titled "Identity, Diversity, and Community," where students explore differences and consider the ways in which technologies available to the few in a resource-rich healthcare system can modify or limit diversity within society, not by caveat or eugenics laws, but through the ultimate reign of unfettered individual choice and control. We also consider how living well depends on the ability to achieve a measure of good health, which is always shaped in part by how health and well-being are defined and by whether people have access to the things they need, such as adequate nutrition, potable water, a safe environment, medicine, and various healthcare technologies. We also ask how the freedom to live authentically in our uniquely sexual, gendered bodies impacts living well considered holistically.

A significant number of these first-year students enter with the hope of joining the health profession, many as physicians. While "making a good living" may be an aspect of their desires, most students think of the medical profession in terms of a vocation that is rooted in compassion. Through readings, discussion, and a weekly community-based learning experience, the seminar provides an opportunity for these students to consider how our socially constructed selves assume and presume that other communities are either exactly like us or radically different from us, depending on the particular issue at hand. I have found that, through the lens of disability theology and ethics, students gain access to perspectives that they may not have considered. They reflect on the world from the point of view of those who are marginalized, in settings such as nursing homes, centers for refugees and immigrants, underresourced elementary schools, or transition programs for young adults with disabilities. With the challenge of Chimamanda Ngozi Adichie's "The Danger of a Single Story,"[27] Greg Boyle's "circle of compassion,"[28] and Brené Brown's "The Power of Vulnerability,"[29] at the beginning of the year, students learn to see the world from the outsiders' perspective, and discover that embracing vulnerability offers a possible pathway to connection. The interpretation of their personal experiences within community-based learning settings is challenged by and reflected upon through the lens of human flourishing and Catholic social thought. The interplay between experience and reason in an academic setting can open up the possibility of a profound intercultural dialogue where what we hold in common is understood through a deeper understanding of our differences.

In many ways, this approach to learning (and teaching) is reflective of Cahill's overall approach to ethics. As she wrote in "Reframing Catholic Social Ethics,"

> Human beings share certain basic physical, psychospiritual, and social needs, such as for food, physical safety, human companionship, ritual connection to the transcendent, and political participation. However, the refinement of these goods in the concrete requires inductive experience, as well as cross-cultural elaboration and correction.[30]

The seminar reaches into bioethical areas about which Lisa has written extensively, as well as other issues that have not as yet been a focus of her attention. But the class is in every way a reflection of what some of her former students call the "Cahill DNA." Whatever healthcare profession students in my seminar pursue in the future, they are (hopefully) challenged to consider what runs deepest through Cahill's work over the last forty years:

> The substantive center of Christian ethics is Jesus's ministry of the kingdom or reign of God, and its preferential inclusion of the poor,

---

[27] Chimamanda Ngozi Adichie, "The Danger of a Single Story," *TED Talk* (July 2009), https://www.ted.com/talks/chimamanda_ngozi_adichie_the_danger_of_a_single_story?language=en.

[28] Greg Boyle, "The Voice of Those Who Sing," *Spiritus: A Journal of Christian Spirituality* 5, no. 1 (2005): 79–87.

[29] Brené Brown, "The Power of Vulnerability," *TED Talk* (June 2010), https://www.ted.com/talks/brene_brown_the_power_of_vulnerability?language=en

[30] Cahill, "Reframing Catholic Social Ethics," 4.

the outcast, and the sinner. What defines gospel-based bioethics is a hopeful, practical commitment to improve the health of those who are most vulnerable to illness and early death because they lack basic needs. This commitment is distinctive of Christian bioethics, if not "unique" in the sense that no other bioethical approaches or traditions share it. To succeed in reducing disparities in access to health care requires cooperative social action with members of multiple moral and political communities, meaning that there is no strict boundary between secular and Christian bioethics at the practical, political level, the level of applied Christian social ethics.[31]

The middle way has been Cahill's geographical and existential place in theological bioethics, and it has provided us with a perspective that is both realistic and hopeful. In that space she has challenged herself and her students to take in the experiences and perspectives of others and see our differences as well as our common desires and struggles. She has been a builder of bridges and a restorer of breaches, as Isaiah demands of us:

> If you remove the yoke from among you,
>> the pointing of the finger, the speaking of evil,
> if you offer your food to the hungry
>> and satisfy the needs of the afflicted,
> then your light shall rise in the darkness
>> and your gloom be like the noonday.
> The Lord will guide you continually,
>> and satisfy your needs in parched places,
>> and make your bones strong;
> and you shall be like a watered garden,
>> like a spring of water,
>> whose waters never fail.
> Your ancient ruins shall be rebuilt;
>> you shall raise up the foundations of many generations;
> you shall be called the repairer of the breach,
>> the restorer of streets to live in.[32]

The body of Lisa Sowle Cahill's work has given us the ethical vision and challenge to work for accessible streets we can all live in, air we can breathe, water we can drink, and bodies we can inhabit without fear of violence. It is a vision and challenge with enduring value for the future.

---

[31]Cahill, "Bioethics, the Gospel, and Political Engagement," 246.
[32]Is 58:9b–12.

The Courageous "Middle Way"

Lisa Sowle Cahill's Contribution to Healthcare Ethics

Hoa Trung Dinh, SJ, and Stephanie C. Edwards

Spanning the last four decades, Lisa Sowle Cahill's works engage a wide range of health issues, from abortion to euthanasia, from in vitro fertilization and embryo experimentation to genetics and genomics. Cahill offers a distinctive approach to the public debates on these highly contentious issues against the background of Catholic moral discourse. People who look to her for clear, simple, definitive answers amid the competing views on individual autonomy, freedom of choice, and sanctity of life will be disappointed. Pro-life activists, Catholics or otherwise, will be frustrated if they look to Cahill for ammunition against their opponents. Pro-choice activists will end up equally frustrated if their goal is polemical firepower. Cahill's approach is not to side with one camp against the other, nor to give people clear, firm instructions lest they be swayed by the clever and fallacious reasoning of their opponents. Cahill offers a learned, balanced approach that appreciates the values promoted by each side of the debate and points to the possibility of common ground. While not dismissing the validity of either position out of hand, Cahill frequently points out the shortcomings of certain arguments and raises further questions for advocates on each side to consider in order to be consistent with their own professed values and commitments.

Throughout her lifetime of work, Cahill proposes a type of "middle way" that holds the potential to overcome the stagnation too often present in Catholic moral discourse generally, and healthcare ethics debates in particular. Instead of providing fuel to the debate fires, Cahill provides a model of respectful and empathetic participation in public discourse. Yet this is not to suggest that her method is meek. In fact, just the opposite:

this middle path is fueled by a fierce commitment to the "truth in love," in a hope that Christian faith can provide a particular and necessary imagination to healthcare debates that can bring about justice.[1]

As such, this chapter engages with Cahill's methodology as a courageous "middle way"[2] within three specific fields of moral discourse: (1) Catholic moral discourse and Catholic case-based healthcare provision; (2) the broader, secular civil discourse on healthcare ethics; and (3) concrete public policy in both the American and global contexts. While Cahill's contribution to these areas is often framed in terms of the "common good," this orientation emphasizes the ends over the process. Cahill's thought *is* definitively oriented by just ends, but it also contains a rich contribution to how we achieve those outcomes. The challenges of global healthcare are multiple, controversial, and ongoing. We hope that, by reflecting upon the conceptual, measured, and indeed courageous process-oriented framework of engagement that we draw from Cahill's work, healthcare practitioners, scholars, and policy makers alike can discover more fruitful and, indeed, healthy ways forward.

Catholic Moral Discourse and Catholic Healthcare Provision

Since the Second Vatican Council, Catholic moral discourse has largely reflected the "culture wars" between two broad camps, painted as conservatives and progressives, within the Church. There seem to be insurmountable disagreements among scholars, ministers, and advocates about the nature and role of the teaching office of the Church, the role of individual conscience as a moral guide, and whether moral norms can be derived a priori from timeless moral truths. Over the last five decades, the most heated disputes have been around artificial contraception, the ordination of women, same-sex marriage, assisted reproductive technologies, and communion for divorced and remarried Catholics. Some disputes were so fierce they required a declaration from the Congregation for the Doctrine of the Faith or a papal document to "settle." In *Veritatis Splendor*, John Paul II's declaration on proportionalism aimed to resolve the dispute in favor of the so-called conservatives, while Francis's directive on communion for remarried Catholics in *Amoris Laetitia* was seen by some as an intervention in favor of the so-called progressives. Yet even

---

[1] Lisa Sowle Cahill, "Theological Ethics as Political Ethics: A Conversation with Raymond Guess," *Studies in Christian Ethics* 25, no. 2 (2012): 153–59, at 154.

[2] We are borrowing this apt designation from William Bole's insightful article, "No Labels, Please: Lisa Sowle Cahill's Middle Way," *Commonweal* 138, no. 1 (January 14, 2011): 9–15.

with papal decree, these issues (and many more) remain lightning rods for further debates within the Church.

Catholic culture wars have claimed many victims and consumed much energy and resources over the decades. Similar to other internal conflicts, each side tends to consider itself the authentic bearer of tradition, while the other is seen as an adversary whose view would mislead or undermine the integrity of that tradition as bearer of truth. In such a moral landscape, Catholic scholars often position themselves by declaring where they stand on certain issues, and consider others as friends or foes depending on their stances on these same issues. One is to pick a side and defend it unfailingly. In this context, Cahill's works stand out. Her voice is not a clarion call for either "side"—instead she can draw ire from all involved, at times being critiqued by some Catholic scholars precisely because of her middle way.[3]

As unsettling as it may sound, the Catholic culture wars are not behind us, and not likely to end anytime soon. Quite the opposite, they are likely to continue for as long as the Church exists, for they reflect the faith-filled people's vigorous commitment to certain visions of Catholicism against rival claims. If that is the case, the right response might not necessarily lie in an attempt to settle every dispute, but instead to cultivate the right attitude when there is disagreement. In any situation, it is important to avoid hostility toward the other, and to refrain from blaming the other for all the existing problems in the Church. In his 2014 address to the College Theology Society, Archbishop Joseph Tobin made a similar point when he warned against the "balkanization" of the faithful into progressive and traditionalist factions that pointed fingers at each other.[4] Archbishop Tobin cautioned against the infighting that has increasingly polarized the Church and the tendency to "oversimplify what are really complicated questions in the hope of discovering who to blame."[5] Yet how do we cultivate such a habit of respectful engagement in the face of complex, embodied, life-defining moral issues?

Within this context, Cahill's middle way offers a valuable alternative to hostility and finger pointing. Writing on disputed issues, Cahill frequently points to the common ground she sees between divided positions,

---

[3] See, for instance, Jason T. Eberl's review of Cahill's *Theological Bioethics: Participation, Justice, and Change*, in *American Catholic Philosophical Quarterly* 83, no. 4 (2009): 615–18; Leslie Woodcock Tentler's review of Cahill's book, *Family: A Christian Social Perspective in Church History*, in *Church History* 71, no. 2 (2002): 448.

[4] Joshua J. McElwee, "Archbishop Warns of 'Balkanization' in US Church," *National Catholic Reporter*, June 2, 2014, https://www.ncronline.org/news/politics/archbishop-warns-balkanization-us-church.

[5] Ibid.

ground that is often sacrificed for the sake of winning an easy "point" or performing public shame on the other side. Cahill challenges Catholics to look beyond the culture wars and attend to the broader, more fundamental ethical concerns as demanded by the Catholic tradition. In 2005 the death of Terri Schiavo in the United States prompted fresh debates on the duty of care toward persons in postcoma unresponsiveness. Cahill pointed away from the vitriol ruling public discourse and toward moral markers that should have been the priority for Catholic leaders: the importance of family and community support, the role of interpersonal and spiritual values in end-of-life decisions, and the values of solidarity and justice in the allocation of basic healthcare to all sectors of society.[6] On the issue of life-sustaining treatment at the end of life, Cahill proposes an integrated approach that seeks to balance often competing factors. Her argumentation is deft and delicate, reaching toward a broader vision for care rooted in the following: (1) a rejection of both individualist and utilitarian views of the person, (2) a clarification of the traditional Catholic definition of extraordinary means to take account of the burden to self and others, (3) an understanding of individual rights *and duties* in relation to the common good, and (4) the need to foster equitable distribution of healthcare resources, with special attention to those who lack access to the most advanced medical technology.[7] This may seem like a burdensome task when dealing with a particular case, especially one as public as Schiavo's, but Cahill maintains that it is only when we honor the complete constellation of ethical issues surrounding a particular case that we are truly doing our due diligence not only as ethicists but as proclaimers of the gospel. The particular ability to frame ethical debates with clarity and faithful purpose, especially for commentators removed from the direct care provision in a case, is one of Cahill's most lasting methodological contributions.

Healthcare in Civil Discourse: A Model of Participation

No matter the case, Cahill offers a distinctive approach to the civil, as well as church-based, debates on these highly contentious issues. Operating against the background of Catholic moral discourse and bringing its tools to bear on public discourse, she illuminates key values and commitments

---

[6]Lisa Sowle Cahill, "Catholicism, Death and Modern Medicine," *America* 192, no. 15 (April 25, 2005): 14–17.
[7]Lisa Sowle Cahill, "Sanctity of Life, Quality of Life, and Social Justice," *Theological Studies* 48, no. 1 (1987): 105–23, at 123.

on all sides, cultivating the opportunity for common ground. Always, her voice is clarifying, not condemnatory. In a 1987 article on abortion, for example, Cahill wrote,

> For many persons on both sides, points of at least tacit agreement are that contraception is preferable to abortion, that not every reason for abortion is morally equal, and that late abortions are morally worse than early ones. However, these points of agreement and the valid concerns of opponents tend to become submerged in polemic.[8]

While a public consensus on abortion policy remains elusive, Cahill deftly identifies the common ground that the seemingly polarized groups share. It is this common ground, if they choose to see it, that is a safe base from which Cahill believes people can engage, not as adversaries but as participants in a respectful dialogue with each other. True dialogue begins when participants see the other not as an enemy but as a responsible fellow citizen whose active participation would contribute positively to the common good in a democratic society. If public debates on health issues frequently lead to polarization and entrenchment, Cahill's approach offers a viable alternative: a pathway through which a consensus can emerge based on the natural equality of persons. Underlying Cahill's methodology is the belief grounded in Thomistic natural law tradition that a consensus is possible through respectful dialogue in a civil society. Within a pluralistic democracy like the United States, Cahill believes that public policy must reflect the moral consensus of the community, and that Catholic moral teachings can influence public policy only to the extent that they can be made accessible and convincing to the general public.[9]

Though rarely dismissive of the position of either "camp" out of hand, Cahill frequently points out the shortcomings of certain arguments and raises further questions for advocates on each side to consider in order to be consistent with their own professed values and commitments. On the eve of the abortion pill RU486 becoming legally available in the United States, a seeming victory for the pro-choice advocates, Cahill pointed to the moral question that remained for abortion defenders to consider: "The price of early abortion availability might be lessened moral sensitivity to the reality of a choice to cause the embryo's death, and thus a diminished sense of moral responsibility to avoid unwanted pregnancy in preference

---

[8] Lisa Sowle Cahill, "'Abortion Pill' RU 486: Ethics, Rhetoric, and Social Practice," *Hastings Center Report* 17, no. 5 (1987): 5–8, at 7.

[9] Lisa Sowle Cahill, "Catholicism, Ethics and Health Care Policy," *Catholic Lawyer* 32, no. 1 (1988): 38–54.

to ending it."[10] Cahill does not condemn their position, but rather urges the pro-choice camp to interrogate its larger commitment to its stated goals. It is worth noting that this same position is also applied to the pro-life camp, urging a commitment to women's voices, an attention to case details, and an equally ardent commitment to the practical needs of women's health as its focus on the embryo.[11] In the U.S. debate over stem cell research, where the conversation focused exclusively on the status of the embryo, Cahill called attention to the economic incentives behind such research, and thus the need to situate and regulate stem cells in the context of other healthcare needs, with vigorous peer review and legal oversight.[12] Cahill reminds us, again and again, that in healthcare there are no easy, universal answers, and that there is always more at play than a purely polemical stance can take into account. Instead of providing righteous fire and shouts of shame, Cahill offers a model of respectful and empathetic participation in public discourse on contentious issues. In acknowledging the goodwill on the part of other interlocutors and the genuine values that they want to promote in the debates, Cahill's approach can help overcome the gridlock frequently encountered in public debates on life-and-death issues.

It is nearly banal at this moment in time to criticize civil discourse for its embrace of anything but civility. Yet the moral orientation of Cahill's work does not allow for a retreat into sectarian safe zones in the public sphere, just as it urges engagement within the Church itself. Instead, she urges us all forward toward the hard work of participation, of entering a fraught public array where one may leave, at best, singed on the edges if not burned completely by the brutality of ad hominem attacks and strawman arguments that crowd our common debate platforms. Yet for Cahill it is not some crusader mentality or popularity contest that urges her toward engagement despite the dangers. It is instead a complete and faithful adherence to the gospel call to serve the poor. For example, Cahill leans on both liberation theology and Pope John Paul II to illuminate how fundamental theological commitments demand concrete action on behalf of the poor, particularly in healthcare.[13] While maintaining that

---

[10]Cahill, "'Abortion Pill,'" 7.

[11]Cahill models this type of thinking in her response to the excommunication of Sr. Margaret McBride in Phoenix, Arizona, in 2010: "There was no good way out of it. The official church position would mandate that the correct solution would be to let both the mother and the child die. I think in the practical situation that would be a very hard choice to make" (NPR, "Nun Excommunicated for Allowing Abortion," *All Things Considered*, May 19, 2010, https://www.npr.org/templates/story/story.php?storyId=126985072?storyId=126985072).

[12]Lisa Sowle Cahill, "Social Ethics of Embryo and Stem Cell Research," *Women's Health Issues* 10, no. 3 (2000): 131–35, at 135.

[13]Lisa Sowle Cahill, "Theological Bioethics: Participation, Justice, Change," October

just positions on healthcare issues can be revealed and communicated through reason to all parts of society, she urges Catholics in particular to attend to the motivational underpinnings of faith in the resurrected Christ to support the arduous and long-term work of cultivating not only hope but practical change, to benefit all people at the margins, no matter their ethnicity, faith, geographic location, nationality, gender, ability, or any other characteristic. This dogged commitment to all persons made in the image of God motivates all of Cahill's interventions in secular healthcare debates, and offers a model of courageous, positive engagement that holds the potential of transforming real lives.

Repeatedly Cahill challenges the "moral ranking" that too often occurs within religious debates (e.g., concern for stem cell research must necessarily be met with a similar fervor for basic access to healthcare) and applies the same method to civil discourse. She argues that the rationale to serve the poor is not particularly special, that any good society seeks to do so, but that the Christian imagination can reveal a special motivation as well as introduce an expanded moral imagination to the conversation through the faith's paradigmatic imagery, parables, and symbols.[14] These two factors, motivation and imagination, are particularly necessary in secular civil healthcare debates, as we may all agree that healthcare is a good, but we have extreme difficulty in achieving universal and just access. Cahill urges the faithful toward engagement that does not encourage "neutral language" or shy away from what "commands our absolute loyalty."[15] She argues instead that as Christians are involved within public processes, these convictions have the power to not only awaken a shared moral imagination but also to encourage and sustain the believer as they work to transform the world. It is the paradigmatic belief in the Resurrection that can and should be carried into the public sphere, the belief in a power that can indeed make all things new.

For example, parables of an inclusive kingdom of God proclaim a new reality that exists already among us if we have the courage to grasp and enact it.[16] Cahill reminds us,

---

11, 2012, Lecture at Loyola University Chicago Stritch School of Medicine, https://www.youtube.com/watch?v=-m_YKfA8aTE. See also Cahill, "Sanctity of Life," 115.

[14] Cahill, "Theological Bioethics," lecture: "Healthcare justice is not a duty for Catholics only or for Christians. Justice does not gain its mandatory character by being a revelation of Scripture or of Church authority. Justice, including access to basic healthcare, is a minimum requirement of human dignity and of any good society. Hence Christians can and should advocate for access to healthcare as a basic duty of any good society and a basic right of the members of all societies" (https://www.youtube.com/watch?v=PpiQh7oDFKQ).

[15] Ibid.

[16] Cahill, "Theological Bioethics," lecture, part 3, https://www.youtube.com/watch?v=PwafzMajmxU.

Christian hope is a practical virtue: one that requires work . . . imagination, and commitment. Hope feeds on action undertaken with courage to change difficult situations. Hope does not require guarantees of future success nor even a balance of success over failure. Hope comes from solidarity in action that makes a difference, enabling participants to realize a different future is possible.[17]

Hope within healthcare justice comes from working to enact concrete initiatives. Cahill balances this overarching hope with very practical and pragmatic steps, from micro to macro levels, grounded in ongoing participation. Within this work, "Middle axioms are the instruments by which religious values and theological interpretation seek common ground with companion moral traditions and practices, yet also press along that ground toward a deeper or higher level."[18]

Public Policy

Contributions to discourse both within the Church and in the public sphere are not conversations as thought exercises for Cahill, but dialogues intended to have concrete outcomes in public policy. Indeed, "Elite academics are not entitled to declare the struggle for justice naïve, unimportant, or impossible. People existing on less than a dollar a day, being raped in a conflict zone, or tortured in a prison cellar [or denied even basic healthcare] have the prerogative to say if the way of the eucharist or the cross entails abdication of politics."[19] Although Cahill's arguments can find traction and application in any context, we here offer a brief reflection on her two broad contexts: the American context with an emphasis on dialogue, and the global context with an emphasis on care for the most vulnerable. Both are fundamentally ongoing tasks, for "engagement rather than completion fulfills the meaning of the common good."[20]

Healthcare in the American Context: Commitment to Dialogue

While Cahill's methodology is one of engagement and precise moral thinking, she cedes no ground in the centrality of healthcare justice to Catholics in the American context: "Healthcare access is an issue for all

---

[17]Ibid.
[18]Lisa Sowle Cahill, *Theological Bioethics: Participation, Justice, and Change*, Moral Traditions, ed. James F. Keenan, SJ (Washington, DC: Georgetown University Press, 2000), 253.
[19]Cahill, "Theological Ethics as Political Ethics," 156.
[20]Cahill, *Theological Bioethics*, 254.

of us, a moral issue, and we must make it central in whatever party we support."[21] With the U.S. Conference of Catholic Bishops and an emphasis on the "consistent ethic of life," Cahill passionately argues for equal support of all "life" issues beyond a certain person's or group's preferred "ranking" of issues. Of course, she admits, not all issues are the same, but "distinctions cannot be an excuse to dismiss or excuse other moral evils";[22] care for the unborn, the immigrant, and the poor are not optional but rather coequal concerns. This is rooted in a foundational understanding of embodiment from the Christian lens. If we are to take the body of Christ seriously, we are knit together in a shared, socially significant embodiment that should be determinative of our commitments to one another. If one takes this existence as truth, the healthcare debates might be transformed. Cahill observes,

> It is the challenge to create a community of solidarity in which suffering and death are healed and avoided when possible, and are recognized as constitutive of human selfhood even after they are not. In such a community, the suffering and dying self would not experience dependency as defilement, but as an extenuation and deepening of the self's social destiny. All persons in such a community might learn to take their own bodily vulnerability as an occasion for self-transcendence through compassion for the vulnerability of others and in openness to the sustaining communion of being which Christians symbolize as "resurrection life."[23]

This is the distinctively Christian task: to cultivate and model the love command, particularly as imaged in the Good Samaritan. This parable is interpreted by Cahill as central to the healthcare debates, as the Samaritan is in a position to show mercy to one in need and does not just observe this capacity, but *follows through on the opportunity to do so*. To "go and do likewise" is the fundamental task that the gospel demands.[24]

While some might balk at this clarity of faith origins within the public healthcare debates, Cahill argues that we are inauthentic and less effective if we ignore the root of ourselves and our motivations. As such, Cahill reminds us that "it is best to construe 'public discourse' not as a

---

[21] Cahill, "Theological Bioethics," lecture, https://www.youtube.com/watch?v=-m_YK-fA8aTE.

[22] Ibid.

[23] Lisa Sowle Cahill, "'Embodiment' and Moral Critique: A Christian Social Perspective," in *Embodiment, Morality, and Medicine*, ed. Lisa Sowle Cahill and Margaret A. Farley (Boston: Kluwer Academic Publishers, 1995), 199–215, at 214.

[24] Cahill, "Theological Bioethics," lecture, https://www.youtube.com/watch?v=-m_YK-fA8aTE.

separate *realm* into which we can and ought to enter tradition-free, but as embodying a *commitment* to civil exchanges among traditions, many of which have an overlapping membership, which meet on the basis of common concerns."[25] Christians' participation in the broader discourse around healthcare and bioethics is neither about translation to a dominant way of speaking, nor demands conformation to certain behaviors only defensible on faith. Instead, Christians are called to the "formation of socially radical communities that challenge dominant values and patterns of social relationship, not by withdrawing from the larger society, or by speaking to it from outside, but by participating in it in challenging and even subversive ways."[26] As Cahill points out, while we may not be personally responsible for all actions of the social body politic, we are morally responsible for the actions we take or fail to take. As Christians we can choose to be both a pilgrim and a prophet, and know when to engage in either mode, depending on the situation and the probable effect.[27] In this measured but passionate and committed frame, Cahill urges all within the American context to take their various roles seriously, to engage in dedicated, clear dialogue in recognition of shared embodiment and implementing the vision of the gospel.

Healthcare in the Global Context: Advocacy for the Most Vulnerable

Cahill's advocacy for the most vulnerable is another distinctive feature of her approach to healthcare that is particularly salient in her focus on global healthcare. In a 1982 article she explains that the duty to care for the most vulnerable is grounded in the Thomistic view of the common good and the interdependence of human persons within society:

> Persons are by definition interrelated in a social whole whose fabric of reciprocal rights and duties constitutes the very condition of their individual and communal fulfillment. In such a view one indeed has a duty, premised on the mutual interdependence and obligations implied by common humanity, to help another person when to do so involves relatively little self-sacrifice and a proportionate gain for the other.[28]

---

[25]Lisa Sowle Cahill, "Can Theology Have a Role in 'Public' Bioethical Discourse?," *Hastings Center Report* 20, no. 4 (1990): 10–14, at 12.
[26]Ibid., 12.
[27]Lisa Sowle Cahill, "The Call of the Catholic Citizen: Theologians and Other Scholars Respond to Cathleen Kaveny," *America* (November 1, 2010), https://www.americamagazine.org/issue/753/100/call-catholic-citizen.
[28]Lisa Sowle Cahill, "Abortion and Argument by Analogy," *Horizons* 9, no. 2 (1982): 271–87, at 286.

For example, the fact that the unborn fetus is totally and solely dependent on the mother for survival is an ethically relevant factor for moral consideration. Cahill suggests that "the special, unique, natural, and essential dependence of the fetus on the mother is a sufficient condition of some duty of nurturance on her part and on that of the community of which they are both members."[29] Note that, in this view, it is not the mother alone, but the community of members, codependent, who nurture one another and care in particular for the members most at risk.

On this basis, when encountering other forms of vulnerability in healthcare, Cahill suggests that we reconcile ourselves to the fact that we are dependent on each other and, for that very reason, are responsible for each other's well-being.[30] Most passionate is her pleading for greater access to basic healthcare on behalf of the most disadvantaged in our world. Cahill insists that at both the national and the global levels, healthcare is a collective responsibility.[31] Citing John Paul II, Cahill insists that Catholics are to take an active role in urging governments at home and abroad to provide for the healthcare needs of those who do not have a voice, and ensure that healthcare be driven by the spirit of solidarity and charity rather than profit.[32] She laments that the United States and Europe spend far more money on ice cream, cosmetics, perfumes, and pet food than what the developing world would need to provide water and sanitation for all, medical care for women in pregnancy and childbirth, and basic health and nutrition to its citizens.[33]

It is only this type of global intervention that can even begin to address the most fundamental right to healthcare and help protect humanity from the pandemics that have become all too frequent. For example, in 1988, when there was much prejudice against HIV/AIDS sufferers in the United States, Cahill argued that these patients should be afforded compassionate medical, social, psychological, and spiritual assistance as demanded by justice and the common good.[34] In 2000 Cahill identified poverty as the primary cause of the spread of HIV/AIDS at the global level, compounded by racism, the low status of women, and the exploitative global economic system.[35] Cahill especially highlighted the vulnerability of women globally

---

[29]Ibid., 287.
[30]Cahill, "'Embodiment' and Moral Critique: A Christian Social Perspective," 214.
[31]Lisa Sowle Cahill, "Catholics and Health Care: Justice, Faith and Hope," *Journal of Catholic Social Thought* 7, no. 1 (2010): 29–49, at 29.
[32]Ibid., 46.
[33]Ibid., 47.
[34]Cahill, "Catholicism, Ethics and Health Care Policy," 52.
[35]Lisa Sowle Cahill, "AIDS, Justice, and the Common Good," in *Catholic Ethicists on HIV/AIDS Prevention*, ed. James F. Keenan, SJ, with Jon D. Fuller, SJ, Lisa Sowle Cahill, and Kevin Kelly (New York: Continuum, 2005), 282–93, at 282.

because women are the poorest among the poor, often having no say in the sex life of husbands, being forced into sex work, and in many cases cast out by family when they develop AIDS. In this context, a more adequate political and ecclesial response to the AIDS pandemic would be to not only address the immediate need but to help eradicate dire poverty and empower women in affected communities rather than to focus solely on volatile issues like sex outside marriage and condoms.[36]

Conclusion: The Call for Catholic Healthcare Activism

Cahill's methodology challenges scholars, practitioners, and laypeople alike to look beyond their entrenched positions, even on controversial issues, and consider the views of other interlocutors with some measure of respect. At least one can give one's opponent the benefit of the doubt—but this is no easy task, for it requires a certain conversion of heart or a process of de-identification with one's moral position. Cahill distinguishes herself as a peacebuilder among Catholic scholars and directs people's attention to where it rightfully belongs: the plight of the disadvantaged in their own society and beyond. From this orientation, Cahill admits to the ongoing need for creativity and open engagement. For example, while she maintains a deep commitment to the critique of the "human body into a cog in the wheel of scientific and economic advancement,"[37] she also admits to an often overly simplified examination of market dynamics and the potential good uses of the market when defined by moral constraints.[38] By recognizing oneself within these processes, Cahill argues that all moral imaginations can be expanded, even or especially for those rooted in the Christian narrative where "priority of access for all to basic social and material goods can get marginalized in the quest for renewed Christian identity.... Yet the mandate to work for just global conditions has been a resounding theme" of the Church and Catholic organizations.[39]

Building on the concepts of the dignity of the person and the common good from Catholic social teaching, Cahill calls for Catholic activism on behalf of the least well-off and most vulnerable in particular contexts and

---

[36]Ibid., 283–85.
[37]Aline Kalbian, "Considering the Risks to Economically Disadvantaged Egg Donors," *American Journal of Bioethics* 11, no. 9 (2011): 44–45, at 45. Kalbian is drawing on Cahill's now foundational work, *Theological Bioethics: Participation, Justice, and Change.*
[38]Cahill, "Theological Bioethics," lecture, https://www.youtube.com/watch?v=-m_YK-fA8aTE.
[39]Cahill, "Theological Ethics as Political Ethics," 154.

at the global level.[40] As she explains, Catholic social teaching is not just a theory but a vibrant tradition of Catholic social action. The processes of participatory healthcare activism are locations for real and fundamental change. Cahill argues that "beyond providing principles and ethical analysis, Christian ethics supports sites where solidaristic respect and inclusion are enacted, forming members to carry reordered relationships and practices into their social worlds, increasingly comprising global networks."[41] From this, "realistic optimism that change is really possible" can be cultivated and sustained.[42] Cahill insists that "across all levels of society and politics, everyone committed to health care justice should become an advocate for more just national and international policies and practices."[43] Cahill sums up the mandate and method for Catholic activism in this way:

> A Catholic ethic for global health care must respect the dignity and empower the agency of all those affected by poverty and disease. It must involve local, regional, national, international, transnational, and global actors to act in solidarity with those who suffer. And it must mobilize Catholics at every level to act for the global common good by affirming health care as a Christian duty and a human right and by adopting the option for the poor as the first step toward global health justice.[44]

As the Catholic culture wars rage on, and entrenched case-based analysis dominates healthcare debates, Cahill challenges Catholic faithful and civic leaders on all sides to look beyond their differences to uncover a "middle way" that inspires action on behalf of the most vulnerable and disadvantaged in our world. That sounds like a prophetic, courageous voice for our Church and our world today.

---

[40] Lisa Sowle Cahill, "Global Health and Catholic Social Commitment," *Health Progress* 88, no. 3 (May–June 2007): 55–57, at 55.
[41] Cahill, "Theological Ethics as Political Ethics," 158.
[42] Ibid., 154.
[43] Cahill, "Global Health and Catholic Social Commitment," 55.
[44] Ibid., 57.

An Environmental Ethics of Hope and Creativity

Jill Brennan O'Brien

Although Lisa Sowle Cahill has rightly been called "the ultimate utility player in Catholic academic theology,"[1] her writings on environmental ethics are still somewhat limited. Nevertheless, ecological concerns are clearly evident in her work on social ethics and justice.[2] For instance, she notes, "Though I will not assess specific examples, the magnitude of an environmental problem like climate change is enough to signal the urgency of a creation-wide extension of moral responsibility."[3] Moreover, her works on creation (and our responsibility toward it) and justice offer applicable insights, as does her emphasis on the need for creativity and inclusion in theological ethics. Consequently, an environmental ethics drawn from Cahill's scholarship would include, but not be limited to, the following emphases: (1) the relationship between concrete considerations and abstract theories, (2) topical and interdisciplinary inclusivity, and (3) a moral obligation to protect the natural world derived from the creation stories in Genesis. In this chapter we explore each of these points in turn.

First, note that, while Cahill's academic formation under her primary mentor, James Gustafson, is evident in her writing—particularly when she addresses imagination, possibility, paradox, and ambiguity—unlike Gustafson, she is more willing to express hope in our ecological future. The concluding section of the chapter therefore presents ways in which her

---

[1] William Bole, "No Labels, Please: Lisa Sowle Cahill's Middle Way," *Commonweal* 138, no. 1 (January 14, 2011): 9–15, at 9.

[2] For example, in spring 2020, in a series of lectures in the United Kingdom, Cahill engaged the environmental crisis by focusing on Pope Francis's encyclical letter *Laudato Si'* (2015, www.vatican.va) and on women's contributions.

[3] Lisa Sowle Cahill, *Global Justice, Christology, and Christian Ethics*, New Studies in Christian Ethics, ed. Robin Gill (New York: Cambridge University Press, 2013), 280.

moral creativity and openness to possibilities offers a "hopeful realism"[4] that is simultaneously grounded and anticipatory.

Concrete and Abstract in Reciprocal Relationship

In a 2002 article on global ethics, Cahill highlights the need for "boundary-crossing creativity"[5] and argues that "the possibility of global ethics, then, should not be pondered in the realm of abstract or deductive reason alone, but through engagement with practical, political affairs."[6] Willis Jenkins echoes her concerns, noting that "the concepts and norms of global ethics arise from practices that move across significant human boundaries in order to create solidarity in bearing one another's problems."[7] Indeed, he states, "Ethics happens by participation."[8]

Speaking specifically about environmental ethics, Cahill notes, "As in human affairs, practical wisdom or prudence is key to ecological morality. Specific decisions must and can be gauged to the conditions, needs, capabilities, and well-being of concrete beings and relationships."[9] She points to the work of ecotheologian Celia Deane-Drummond to support this claim, noting that "Deane-Drummond agrees that prudence is necessary to make decisions in the face of uncertain future scenarios, to adjudicate between the human needs of the poor and species extinction, to decide specific policies that will reduce climate change, and so on."[10] Cahill also highlights Deane-Drummond's suggestion that, "although the market-based political economy that has led to poverty and environmental injustice needs radical reform, it might be best to seek interim mediating strategies that will address the more pernicious effects of liberalism and

---

[4] See, for example, Douglas F. Ottati, *Hopeful Realism: Reclaiming the Poetry of Theology* (Eugene, OR: Wipf & Stock, 2009). Ottati defines *hopeful realism* as "a practical stance and attitude that challenges many sensibilities and viewpoints, and that also has implications for how we may understand the church and its ministry. Hopeful realism refuses both easy optimisms and cynical pessimisms. It suggests that we do not really know ourselves when we concentrate on our abilities apart from our limits and our faults. However, it also claims that we do not truly know ourselves when we consider our limits and our faults apart from our abilities and apart from the traces of true communion in community that we encounter in God's world" (3).

[5] Lisa Sowle Cahill, "Toward Global Ethics," *Theological Studies* 63, no. 2 (2002): 324–44, at 330.

[6] Ibid., 335.

[7] Willis Jenkins, *The Future of Ethics: Sustainability, Social Justice, and Religious Creativity* (Washington, DC: Georgetown University Press, 2013), 127.

[8] Ibid., 128.

[9] Cahill, *Global Justice, Christology, and Christian Ethics*, 284.

[10] Ibid.

capitalism, while not giving up on deeper long-term changes."[11] Here, Cahill appears to support the argument that ecotheologians should focus on Niebuhrian, proximate goals, rather than getting mired in efforts toward comprehensive, worldwide political reform.[12] Indeed, she notes, "Enforceable global conventions and norms are certainly needed, but they will have to be achieved in a pragmatic, piecemeal, and strategic manner, requiring a huge level of grassroots pressure on public representatives, governments, and businesses, especially those in regions harboring the major agents of environmental destruction."[13] She also applauds Pope Francis's recognition in his 2015 encyclical *Laudato Si'* that Catholic social teaching must not continue to rely solely upon world authorities like the United Nations to achieve its goals. She writes,

> Whereas popes from John XXIII to Benedict XVI have looked to the U.N. to settle international disputes and resolve global injustices, the actual power of the U.N. is not now equal to the task, if ever it was. While *Caritas in veritate* tacitly alluded to this fact by championing alternative types of social agency, Francis recognizes it explicitly in respect to international environmental agreements. The further development required is to move CST explicitly to a framework in which a variety of national, international, and transnational actors can be named, if necessary shamed, and called to moral account.[14]

Notably, Cahill also emphasizes the possibilities revealed in the gospel stories as a resource for new ethical modalities, as when she writes: "Moral theologians must be engaged participants in the moral and social challenges they describe. As theologians, we must name oppressive conditions as sin, confront sin with the transforming narratives of the gospel, and seek concretely to enact the new relationships those narratives depict."[15] Her concern for the dangers of an ethics that doesn't reflect the "transforming" quality of the gospel stories is also supported by Jenkins. He

---

[11] Ibid.

[12] Reinhold Niebuhr cautions, "Overconfident moral idealism is more confusing than it is helpful, because its goals are so unattainable as to make its postulation nearly irrelevant," in *Moral Man and Immoral Society: A Study in Ethics and Politics*, Library of Theological Ethics (Louisville, KY: Westminster John Knox Press, 2001), 116.

[13] Cahill, "*Laudato Si'*: Reframing Catholic Social Ethics," *Heythrop Journal* 59, no. 6 (2018): 887–900, at 893.

[14] Ibid., 888.

[15] Lisa Sowle Cahill, "Moral Theology: From Evolutionary to Revolutionary Change," in *Catholic Theological Ethics in the World Church: The Plenary Papers from the First Cross-Cultural Conference on Catholic Theological Ethics*, ed. James Keenan, SJ (New York: Continuum, 2007), 221–27, at 227.

observes that "Christian ethics should imagine the practice of faith less in terms of a worldview with ideals ready to apply and more in terms of a movement constantly trying to open possibilities of living the tradition of Jesus in unexpected conditions."[16]

Cahill and Jenkins are far from alone in their critique of the inadequacies of a theory-based ethical modality. Another theologian calling for a more integrated model of doing Christian ethics is Traci West, who notes that "in the field of Christian ethics (as in most academic work), conceptualization is too often divorced from the practical realities of situations."[17] She specifically addresses the reciprocity required for a cohesive and comprehensive ethical methodology:

> Some social ethicists emphasize concrete practices because theory seems tedious and irrelevant. Others emphasize theory because concrete practices seem too idiosyncratic and transitory. I contend, however, that both theory and practice, and a fluid conversation between them, are most fruitful for conceiving Christian social ethics. Theory needs practice in order to be authentic, relevant, and truthful. Practice needs theory so that practices might be fully comprehended.[18]

Like Cahill, West alludes to the need for innovation in the development of efficacious social ethics practices: "Creative strategies promoting human well-being can be discovered in concrete practices as well."[19] Theory and practice, if viewed from a perspective of openness to new possibilities, can thus inform and transform one another.

Cahill also argues that the practical component of theological ethics entails collaboration if it is to be transformative, stating that "we seek knowledge within our theological discipline, but we also can help sustain hope at the practical level by fostering action that unites people around common objectives."[20] And this collaboration must also be inclusive: "Christians can and must join with members of many moral, religious, and cultural traditions to relieve human suffering, enable human agency, and build just institutions."[21] She explains, "The kind of universality that

---

[16] Jenkins, *The Future of Ethics*, 69.
[17] Traci C. West, *Disruptive Christian Ethics: When Racism and Women's Lives Matter* (Louisville, KY: Westminster John Knox Press, 2006), xvi.
[18] Ibid., xvii.
[19] Ibid.
[20] Cahill, "Moral Theology: From Evolutionary to Revolutionary Change," 227. See also Cahill, "*Laudato Si*': Reframing Catholic Social Ethics," 894–95.
[21] Cahill, *Global Justice, Christology, and Christian Ethics*, 30. Elsewhere, Cahill notes

is dialectical and hybrid also depends on real practices of interconnection and recognition, in the sorts of mediating structures and institutions that have proliferated in the age of modern communication."[22] Her concern for the need to intertwine theory and practice is borne out particularly clearly in the realm of environmental ethics, given its often future-oriented focus and the massive scale of the issues it treats.

Topical and Interdisciplinary Inclusivity

In his 2015 encyclical *Laudato Si'*, Pope Francis argues that "the human environment and the natural environment deteriorate together" (*LS* 48), and thus "a true ecological approach always becomes a social approach" (*LS* 49). Cahill echoes this argument through her resistance to silo-ized foci within ethical subfields, arguing that environmental ethics isn't just a concern for "nature"—rather, it should include discussions of connected issues such as gender, justice, and poverty. Drawing from Leonardo Boff and Virgilio Elizondo,[23] she asserts that "environmental degradation wreaks suffering on the poor first and most of all. The process of naming ecological goods and responding to ecological dangers should be inclusive of all those affected."[24] Or as Margaret Farley notes, "There is a link between our exploitation of the earth and our injustice to human beings. The poor suffer disproportionately from environmental destruction, and racism and sexism have ecologically distorted faces."[25]

Cahill highlights the connection between gender, environmental ethics, and Catholic social teaching, in particular. For example, *Laudato Si'*, she notes,

> provides an opportunity to uplift the role of women in accomplishing this goal. Women globally are more affected than men by environ-

---

that Pope Francis "has by his personal style, and his prophetic yet nondogmatic stances on a number of other social issues, earned a tremendous amount of moral capital across religious, cultural, and political traditions," and that "Initiatives from other religious traditions (especially the Abrahamic faiths), in direct response to *Laudato Si'*, were forthcoming" (Cahill, Laudato Si': Reframing Catholic Social Ethics," 895, 896).

[22]Cahill, *Global Justice, Christology, and Christian Ethics*, 30.

[23]Cf. Leonardo Boff and Virgilio P. Elizondo, eds., *Ecology and Poverty: Cry of the Earth, Cry of the Poor* (Maryknoll, NY: Orbis Books, 1995).

[24]Cahill, *Global Justice, Christology, and Christian Ethics*, 281.

[25]Margaret Farley, "Religious Meanings for Nature and Humanity," in *The Good in Nature and Humanity: Connecting Science, Religion, and Spirituality with the Natural World*, ed. Stephen R. Kellert and Timothy J. Farnham (Washington, DC: Island Press, 2002), 103–12, at 111.

mental degradation, since women typically are responsible for the daily sustenance of their families and communities. In many regions, women cultivate the land more than men. Women are at the vanguard in resisting damage to their local environments. Local action, connected to networks of activists, theorists, and policy-makers, lends momentum to the global cause of eco-justice. The framework of Catholic social teaching as recast by *Laudato Si'* makes it especially clear that it is both necessary and possible to engage women's agency, worldviews, and theologies in efforts toward environmental justice.[26]

She laments, however, the lost opportunity in that "women's activism is not mentioned in *Laudato Si'*, is not highlighted in Catholic social teaching, and has not emerged as a priority in faith-based organizing around environmental goals."[27] Nevertheless, she gleans the significant insight that "no Christian ethics of environmental or gender justice can afford to neglect interdisciplinary, intercultural, and interreligious resources, as Pope Francis's ecology encyclical well displays."[28] In other words, theologians cannot do environmental ethics in a vacuum—we must expand beyond the boundaries of theology to draw from other disciplines, cultures, and epistemologies if we are to make inclusive and broad efforts toward ecological justice and all it entails.[29]

While some may argue that interdisciplinary analysis waters down the unique contribution of theology, Cahill emphasizes theology's undeniable relevance amid secular policy formation. She notes, for example, that "Catholic thought can call societies to achieve a balance between rights and obligations and to curtail the excessive claims of individual rights."[30] Furthermore, insights from Christianity, in particular, can unearth ethical

---

[26]Lisa Sowle Cahill, "The Environment, the Common Good, and Women's Participation," in *Theology and Ecology across the Disciplines: On Care for Our Common Home*, ed. Celia Deane-Drummond and Rebecca Artinian-Kaiser, Religion and the University Series 5 (London: Bloomsbury T&T Clark, 2018), 135–48, at 135.

[27]Ibid.

[28]Ibid.

[29]As James Gustafson wryly notes, "To speak about environmental ethics in a distinctive voice is difficult, if not impossible. Environmental ethics certainly competes with bioethics and business ethics in the market of what I have called 'Ethics: An American Growth Industry" (Gustafson, *A Sense of the Divine: The Natural Environment from a Theocentric Perspective* [Cleveland: Pilgrim Press, 1994], 15). Or, as Margaret Farley points out, "It is not sufficient simply to look at theologies of nature and humanity, since these are intertwined with, for example, theologies of God, creation, freedom, and sin" (Farley, "Religious Meanings for Nature and Humanity," 105).

[30]Lisa Sowle Cahill, "Genetics, Theology, Common Good," in *Genetics, Theology, and Ethics: An Interdisciplinary Conversation*, ed. Lisa Sowle Cahill (New York: Crossroad, 2005), 117–36, at 125–26.

values in the secular realms of economics and politics: "The universalizing tendency of the love command may remind us to reexamine the moral values already embedded in policies about access to care and can challenge the broader society to be more accountable to values that are easily submerged by a market ethos, though in principle recognizable to all."[31]

One practical issue that arises in nearly every discussion of environmental ethics is the difficulty in adjudicating among competing claims for ecological justice and social (i.e., human) justice. For example, Jenkins asks, "Do we understand those right relations within creation in reference to a just human society or to ecological wholeness? Which takes priority in a pastoral strategy: are environmental problems matters of social injustice or ecological injustice?"[32] Cahill's demand for inclusivity enables her to hold together competing claims. For example, she asserts that potential policies on embryonic stem cells "must be accountable to diverse values, such as the good of scientific research, the value of the embryo, and the value of maximizing the benefits of health expenditures for the least well-off."[33] Addressing environmental ethics specifically, she writes,

> It is inevitable that some circumstances will be difficult and some needs will conflict. It is not only inevitable, it is obligatory, to decide priorities among needs and, in the natural world, to prefer the good of some creatures to that of others in cases of conflict. Yet respect for the goods proper to every creature, and the value in principle of the access of every being to the goods proper to it, create a moral obligation to reduce suffering and enhance well-being as much as possible. The virtue of humility will lead humans to acknowledge limits and repent of failures.[34]

A theological basis for this "moral obligation to reduce suffering," including in the natural world, can be found in her discussion of the doctrine of creation, as we note in the next section.

---

[31] Ibid., 126. As Farley observes, "Conversion and repentance may come only when the face of suffering and loss becomes visible to us—in nature and in humanity—and it is in part the task of theology to make visible that face" (Farley, "Religious Meanings for Nature and Humanity," 111).

[32] Willis Jenkins, *Ecologies of Grace: Environmental Ethics and Christian Theology* (New York: Oxford University Press, 2008), 63.

[33] Lisa Sowle Cahill, *Theological Bioethics: Participation, Justice, and Change*, Moral Traditions, ed. James F. Keenan, SJ (Washington, DC: Georgetown University Press, 2005), 145.

[34] Cahill, *Global Justice, Christology, and Christian Ethics*, 284.

Humanity's Moral Obligation to Creation

Cahill's mentor, James Gustafson, emphasizes the ambiguity inherent in theological ethics, including environmental ethics: "Moral ambiguity pervades medical and economic choices as well, but in ecological issues it has particular dimensions. Living with moral ambiguity is a fact of life as humans intervene in the natural world, and while it is the task of ethics to seek to reduce, if not eliminate it, our success is limited."[35] Cahill acknowledges the ethical uncertainty caused by human finitude, but nonetheless emphasizes that, in keeping with her reading of the doctrine of creation, we are responsible for sin and suffering, including in the natural world, and that we are thus responsible for reversing them.

More specifically, based on her analysis of the Genesis accounts of creation, she asserts,

> The "curses" should be read as declarative rather than prescriptive statements; in them, God announces the consequences of human action. God certainly does not demand that future human action refrain from attempting to rectify the broken situation caused by sin. In fact, the opposite seems to be required if we take seriously creation's original goodness and the divine distress at its despoilment suggested by God's persistent questioning of the offending pair (Gen 3:9–18).[36]

She explicitly includes nonhuman nature in her mention of creation's "despoilment" and thus as within the purview of what humans should attempt to "rectify," stating,

> The doctrine of a good creation in contemporary theology implies that humans have an obligation to undo the evil effects of their sin on the human body, human relationships, and the created environment. While sin cannot be conquered by human effort alone, and while final victory over evil is eschatological, humans still have an ethical obligation to reduce evil in the world.[37]

---

[35] Gustafson, *A Sense of the Divine*, 17–18.
[36] Lisa Sowle Cahill, "Creation and Ethics," in *The Oxford Handbook of Theological Ethics*, ed. Gilbert Meilaender and William Werpehowski (Oxford: Oxford University Press, 2007), 7–24, at 13.
[37] Ibid.

In a later writing, Cahill returns to this analysis, noting that "to live in 'the image of God' (Gen. 1:28) means to exist in relationship to God and to other creatures, healing misery and exercising providence for the well-being of all to the extent that we are able."[38] In living out this vocation, we may turn again to her doctrine of creation, in which she states, "The healing of humanity and the earth demands practical political, religious, and theological co-operation among the world's faiths and cultures,"[39] arguing that "to correct human abuses of creation and the injustice toward other humans that follows, an ethic of sacrifice and restraint will be necessary on the part of the privileged."[40]

She is careful to note that an emphasis on the creation narratives does not imply a watered-down "minimum of human morality" that can be used to "provide a natural basis for social life," thus relinquishing the value of a specifically Christian environmental ethics.[41] On the contrary, she states, "To invoke creation is not to bracket religious identity while pursuing common human moral values. Rather, creation is a symbolic point of unity among religious traditions. It can underwrite religious commitment to uphold continuities and commonalities in human moral experience and obligation across traditions."[42]

From her reading of Genesis and her statements on the doctrine of creation, she clearly believes that humans have responsibility in the healing of the created world, even if the path to do so remains ambiguous due to "human finitude and fallibility," to use Gustafson's words.[43] This ambiguity is also due to the reality that, as Gustafson notes, "The Almighty has his own purposes"[44]—or as Gustafson often notes, "God will be God."[45] While Gustafson insists on a vigilant recognition of human limits, however, Cahill acknowledges those limits and, at the same time, expresses a certain *hopefulness* about the ability of humanity to work together toward the healing of the suffering of human and nonhuman creation—an aspect of her environmental ethics that we explore next.

---

[38]Cahill, *Global Justice, Christology, and Christian Ethics*, 285.
[39]Cahill, "Creation and Ethics," 22.
[40]Ibid., 15.
[41]Ibid., 8.
[42]Ibid.
[43]James M. Gustafson, *The Contributions of Theology to Medical Ethics*, the 1975 Pere Marquette Theology Lecture (Milwaukee: Marquette University Press, 1975), 67.
[44]James M. Gustafson, *An Examined Faith: The Grace of Self-Doubt* (Minneapolis: Augsburg Fortress, 2004), 109.
[45]Gustafson, *A Sense of the Divine*, 149; James M. Gustafson, *Ethics from a Theocentric Perspective: Ethics and Theology*, vol. 2 (Chicago: University of Chicago Press, 1984), 320, 321, 322.

Creativity and Hope

As noted at the beginning of this chapter, Cahill possesses a unique aptitude for moral creativity that goes beyond the thoughts expressed by Jenkins and Gustafson and gives her ethical writings relevance and incisiveness. Far from being naive, she presents a "hopeful realism"[46] that is cognizant of human limits while still allowing for the "impossible possibility"[47] of transcending those limits. For example, she links creativity to her emphasis on the inclusion of practical experience in ethics:

> A public Christian theology today must work in the practical spaces linking church and polis in and through the multiple identities and activities of its members, local, midlevel, and global. The interaction of theology, ethics, and politics in these practical spaces likewise transforms theology. True understanding of God and of humanity before God may inform practice before it is recognized theologically; critical practices motivate the revision of theological claims. In fact, changing global patterns of social interaction and the liberation movements they have birthed are challenging Christian beliefs and institutions in a way that theology has yet to absorb fully.[48]

Jenkins echoes this sentiment, focusing on the value of the immersion of the theologian into the practical spaces that ethical insights both emerge from and impact. He asserts, "I hold that faith in a transformative God appropriately drives moral creativity. I do not claim that moral creativity requires faith in God or the transcendent, but I do demonstrate why ethicists might expect extraordinary moral creativity from communities that believe that in facing their problems they give answer to a transcendent and transforming God."[49] He also claims that "religious ethicists sometimes overestimate the practical importance of religious beliefs and cultural worldviews while underestimating the moral creativity in religious reform projects."[50]

Even Gustafson expresses an element of hope, at times, observing that "it is premature to close the knowledge and insight of our sources before we have explored new sources of capacities and powers to act. Agents are

---

[46] Ottati, *Hopeful Realism*.
[47] Reinhold Niebuhr, *An Interpretation of Christian Ethics* (New York: Harper & Brothers, 1935), 109.
[48] Cahill, *Global Justice, Christology, and Christian Ethics*, 30.
[49] Jenkins, *The Future of Ethics*, 11.
[50] Ibid., 5.

not limited to access to one form of power or capacities."[51] He doesn't actually use the words "creativity" or "possibilities," but his reference to "new sources of capacities and powers to act" certainly implies openness to positive social change.

Cahill's writings on Christology also offer insights that can be extended to environmental ethics, in terms of having hope while working for ecological justice. See, for example, her observations on how the expression "what God has done in Christ" allows for the possibility of humans to transcend the limits imposed by their finitude and fallibility. Echoing liberation theology, she writes,

> "Resurrection life" will never be fully available in history itself. Nevertheless, theologians of the nineteenth-century Protestant "social gospel," popes of the same era who inaugurated the tradition of Catholic social encyclicals, and liberation theologians who later advocated a "preferential option for the poor," all agree not only that Christians have the *obligation* to challenge sinful social structures but that Christians can *hope* that social transformation is really possible in light of what God has done in Christ.[52]

Moreover, she notes that Christ's dual nature as human and divine is precisely what allows for the possibility of humanity transcending its limits:

> According to Nicea, God did not send any lesser being as an intermediary to participate in the human condition; the love of God for humanity was great enough to draw God directly into humanity's own being, marred though it is by sin and death. It is God alone who can and does save us from this condition. If human life is so united to God that it is lifted into the very reality of God, then transformation of our condition is possible.[53]

In a later work, she explicitly invokes liberation theology to bolster her argument for the "impossible possibility" of humanity achieving some measure of social transformation this side of the eschaton, as when she writes, "Just as Jesus' resurrection is a historically 'impossible' act of God, so the resurrection life of Christians in history must express what is 'historically impossible.' Christians must bring about the impossible,

---

[51] Gustafson, *A Sense of the Divine*, 148.
[52] Lisa Sowle Cahill, "Christology, Ethics and Spirituality," in *Thinking of Christ: Proclamation, Explanation, Meaning*, ed. Tatha Wiley (New York: Continuum, 2003), 193–210, at 194.
[53] Ibid., 200.

albeit partially, testifying that 'the impossible has become possible.' "[54]

But like her mentor, Cahill is a realist, not an idealist. Quoting Gustafson, she asserts, "It is right to beware of 'exaggerated religious rhetoric that makes promises that God probably cannot keep; assurances of a cosmic hope, but not much attention to the small possibilities for some tiny improvements in the complexities of individual, interpersonal, and public life.'"[55] Furthermore, she writes, "Hope is not the same thing as optimism about general upward trends in global justice," and it is also "not unrealistic about what can be accomplished,"[56] though she would likely affirm that more than "tiny improvements" are possible. Hope, she argues,

> takes root in actual work to change conditions, work in which we find solidarity with others, experience successes as well as discouragements and failures, and develop the fellowship and the courage that enable us to go on working toward the better future we envision.[57]

Cahill describes the role of hope in Christian ethics and theology as "a virtue of the will that disposes us to act for a future good that is difficult to attain, but not impossible."[58] She continues,

> Hope is not blind trust that "everything will work out for the best," despite all evidence to the contrary. It is more than the expectation of rewards in eternal life, for the sake of which we endure life's burdens. Hope also does not require absolute assurance that human life and history are getting better, or that the world is safely on the road of progress.[59]

She also emphasizes the role of human agency in sustaining hope. Noting that Aquinas "calls hope an 'infused' virtue, meaning that it comes from God," she responds, "But this virtue is not detached from human efforts, nor does it come to us apart from our experience of community."[60] Hope, she argues, "depends on practical action, steps that are taken to change situations of difficulty or despair—steps that are taken together, bear up

---

[54] Cahill, *Global Justice, Christology, and Christian Ethics*, 292.
[55] Ibid., 290, quoting from Gustafson, *An Examined Faith*, 107.
[56] Ibid., 292.
[57] Ibid., 292–93.
[58] Lisa Sowle Cahill, "A Theology for Peacebuilding," in *Peacebuilding: Catholic Theology, Ethics, and Praxis*, ed. Robert J. Schreiter, R. Scott Appleby, and Gerard F. Powers (Maryknoll, NY: Orbis Books, 2010), 300–331, at 324.
[59] Ibid.
[60] Ibid., 324–25.

those who lack strength, and form a corporate identity around a vision of the future in which all can share."[61] Furthermore, she concludes, "Hope requires both imagination and action to grow."[62]

Many of Cahill's writings and public statements reveal her moral imagination. As one journalist noted, Cahill's contribution lies in "Building bridges, enlarging contexts, standing up against reductionism—all that may add up to a prophetic vocation for one inclined, by nature and conviction, to see the other side."[63] Cahill's ability to consider multiple viewpoints and paradoxical realities is key to her efficacy as an ethicist. Her moral creativity allows her to transcend despair as she pushes the boundaries of the ethical and theological imagination to include insights, methods, and actions in support of goals previously deemed unattainable.

---

[61]Ibid.
[62]Ibid., 325.
[63]Bole, "No Labels, Please," 15.

Part III

The Future of Christian Ethics

Anticipating the future directions of Christian ethics is, to be sure, a daunting exercise. Reflecting critically on challenges that characterize the discipline presently, therefore, may be a more manageable if not preferable enterprise. The richness and diversity of perspectives shaping Christian ethics today add further elements of complexity to the challenge of forecasting the future directions of the field. Can we find clues to how Christian ethics ought to move forward in the four-decade-long track record of Lisa Sowle Cahill's scholarship?

Relying on Cahill's contributions to Christian ethics as a guidepost, the four chapters of this concluding part of the book examine methodological and thematic directions that ought to inform Christian ethics as a discipline moving forward:

- a chapter that demonstrates how Cahill's work calls us to strive for a Christian ethics that privileges the point of view of the marginalized and radical solidarity with the poor
- a chapter on the lessons to be drawn in our globalized world from Cahill's sustained support of theological scholarship and networking emerging around the globe, particularly in the Global South
- keeping in mind her ecumenical theological training and commitment, a chapter that underscores the wisdom of fostering and strengthening dialogue with Protestant authors, and their theological roots, themes, and perspectives
- a chapter that takes stock of the influence of the Second Vatican Council on Cahill's theological ethics and its implications for the renewal of Catholicism today and into the future

These four essays underscore the critical relevance of Cahill's scholarship in contemporary Christian ethics and indicate pathways for creative engagement with new and emerging ethical challenges.

Ethics from Marginalized Perspectives

Nichole M. Flores

It was a Friday morning in spring 2009. I was on my visit as an admitted student to the Boston College theological ethics program. Lisa Sowle Cahill had invited accepted students to sit in on the biweekly doctoral colloquium. ("It's a colloquium, not a seminar!" as she would remind us when we employed the incorrect terminology.)

As always, two thought-provoking papers were presented and two thoughtful respondents offered initial questions and comments. Of course, the discourse was rigorous, challenging, and pursued in the spirit of collegiality. After allowing students and other faculty members to weigh in on one of the papers, Cahill (who was moderating the discussion) offered a comment of her own. "Looking at your bibliography," I remember her saying, "I didn't see any women or people of color." Without castigating or embarrassing the presenter, she emphasized the necessity of engaging these voices in the presenter's work going forward. The presenter nodded enthusiastically and jotted down the critique. The rest of us did as well.

Cahill's intervention delighted me as a new doctoral student, and especially as a Chicana in the theological academy. Before coming to Boston College I had been fortunate to have scholars of color as teachers and mentors. They had instilled in me the necessity of reading works by nonwhite, nonmale authors as I formed my own arguments and forged my own research agenda. These teachers also conveyed to me that I would have to advocate for including scholarship written from the margins, and maybe even fight against professors, mentors, and university structures to defend the inclusion of this work in my education. As a master's-level student, I had already challenged white professors who believed that scholarship from marginalized perspectives was not essential to ethical discourses on love, justice, or community. My interest in the arguments about love in the *mujerista* ethics of Ada María Isasi-Díaz, for example, was considered interesting and perhaps informative, but certainly not the substance of excellence that would warrant the field's sustained attention.

Up until that moment, I had had very few encounters with white women—including white feminists—who were willing to advocate, and even to fight, alongside me in clearing space for the perspectives of racially and ethnically minoritized scholars in Christian ethics. But here was Lisa Sowle Cahill, a luminary of the field of Christian ethics with influence in the highest levels of our discipline and academy, arguing that excellence in Christian ethics demands engagement with the scholarship, experiences, and voices of marginalized people and communities.

Her advocacy for the inclusion of marginalized perspectives is rooted in her appreciation of the significance of social location in ethical reflection. Referencing the significance of culture in the ethical methodology of her own mentor, James M. Gustafson, Cahill explains, "The importance of social location has become more and more clear to me over the years, although I remain just as firmly dedicated as ever to the (typically Roman Catholic) view that there are in fact moral values that are in some sense objective because they are rooted in common human needs and purposes."[1] Her intervention during that colloquium was only the first time that I saw her advocate for the inclusion of marginalized voices in the field. Whether in classes, colloquia, or office hours, she invites her students and colleagues to see beyond their own preferred discourse and perspective, even when they differ from the students'.

How did marginalized voices become central to Cahill's scholarship and teaching? Her engagement with perspectives at the margins must be read in the context of her experiences *both* of marginalization *and* of privilege within the theological academy. While it is now taken for granted that women are leading voices in ethics, this was not the case during the earliest years of Cahill's career. Much of her early career was spent creating space for her own contributions in a field that was even more hostile to women's perspectives than it is today. At the same time, Cahill was cognizant of her own privilege as a white woman. A personal anecdote illustrates her keen awareness of this privilege:

> In the times when my parents were growing up in Michigan, and even when I spent idyllic summers playing with cousins there in the 1950s, lynchings were widespread in the South. In the insulated world of my childhood, I was unaware of this violence. The institutions of civil society furnished my protections just as, by binding our attention, fellowship, and loyalty so close to home, such institutions enabled the violence that transpired in equally intimate associations elsewhere.[2]

---

[1] Lisa Sowle Cahill, *Family: A Christian Social Perspective* (Minneapolis: Fortress Press, 2000), xiii.
[2] Ibid., 12.

Cahill's critical reflection on her own upbringing demonstrates the structural harms caused by white supremacist social institutions, including insular family arrangements that bind the interests of the most privileged members of society too close to those who share their economic, social, political, and religious backgrounds. Cahill thus identifies the insularity and ignorance of her community during a time of social turmoil even as she experienced marginalization as a woman within this traditional nuclear family structure. In so doing, she models a posture that is essential to the study of social ethics today: it is necessary to attend to the voices of those of the fringes of the Church, society, and academy to develop a realistic view of the world in which we study and practice ethics.

In this chapter I examine how Cahill's simultaneous awareness of her own marginalization and privilege informs her ethical method. I do so by outlining her engagement with marginalized voices in three of her influential texts: *Family: A Christian Social Perspective* (2000); *Global Justice, Christology, and Christian Ethics* (2013);[3] and *Theological Bioethics: Participation, Justice, and Change* (2005).[4] Examination of these books demonstrates the development of Cahill's inclusive methodology over time as well as across the range of practical topics that she has addressed during the course of her career. I also argue for a more dynamic interaction between the discrete subfields of Catholic theological ethics, Christian social ethics, and religious ethics (all three areas to which Cahill has contributed over the course of her career) toward a more robust engagement with marginalized voices in social ethics. I conclude with a comment on the model of scholarship, teaching, and mentoring that Cahill offers to her students—a model that requires awareness both of one's own marginalization and one's own privilege.

Family Ethics from the Margins

Published at the turn of the millennium, Cahill's *Family: A Christian Social Perspective* advances a culturally attuned methodology for normative reflection on the family. Concerned that families are undermined by "condemnatory and punitive attitudes and policies toward nonconforming families," Cahill aims to rearticulate a Christian vision of family that is more responsive to structural injustices that harm marginalized individuals

---

[3]Lisa Sowle Cahill, *Global Justice, Christology, and Christian Ethics*, New Studies in Christian Ethics, ed. Robin Gill (Cambridge: Cambridge University Press, 2013).

[4]Lisa Sowle Cahill, *Theological Bioethics: Participation, Justice, and Change*, Moral Traditions, ed. James F. Keenan, SJ (Washington, DC: Georgetown University Press, 2005).

and communities.[5] Specifically, she seeks to replace an insular notion of nuclear family with one that is more attuned to the Church's social tradition. The model of a strictly nuclear family, she argues, is antithetical to the social mission of the Catholic Church. She explains, "In my view, the Christian family is not the nuclear family focused inward on the welfare of its own members but the socially transformative family that seeks to make the Christian moral ideal of love of neighbor part of the common good."[6] This thesis becomes the foundation of her methodological intervention, which turns to practices and structures in African American families as a site for normative ethical reflection.

Cahill anchors her contributions to family ethics in a compelling description of her own horizon shift resulting from the experience of adopting and raising children in an intercultural context. While she describes her own childhood familial context as socially insular, adopting three of her five children from Thailand (and subsequently forming close bonds with people and institutions in that country) transformed her understanding of the family structure, which is open to many possibilities beyond the traditional nuclear model that orients much theological and social scientific reflection on this institution. She writes, "As a result of my family's adoption experience, and as more and more feminist theologians from the 'Third World' and from Latina and African American traditions on this continent become highly visible in the mainstream discourse of the North American theological academy, I began to see how to place my original concerns in a more intercultural framework."[7] Intercultural engagement opened her ethical reflections on family to a range of practices beyond those of the white nuclear family idealized in U.S. society. These practices can instruct us on how to cultivate families that are more responsive to the social dimension of our humanity.

In a keen methodological move, Cahill turns to reflection on the commitments and practices of African American families to respond to the problem of social insularity in constructions of the nuclear family. Cahill begins her analysis with an essential recognition of the tendency to pathologize black families in social sciences as well as ethics and other forms of normative inquiry. While some would disqualify African American families from normative reflection due to the strains on the community from persistent poverty and domestic violence, Cahill correctly asserts that families from all backgrounds face these kinds of challenges as well. Of interest to Cahill is the manner in which African American families draw

---

[5]Cahill, *Family*, xi.
[6]Ibid., xii.
[7]Ibid., xiv.

upon the resources of their faith, culture, and community to respond to these challenges. Indeed, African American family practices elucidate the ethical priority of attending to the state of families beyond the four walls of one's own home: "the well-being of these families, and especially their children, is everybody's problem," writes Cahill.[8]

While Cahill sees African American families as a source of normative reflection, her method is pursued in an interrogative mode rather than a merely prescriptive one:

> My aim is . . . to begin to absorb the lessons about family life that African American experience can teach those of us who come from other segments of America and who tend to approach the situations of families in this country primarily from the standpoint of the "traditional," middle-class nuclear family, relatively privileged by class and socioeconomic standing.[9]

Specifically, Cahill is interested in "community solutions" cultivated within black families in response to challenges foisted upon the community through the legacies of slavery and Jim Crow laws that perpetuate economic, social, and political inequality. She identifies the practices of welcoming the children of others within an extended family or adoptive family network, founding black schools and scholarships, and promoting black-owned businesses and economic development as examples of practices that ensure the care for the entire community within the framework of family.[10]

Emphasizing practices of extended or adoptive family, Cahill highlights the resonance between African American family practices and the practice of family as domestic church as articulated in Catholic social teaching and thought. While articulations of domestic church have emphasized the importance of parents serving as "the first preachers of the faith to their children,"[11] Cahill recognizes the rich potential of this ecclesial metaphor to describe the capacity of the African American family to extend care and compassion beyond the boundaries of the nuclear family, and even beyond the biological extended family. She writes, "The black family as domestic church mediates the compassionate love of God through its family spirituality and catechesis, but this love does not reach its

---

[8] Ibid., 99.
[9] Ibid., 112.
[10] Ibid., 120.
[11] Vatican Council II, Dogmatic Constitution on the Church, *Lumen gentium* (1964), no. 11, www.vatican.va.

limit with the closed family circle."[12] Interpreted in the context of black families, the domestic church is a metaphor that helps us to understand family life well beyond the limits of what is concretely lived by parents and their children. In this way, Cahill situates African American families as a source for normative reflection on family ethics, acknowledging the potential for normative authority of communities that have been unjustly relegated to society's margins.

Christological Ethics from the Margins

Despite the influence of her own experience of family belonging in a global context, Cahill's reflections in *Family: A Christian Social Perspective* emphasize the U.S. context. Still, her insistence on the interrogation of white normativity from marginalized perspectives is also crucial to her contributions to ethics in global context. Specifically, Cahill's attention to the relationship between theology and practices allows for a capacious theological method that can reflect on culture in a rigorous way without forgoing the relevance of normative claims. As Cahill explains,

> Modern ideals of equality, respect, and compassion inform Christians' moral judgments and call their attention to universal realities of human well-being that sit in judgment of particular cases. Yet Christians also locate their moral and political convictions within the practices of the church. Informing the life of the church—when it is authentic—is the present experience of resurrection life in the Spirit of Christ.[13]

Here, Cahill gestures to the role of practices in embodying our theological beliefs. In the Church, for example, sacramental and liturgical practices are theological expressions. Similar to her methodological approach in *Family: A Christian Social Perspective*, Cahill insists upon the necessity of attending to the sacramental and liturgical practices of those on the margins of society to recognize and acknowledge the theological insights manifest in those communities. Cahill's methodological priority of practice thus invites attention to those who have been excluded for economic, social, political, and ecclesial structures—and it calls for conversion.

Cahill's contributions to the study of Christology and ethics offer a preeminent example of this method. In *Global Justice, Christology, and*

---

[12]Cahill, *Family*, 122–23.
[13]Cahill, *Global Justice, Christology, and Christian Ethics*, 24.

Christian Ethics, she draws on the work of Chicana theologian Nancy Pineda-Madrid to highlight how the theological and liturgical practices of those on the margins of both church and society ought to inform our common faith as Catholics. In her essay "Traditioning: The Formation of Community, the Transmission of Faith," Pineda-Madrid offers a theological account of the devotion of *cantineras* (barmaids) to La Virgen de Guadalupe.[14] The *cantineras* are outcasts in their community, looked down upon for their work regardless of the unjust social circumstances that condition their economic and moral decision-making in a global economy that views them as *mujeres desechables* (disposable women). Nonetheless, they come to the Guadalupe feast-day liturgy bearing *flores y canto*—flowers and song that are signs of their devotion to the Virgin and her son. Pineda-Madrid argues that their participation in the liturgy is disruptive both in the sense that it is not an "official" part of the liturgy and in that it undermines false notions of purity and propriety that are often present within church communities. Nonetheless, the *cantineras* approach the liturgy in a doxological posture, offering praise to the God who dined with the disposable members of the society in which God became incarnate.

Responding to Pineda-Madrid's account of the participation of the *cantineras*, Cahill argues that their liturgical practice is instructive for an ecclesiology that conveys a truly Christian soteriology:

> Through their intrusive presence at the annual celebration, the *cantineras* affirm their own dignity and that of others whose poverty had pushed past the margins of social respectability. In enacting their relationship to Guadalupe as protector and benefactor, they expose publicly the question of their role in the Church and the justice of their circumstances. The other members of the congregation could not avoid them. These women strategically manipulated a local ritual practice to transform their experience of self, challenge and alter community relations, and restore their own agency and authority.[15]

Cahill's ethical reflection on Pineda-Madrid's theology of the *cantineras* gestures to the role of practices in illustrating the radical and comprehensive scope of Christ's redeeming work. "This is the issue of who does and does not belong to the community of salvation, who is or is not recognized

---

[14] Nancy Pineda-Madrid, "Traditioning: The Formation of Community, the Transmission of Faith," in *Futuring Our Past: Explorations in the Theology of Traditions*, ed. Orlando O. Espín and Gary Macy (Maryknoll, NY: Orbis Books, 2006), 204–26.
[15] Cahill, *Global Justice, Christology, and Christian Ethics*, 26.

in the community's practices," Cahill explains.[16] The witness of these women on the margins of the Church is thus theologically indispensable.

Despite the establishment of theological and ethical discourses by minoritized racial and ethnic communities over several decades, the expertise of these scholars is still often overlooked, uncited, or undersold. This has been a persistent challenge in historical, theological, and ethical commentary on La Virgen de Guadalupe in particular, as the work of white male historians such as Stafford Poole, SJ, has been regarded with more authority than the theological and sociological work of Latina scholars such as Jeanette Rodriguez and Socorro Castañeda-Liles.

Beyond Cahill's insight into the reciprocal relationship between theology and practice advanced in her volume *Global Justice, Christology, and Christian Ethics*, her citation of Pineda-Madrid's work—and acknowledgment of Pineda-Madrid's theological authority in this analysis—reflects her methodological priority of marginalized voices. In general, the theological academy still struggles to metabolize the experiences and practices of racially and ethnically minoritized women without objectification or unjust appropriation. In light of this ongoing challenge, Cahill instructs fellow white feminists to read, cite, and highlight the growing body of theological scholarship of racially and ethnically minoritized women to interrogate and transform white Catholic theology.

For white ethicists, including Cahill, much work remains to learn the breadth and depth of theological and ethical contributions emanating from minoritized communities. Nonetheless, Cahill models the necessary practices of rigorous and sustained engagement with this scholarship in a manner that lifts up the vital perspective and unique expertise of scholars exegeting the theological and liturgical practices of their own communities.

Bioethics from the Margins

Cahill's contributions to theological bioethics maintain the methodological priority she places on practice in the pursuit of a bioethics that truly represents the public. In *Theological Bioethics: Participation, Justice, and Change*, Cahill articulates a framework for participatory bioethics in response to questions concerning religious pluralism in a democratic society. Discourses about religion and politics can tend toward abstraction, highlighting theoretical issues that may or may not reflect lived experiences. This approach can obscure the lived experiences of religion that inform daily practices, especially among marginalized communities. By

---

[16]Ibid., 27.

contrast, Cahill advocates for the examination of the practice of religious traditions and their associated beliefs in the concrete reality of particular human communities.

Central to Cahill's method is her argument that bioethics is, in fact, social ethics. She explains, "Even when the focus is what has traditionally been called 'individual' moral decision making, it is now recognized that the knowledge, options, and judgments of individuals have always been highly context dependent. Thus individual bioethical decisions cannot be and never have been separated from social ethics."[17] This approach challenges the prevailing liberal framework that orients the principlist approach to bioethics (otherwise known as the "Georgetown Mantra") as articulated by Tom L. Beauchamp and James F. Childress in their influential text *Principles of Biomedical Ethics*.[18] It is inaccurate to claim that Childress and Beauchamp elevate autonomy as a singular principle at the expense of concerns for relationships and social justice (each of the four principles is prima facie binding). Nonetheless, their method models "thin" engagement with particular human identities and beliefs (including religious beliefs) inflected by a Rawlsian political liberalism, thus tending to situate autonomy as sort of a first principle among equals. The prioritization of autonomy can, if only inadvertently, erode the weight of relational concerns in bioethics in both explicit and implicit ways.

Cahill responds to this risk by advocating for a "thick" engagement with social dimensions of bioethical cases, including theological beliefs and religious practices. While she does not advocate for religious or theological reasoning to govern public bioethical policy in a direct manner as many Catholic and Christian conservatives would, she does emphasize the necessity of engaging with a diverse range of religious perspectives in discerning public approaches to these questions. Permitting thick engagement with religious reasoning helps to generate participation that is essential for an authentically democratic engagement with bioethical questions that challenge society at large. Nonetheless, she does not see broad participation as an end in itself. "The ultimate goal of theological bioethics," she writes, "must be the achievement of social arrangements that are more consistent with the core messages of the involved religious traditions about the uses and limits of liberty and the meaning of the common good and social justice."[19] Participation, including religious participation, must be a means of generating just social arrangements for all members of society. Religious

---

[17] Cahill, *Theological Bioethics*, 2.
[18] Tom L. Beauchamp and James F. Childress, *Principles of Biomedical Ethics*, 8th ed. (New York: Oxford University Press, 2019).
[19] Cahill, *Theological Bioethics*, 61.

participation is thus a means of promoting a more robustly pluralistic and democratic society, not a more homogeneous and theocratic one.

Cahill emphasizes interfaith bioethical organizations as the kind of religious engagement that can bolster democratic participation. She highlights the work of the Interfaith Center for Corporate Responsibility (ICCR), which aims to inform socially responsible investment practices among various religious organizations. This kind of religious activism has had an effect on global health via campaigns against false advertising in the marketing of tobacco, infant formula, and the use of patent prices to make AIDS drugs unaffordable on the African continent and elsewhere.[20] In this way, the ICCR models religious bioethical organizing that promotes a participatory culture necessary for cultivating and sustaining the global common good.

Cahill's participatory approach illustrates the possibility of bioethical practices that attend to the context, experiences, and needs of society's most vulnerable members. This is a holistic approach capable of advocating for the centrality of both autonomy and relationality in bioethical discernment, even as it acknowledges (along with Beauchamp and Childress) the complexity of concrete cases in which they must be weighed and balanced in relation to each other. Furthermore, Cahill's participatory approach is better situated to comprehend the structural dimensions of concrete cases, bringing to bear how legacies of social inequality influence considerations regarding the principle of autonomy, as well as beneficence and nonmaleficence, in the practice of medicine and public health on local, national, and global scales.

Ethics from the Margins and the Turn to Culture

Cahill's contributions have helped define the role of marginalized voices in Christian ethics, yet Christian ethics is not pursued in a vacuum. As a discipline, it both influences and is influenced by adjacent ethical conversations, including Catholic theological ethics / Catholic moral theology and religious ethics, as well as Jewish ethics, Muslim ethics, and the ethical reflections of other religious traditions. Given Cahill's prominence across ethical subfields (specifically Catholic theological ethics, Christian ethics, and religious ethics), her methods and arguments have influenced a broad range of scholars; yet there is evidence that scholars in these fields still struggle to fully see and appreciate advancements made in adjacent ethical conversations that can influence their own work.

---

[20]Ibid., 66.

In 2016 Richard Miller published *Friends and Other Strangers: Studies in Religion, Ethics, and Culture*.[21] Miller argues that religious ethics needs to develop a method that attends to culture in a more rigorous and intentional manner.[22] He writes, "Perhaps if religious ethicists would critically examine the local knowledge and vernacular of traditions of persons who are affected by the claims that religious communities make, they would widen the orbit of their work."[23] This turn to culture requires attention to daily practices as a relevant site of ethical inquiry. "Developing an ethics of ordinary life," he writes, "invites scholars to consider how religious ethics might proceed 'from the bottom up,' drawing on cultural ethnography and social theory as resources for social and cultural criticism."[24]

One might find perplexing that Miller's argument for the engagement of culture in ethical methods does not mention the extensive and substantial arguments that have been made in favor of a turn to culture in adjacent fields, including those authored by Cahill. Perhaps this elision is rooted in Miller's efforts to cultivate approaches to religious ethics that do not function as a de facto extension of Christian ethics. Yet Miller's effort to decentralize Christianity in religious ethics renders invisible the monumental contributions of Christian ethicists from marginalized communities who for decades have been developing culturally engaged ethical methodologies in Christian ecclesial and academic contexts.

Once again, Cahill's methodological interventions suggest a path forward for the problem presented by Miller's work. For too long, the pursuits of Catholic theological ethics, Christian ethics, and religious ethics have been regarded as separate, only overlapping insofar as they all take "religion" and "ethics" as objects of their study. But it is also the case that ethicists, including those from marginalized communities, have been transgressing these modern disciplinary boundaries for many years. In addition to Cahill, ethicists such as Margaret A. Farley, Cathleen Kaveny, and Aline H. Kalbian have made substantial contributions to each of these ethical discourses. Furthermore, the scholarly contributions of ethicists of color such as Emilie M. Townes and Ada María Isasi-Díaz have authored works that are of extraordinary value to multiple ethical conversations, regardless of where the modern liberal disciplinary frameworks would

---

[21] Richard Miller, *Friends and Other Strangers: Studies in Religion, Ethics, and Culture* (New York: Columbia University Press, 2016).

[22] Ibid., 41. Miller defines *culture* as "the total of the inherited beliefs, values, knowledge, and material products that habituate a people, constitute the shared bases of individual and collective identity and action, and provide the milieu in which persons relate to historical knowledge and events" (ibid.).

[23] Ibid., 40.

[24] Ibid.

situate their contributions. Indeed, questioning these frameworks is essential to being able to recognize and engage the contributions of and from minoritized communities to the interdisciplinary, interreligious, and multitraditional work of ethics in a twenty-first-century global context. Cahill's scholarship models this kind of ethical engagement for subsequent generations.

A Pedagogy of Solidarity

Cahill's methodological innovations continue to influence the pursuit of scholarship across multiple ethical discourses. But Cahill's legacy will not be limited to printed publications, either her own or those of her many students. Cahill has instructed us on how to teach and mentor in ways that empower those whom society has attempted to disempower. She has shown us a pedagogy of solidarity, one that "has brought down the powerful from their thrones and has lifted up the lowly" (Lk 1:52 NRSV) toward fostering a more just, equitable, participatory, and authentically inclusive academy.

Cahill has inspired my own practices as a teacher. As a Mexican American woman, I am uniquely positioned to direct my students' attention to marginalized voices in religion, theology, and ethics. At the same time, I also must recognize my own privilege and limitations of perspective. For example, I have much less familiarity with the breadth and depth of scholarship in queer theology. Beyond my academic limitations, I must recognize that my identity as a legally married, cisgender, heterosexual woman limits my ability to recognize and critique unjust social, ecclesial, and academic structures that prevent the flourishing of my LGBTQ+ students and colleagues. My responsibility is to continue to learn from my students, remaining open to their academic interests—but also to their experiences as a center of concern in my own teaching and mentoring. I must be open to allowing their scholarship, advocacy, and experiences to broaden and transform my own perspective. In the process, I must be willing to relinquish privileges that adhere to my sexual identity even as I struggle against affronts to my dignity as a woman from a minoritized racial and ethnic community.

The pursuit of a pedagogy of solidarity can be awkward and difficult, and it is always incomplete. But as Cahill's work has shown us, we must recognize the moral necessity of practicing solidarity in the study of ethics. Indeed, Cahill shows us that solidarity is a lifelong pursuit—one that requires faith, love, hope, and humility.

Doing Ethics in a Global Context

Joseph Loic Mben, SJ

Doing ethics in a global context means incorporating issues other than one's culture, country, or continent into one's moral reflection. As far as culture is concerned, from a Westerner's standpoint it would mean including non-Western perspectives. In terms of places, this means taking into account other countries and continents.

Doing ethics in a global context from a Christian perspective can mean different things. It could mean an intra-Christian inquiry when one realizes the diversity of racial and ethnic backgrounds within the Church. It is not meant to be an ecumenical or interreligious dialogue, although a genuine ethical endeavor in the global context should take different religious sensitivities into account. Ethics in the global context is not limited to religious issues. It cannot be normative, but an applied ethics that looks into the diversity of human experience, trying to discern patterns of morality across contexts.

I want to explore in this chapter how Lisa Sowle Cahill has done theological ethics in a global context. It starts from the awareness that we live in a pluralistic world with its consequences for the practice of ethics. The first section looks at the challenges Christian ethics faces in a pluralistic world; Cahill's strategy here is to look for common ground and not give in to relativism. The second section of the chapter looks at the pervasiveness of evil that one must face at the global level. Third, the search for common ground is substantiated by natural law and the common good. Finally I look at how Cahill does ethics concretely, by considering the specific case of HIV/AIDS.

Ethics in the Face of Pluralism

The nature of the Catholic Church almost mandates doing ethics in a global context—first, because the Church is catholic, that is, universal, and as such believes that Christ's message should be heard in all corners of the world. The fact that the Church is universal means that it is a transversal reality that cuts across various cultures and places. Catholicity refers to inclusivity; it seeks to advance the gospel of Christ, and it means a "reconciled diversity."[1] Cahill embodies this kind of Catholic ethics aimed at the world—a thinking that is truly Catholic, grounded in the Catholic tradition, but also cross-denominational, capable of taking the best from other Christian denominations. An ethics that is truly Catholic cannot be confined locally and needs to open up in order to include global concerns.

Like Catholicism, human reality is characterized by diversity. A majority of human beings is neither Catholic nor from other Christian denominations. Hence, pluralism is much more than simply looking at diversity within Catholicism or Christianity. According to Lisa Cahill, "cultural pluralism" is a "revolutionary challenge" and a "more radical challenge."[2] This challenge demands a reassessment of ethics in general and ethical practice in particular. Indeed, "Moral theology is challenged by the apparent fragmentation of experience into myriad incommensurable value systems, and by the proliferation of 'different' and 'new' voices who assert their right to speak in their own names and for their own contexts."[3] Thus, in today's world the issue is not so much the awareness of cultural pluralism and diversity of experiences, but rather how to deal with these realities. In this postcolonial and postmodern world where any system with universalizing tendencies is suspect, Christian ethics finds itself on shaky ground.

That does not lead Cahill to fall into relativism,[4] be it meta-ethical relativism or normative relativism.[5] Two paradoxical insights guide Cahill's

---

[1] Michael Novak, "The Church Is Catholic," in *The Many Marks of the Church*, ed. William Madges and Michael J. Daley (New London, CT: Twenty-Third Publications, 2006), 48–52.

[2] Lisa Sowle Cahill, "Moral Theology: From Evolutionary to Revolutionary Change," in *Catholic Theological Ethics in the World Church: The Plenary Papers from the First Cross-Cultural Conference on Catholic Theological Ethics*, ed. James F. Keenan, SJ (New York: Continuum, 2007), 222.

[3] Ibid., 223.

[4] She rejects such a stand in her essay "Feminist Ethics, Differences, and Common Ground: A Catholic Perspective," in *Feminist Ethics and the Catholic Moral Tradition*, ed. Charles E. Curran, Margaret A. Farley, and Richard A. McCormick, Readings in Moral Theology 9 (New York: Paulist Press, 1996), 184–204.

[5] *Meta-ethical relativism* claims that no "single moral code has universal validity," and denies that "an assertion that moral truth and justifiability, if there are any such things, are in some way relative to factors that are culturally and historically contingent"; *normative relativism* "holds that it is wrong to pass judgment on others who have substantially different values, or to try to make them conform to one's values, for the reason that their values are as valid as one's own" (David Wong, "Relativism," in *A Companion to Ethics*, ed. Peter Singer, Blackwell Companions to Philosophy [Oxford: Blackwell Publishers, 1997], 442).

approach. The first affirms the contingency of moral truth, which ties in to the diversity of human experience and cultures.[6] The second claims that moral truth is not the result of arbitrariness or whims, but rather it is grounded on the reality of human interdependence and can be objective.[7] Moreover, this claim highlights one of the defining signatures of Cahill's approach to diversity: the search for common ground. Indeed, for Cahill, ethics is "an ability to affirm similarity in difference, and true knowing without reduction."[8]

Pluralism does not prevent the possibility of intelligibility. Actually, ethical and theological discourse can be "intelligible to discourses in other cultural and social settings that are experiencing the same failure of global systems and who are raising the same kind of protest."[9]

Another source of intelligibility is the concrete experience of human persons. In fact, "Human beings everywhere share physical and even psychological characteristics. Every culture and every person values family, food, clean water, shelter, and freedom from fear of violence and illness."[10] At this level, commonalities can be found and agreements can be made. Nonetheless, the search for inclusivity and common ground does not mean complacency or compromising with the truth. Ethics must not be "afraid to be critical, judgmental, persuasive, interventionist, and even coercive."[11] In particular, one cannot compromise on the necessity of basic goods for every human person. This is why she suggests transversalism[12] as the needed approach.

The search for commonality affects the practice of Christian ethics, which cannot be confined to the comfort of the classroom. It must engage with reality not only theoretically but also at a practical level. Hence, in order to "be practically effective, theological and ethical ideals must grip people and communities at more than an intellectual or theoretical

---

[6]Cahill, "Moral Theology," 223.
[7]Ibid.
[8]Cahill, "Feminist Ethics, Differences, and Common Ground," 192.
[9]Lisa Sowle Cahill, *Theological Bioethics: Participation, Justice, and Change*, Moral Traditions Series, ed. James F. Keenan, SJ (Washington, DC: Georgetown University Press, 2005), 63.
[10]Cahill, "Moral Theology," 224–25.
[11]Cahill, "Feminist Ethics, Differences, and Common Ground," 185.
[12]"Transversalism is a process of mutually empathetic and critical communication, in which participants cross imaginatively into one another's territories, express their own values and assertions, listen to others, modify their own claims, try to reach agreement on the moral nonnegotiables, and honestly criticize the shortcomings of all cultural systems" (Cahill, "Moral Theology," 224).

level."[13] This is why, for Cahill, "theory and practice are interdependent."[14] For the ethicist, doing ethics in the global context means opening oneself to others, networking and collaborating with individuals and groups outside of academic circles in order to effect change. And one particular challenge—especially from an African perspective—is how to reach out to the uneducated masses. This calls for a renewal of "the link between theological reflection and argument, and social action for transformative goals."[15] Hence, the ethicist cannot stand as a neutral observer or remain a passive bystander.

The Reality of Evil

Doing ethics in the global context means confronting the difficult and sometimes ugly situations that our world faces, in what Cahill calls the "unprecedented magnitude of global injustice."[16] Today in our world, billions suffer deprivation, violence, epidemics, and insecurity of all kind. This evil can be carried out structurally through group violence that may take the form of xenophobia, racism/ethnocentrism, sexism, stigmatization or scapegoating, exclusion from social goods, discrimination, and various other social ills.[17] Moral theologians refer to this evil reality as *sin*.[18] Identifying evil as sin means first that it is contrary to God's will, and that reality needs to be transformed. Hence, one cannot fall into fatalism, because from a Christian standpoint evil is overcome by Jesus Christ's paschal mystery. In order to offer a relevant ethical reflection and action, one must confront and acknowledge the pervasiveness of evil/sin in human experience. Evil means the disruption of relationships:[19] with God, other humans, oneself, and the nonhuman creation. Evil reveals the inability of human beings to extend love and empathy beyond their intimate circle.[20] Indeed, "Moral evil is the failure to avoid and minimize the harm that plurality and contingency can cause, to manipulate contingent drives and

---

[13] Lisa Sowle Cahill, *Global Justice, Christology, and Christian Ethics*, New Studies in Christian Ethics, ed. Robin Gill (Cambridge: Cambridge University Press, 2013), 6.

[14] Cahill, *Theological Bioethics*, 69.

[15] Ibid., 51.

[16] Cahill, *Global Justice, Christology, and Christian Ethics*, 35.

[17] Ibid., 41.

[18] Cahill, "Moral Theology," 225. The *Catechism of the Catholic Church* (no. 1849) defines *sin* as "an utterance, a deed, or a desire contrary to the eternal law"; the same number adds, "it is failure in genuine love for God and neighbor caused by a perverse attachment to certain goods. It wounds the nature of man and injures human solidarity."

[19] Cahill, *Global Justice, Christology, and Christian Ethics*, 55.

[20] Ibid., 44.

ends for selfish advantage, and to resolve conflicts through domination and perceived competitors."[21]

One example of moral evil is the imbalance in international relations between countries. Their origin is located in the European imperialistic expansion toward the rest of the world since the fifteenth and sixteenth centuries, which resulted in the conquest of the Americas and the colonization of Africa and large parts of Asia.

From an African perspective, colonization has produced enduring effects, such as turning African countries into suppliers of raw materials; continued low wages and salaries and the survival of free, cheap, and forced labor; and Western powers and multinational corporations meddling in the internal affairs of African countries, in terms of coups, weapons supplies, and wars.

Toward a Proper Sense of Our Common Humanity

Commonalities and shared experiences exist between humans, as Cahill claims. However, as she shows, these commonalities are not always actualized in reality, especially at the global level, where relations between nations and international/transnational groups are not generally guided by care for the other and altruism.

There are two key concepts—natural law and common good—that help correct the sense of commonality. Both concepts are pervaded by the notion of justice.

Justice can be understood simply as such or as social justice, contributive justice, or distributive justice. Moreover, justice is "the essential quality and dignity of all human persons."[22] It can also be defined as the "practical recognition of basic human goods, human equality, respect for other species, and participation of all in the common good."[23] More technically, "Justice is an objective criterion of moral relationships that sees persons, groups and communities as interdependent and as having an equal right to share in the material and social conditions of human well-being."[24] Social justice is either defined as "distributive justice and the common good," or as "contributive justice."[25] *Distributive justice* refers to how social public goods are allocated to individuals and groups. This

---

[21]Ibid., 48.
[22]Lisa Sowle Cahill, "Justice, Gender and the Market," *Outside the Market No Salvation?*, *Concilium* 2 (1997), ed. Dietmar Mieth and Marciano Vidal, 133–42, at 134.
[23]Cahill, *Global Justice, Christology, and Christian Ethics*, 3.
[24]Cahill, *Theological Bioethics*, 221.
[25]Ibid., 44, 47.

allocation must be assessed according to its effects on the people whose basic needs are not met.[26] By *contributive justice*, Cahill means "what all persons bring to the common good by their active participation."[27]

Natural Law

In search of common ground, Cahill relies on the (much maligned) notion of natural law as understood by Thomas Aquinas (1225–1274). She acknowledges that natural law ethics "needs to be revised and updated in the global, postmodern world."[28] However, she justifies the recourse to natural law by stating that "the concept of 'human nature' is a way to express what constitutes us as distinctively human, what connects us to other human beings, how humans are related to the rest of the world, what justice requires in those relations, and how and why conversation about justice can be carried on across distances of time, space, culture and religion."[29] There are three dimensions of a revised natural law: the identification of aspects of human nature relevant to moral obligation, the epistemology of natural law, and the notion of moral virtue.[30]

As Cahill notes, "Human nature includes human *characteristics*, human *goods*, and basic human *equality* or '*equal respect.*' "[31] Human nature is subject to change, and natural law affirms the possibility for humans of maintaining certain characteristics while changes occur.[32] With respect to natural law, Aquinas identifies basic spheres of morality: self-preservation; sexual intercourse, procreation, and education of offspring; and knowing the truth and living in society.[33] Any endeavor in social justice in the contemporary world demands the recognition of basic equality.[34] This is a point of contention between cultures.[35] People will not agree with this idea especially in hierarchical societies, where everyone is expected to behave according to their status. However, even in hierarchical societies,

---

[26]United States Conference of Catholic Bishops, *Economic Justice for All: A Pastoral Letter on Catholic Social Teaching and the U.S. Economy* (Washington, DC: United States Conference of Catholic Bishops, 1986), no. 70, http://www.usccb.org/upload/economic justice for all.pdf.
[27]Cahill, *Theological Bioethics*, 47.
[28]Cahill, *Global Justice, Christology, and Christian Ethics*, 250.
[29]Ibid., 249–50.
[30]Ibid., 251–52.
[31]Ibid., 252.
[32]Ibid., 256.
[33]Ibid., 258.
[34]Ibid., 259.
[35]Ibid., 260.

people recognize the inherent value of every human person.[36] This could provide a starting point on which to build.

Concerning the epistemology of natural law or how one can grasp it, Cahill states that natural law is "knowable by reasonable reflection on human experience, especially on the goods which constitute human flourishing, and the institutions necessary to secure, protect, and distribute them."[37] To emphasize the need for moral reflection to be connected to human experience, she states, "moral truth as practical truth is a truth of action."[38] In contrast with the scholastic approach (deductive), Cahill claims that precepts of natural law cannot be known outside of human experience (inductive). This move is strategic in order to avoid the accusation of imparting a hegemonic ideology on others.

Natural law ethics is not limited to a theoretical knowledge of what must be done.[39] The virtues are dispositions that indicate whether a life is ordered or not. As Cahill writes, "The good life is the virtuous life, and the virtuous life is the only life that will guarantee genuine happiness."[40] The virtues simultaneously connect us to the important goods, to God, and to salvation. A virtuous life is conformity and participation in these goods.[41] One may wonder whether, by appealing to virtues, Cahill does not raise the bar too high. One will agree that most societies have a certain understanding of the good and how to achieve it. Every society has a concept of a good life and socializes its members in light of this ideal. Whether the individual chooses to live according to this vision of the good life or not is something that remains to be seen. The society also may not offer all the conditions to help the individual flourish.

Beyond such commonality, Cahill believes that cultures can be intelligible. A particular culture may not articulate the concept of virtue as such but will have an idea of what a good person is and what this entails. For Cahill, "The goods that constitute human flourishing can be known across communities; this is the source of an ethics of natural law."[42]

Indeed, the use of virtue language shows that the search for common-

---

[36] For instance, the Basaa, an ethnic group from Cameroon, in one proverb say that "the sun shines over a village even if it is small," acknowledging the dignity of everyone no matter how insignificant they may be. African cultures in general emphasize interconnectedness between beings to an extent that a smaller being could positively or negatively affect a bigger one.

[37] Cahill, "Feminist Ethics, Differences, and Common Ground," 189–90.

[38] Cahill, *Global Justice, Christology, and Christian Ethics*, 265–66.

[39] Ibid., 267.

[40] Ibid., 268.

[41] Ibid., 270.

[42] Ibid., 273.

ality does not entail settling for minimalist goals or advocate mediocrity (understood etymologically as judging in the middle). The search for commonality is a call for excellence. Human beings are meant to flourish and achieve their full potential. Hence, seeking common ground does not mean watering down the demands of the gospel. It is a common appeal for justice in order to lead to the transformation of human communities so that they will enable their members to flourish and achieve their full potential. This approach indicates that ethics is not just descriptive, but must also reflect on what people ought to do.

By relying on natural law, Cahill tries to discern common traits (provided by experience) and not general traits (abstract and theoretical).

The Common Good

The common good is one of the chief concerns of an ethics done in a global setting. It is a key demand of justice. Cahill's understanding of the common good is indebted to the Church's magisterium.[43] The common good is understood as institutional as well as relational. As institutional, it is "the sum total of those conditions of social living whereby [human beings] are enabled more fully and more readily to achieve their own perfections."[44] This perspective encourages evaluation of the quality of social institutions in their ability to promote the flourishing of individuals. Indeed, "The common good includes the material and social aspect of human flourishing."[45] Such an approach precludes any instrumental use of the person.[46]

The relational or solidaristic understanding of the common good focuses on relationships and interdependence between people and states. The common good here appears as a shared good. Using Aristotle's analogy of friendship, Hollenbach locates this common good at two levels: useful friendship and true friendship.[47] *Useful friendship*, also called *partnership*, allows people to work together in order to attain goods useful to each one of them that they could not have achieved on their own.[48] *True*

---

[43] Lisa Sowle Cahill, "AIDS, Justice, and the Common Good," in *Catholic Ethicists on HIV/AIDS Prevention*, ed. James F. Keenan, SJ, with Jon Fuller, SJ, Lisa Sowle Cahill, and Kevin Kelly (New York: Continuum, 2000), 288–89.

[44] John XXIII, Encyclical Letter on Christianity and Social Progress, *Mater et Magistra* (1961), no. 65, www.vatican.va.

[45] Cahill, "AIDS, Justice, and the Common Good," 288.

[46] Jacques Maritain, *The Person and the Common Good*, trans. John J. Fitzgerald (New York: Charles Scribner's Sons, 1947), 67–68.

[47] Hollenbach, "The Common Good as Participation in Community," 8–11.

[48] Ibid., 9.

friendship is also called *civic friendship* or *true solidarity*.[49] The people or groups involved at this level "seek to promote each other's well-being for moral reasons, having genuine concern for each other's dignity and for the well-being that dignity requires."[50] The common good in the relational perspective emerges in the context of a relationship.

Cahill values both understandings. The raison d'être of the common good is "to enhance the well-being of every member of society, as well as of society as a whole."[51] At the global level, billions do not partake in the common good. Indeed, "Access to goods is typically restricted."[52] Participation in the common good is key to a person's flourishing.[53] In support of an institutional and relational understanding, Cahill notes that people need "the many conditions of social life which make up the common good" and allow "participation of *all* members of society in the common good."[54] In Catholic social teaching, participation is a right and a duty, and being excluded from partaking significantly in social life is an injustice.[55]

At the global level one should speak of a universal common good.[56] The notion of common good allows Cahill to show not only that human beings share commonalities, but they share also the same environment and interact with each other locally and globally. This is why solidarity is closely related to the common good. Pope John Paul II understands the latter as "a firm and persevering determination to commit oneself to the common good; that is to say, to the good of all and of each individual, because we are all really responsible for all."[57] Solidarity highlights the moral responsibility that individuals and groups bear. The achievement of the common good at the global level is closely related to subsidiarity. Subsidiarity is about the relationship of the state with lower or intermediary organizations. It began with a notion of devolution of power from the state within society to lower institutions, and was progressively enriched so as to arrive at an idea of autonomy of intermediary bodies

---

[49] Ibid., 10.
[50] Ibid.
[51] Cahill, "AIDS, Justice, and the Common Good," 288.
[52] Cahill, "Moral Theology," 225.
[53] Cahill, "Justice, Gender and the Market," 136.
[54] Ibid., 140.
[55] Thomas Massaro, SJ, *Living Justice: Catholic Social Teaching in Action*, 3rd classroom ed. (Lanham, MD: Rowman & Littlefield, 2015), 90.
[56] Cahill, *Theological Bioethics*, 47; Cahill, *Global Justice, Christology, and Christian Ethics*, 279.
[57] John Paul II, Encyclical Letter on the Social Concern of the Church, *Sollicitudo rei socialis* (1987), no. 38, www.vatican.va.

and the promotion of the human person and the common good as its ultimate goal.[58]

Cahill is in tune with the magisterium when she affirms that "subsidiarity implies both the relative autonomy of local organizations and the responsibility of government to reign in or modify 'subsidiary' action that is detrimental to the common good."[59] In a global context, "Subsidiarity has to be reconceived so that the vertical dynamic of influence expands to include horizontal and much more pluralistic exercises of authority and efficacy, characterized by collaboration and power sharing."[60] Subsidiarity can function as a tool for the evaluation of "political arrangements and their adequacy for diverse social contexts."[61] Among the questions that should be asked are: To what extent are people at the grass roots involved or not? What is the share of local organizations? Is the activity inclusive and participatory? Does it promote the common good? How are the government and international institutions involved?

Case Study: The Church's Handling of HIV/AIDS

Cahill concretely demonstrates how doing ethics in a global setting worked in the case of HIV/AIDS.[62] HIV/AIDS now primarily affects sub-Saharan Africa, even though it is present in other parts of the world.[63] This distribution led some to wrongly affirm that HIV/AIDS is an African issue. In recent years, a challenge was to find ways to mobilize the rest of the world to act, especially at a time when the pandemic seemed to be under control in the industrialized world. The Catholic Church has been forceful in its advocacy in favor of HIV/AIDS patients: ministering to them, fighting stigmatization against them, and demanding/allowing access to proper medication for patients in poor countries. At the same time, the Church opened its facilities to help HIV/AIDS patients. Moreover,

---

[58]One can see how the notion of subsidiarity evolved in the thought of the following popes: Pius XI, Encyclical Letter on Reconstruction of the Social Order, *Quadragesimo Anno* (1931), nos. 79–80; John Paul II, Encyclical Letter on the Hundredth Anniversary of *Rerum Novarum*, *Centesimus Annus* (1991), nos. 15, 48; Benedict XVI, Encyclical Letter on Integral Human Development in Charity and Truth, *Caritas in Veritate* (2009), no. 57—all at www.vatican.va.

[59]Cahill, *Theological Bioethics*, 4.

[60]Ibid.

[61]Ibid., 45.

[62]From here onward see ibid., 164–68.

[63]According to the latest figures from the World Health Organization, two-thirds of people living with HIV/AIDS live in sub-Saharan Africa; see World Health Organization, "HIV/AIDS: Key Facts," https://www.who.int/news-room/fact-sheets/detail/hiv-aids.

the Church addressed world leaders as well as international pharmaceutical companies, pointing out the injustice of limited access to expensive treatments and the necessity of acting when there was a lack of political will on the matter. Such action was multidimensional. From the ecclesial hierarchy to the grass roots, various bodies at the local, national, and global levels of the Church have been involved in fighting against HIV/AIDS, providing funding, treatment, and spiritual and social support to those afflicted by the disease.

The Church seeks to respond to the demands of Christian discipleship, to emphasize the preferential option for the poor, and to locate and support the common good. The AIDS crisis shows how the work of academics has been supplemented on the ground by religious activism. Indeed, "Theorizing action and holding up the transformative interstices of action, belief and theology are essential tasks of theological scholarship."[64]

In a nutshell, for Cahill, doing ethics in a global setting implies a collaborative effort that requires: being aware of the pluralistic context of today's world and looking for commonalities between various cultures; avoiding the easy way out of relativism that could lead one to cynicism and indifference; building on one's values and ideals; defending ideals and justice for all, especially for the most marginalized; and being able to integrate theory with action.

---

[64]Cahill, *Theological Bioethics*, 168.

The Gift and Virtue of Presence

Catholic and Protestant Dialogue
and the Future of Christian Ethics

Autumn Alcott Ridenour

M. Theresa Lysaught opens the 2018 book *Catholic Bioethics and Social Justice* by describing Lisa Sowle Cahill as the forerunner for justice and the principles of Catholic social teaching within the field of bioethics.[1] Grounding ethics in the practices of concrete communities is a theme across Cahill's various contributions, including *Family: A Social Perspective*; *Bioethics and the Common Good*; *Theological Bioethics*; and more recently, *Global Justice, Christology, and Christian Ethics*, to name a few. As a feminist drawing from relationships, experience, and practice, Cahill asks theological questions in ways that enliven and empower concrete communities on the ground. What theme might unite the various works in their contribution to the field of Christian ethics and its future challenges, particularly those posed by technology and the temptation to escape embodied community and our ethical obligations to the neighbor? Perhaps a theme at the center of Christian community: the gift and virtue of presence.

While much of twentieth-century ethics focused on contention between particular theories, such as whether deontological, utilitarian, or virtue ethics posed the best ethical method,[2] a fresh look at the relational grounding behind Christian ethics rooted as presence or union with Christ through the Spirit might forge a much-needed vision for moving forward in a world of screens and the twenty-first-century challenges that go along

---

[1] M. Therese Lysaught and Michael McCarthy, eds., *Catholic Bioethics and Social Justice: The Praxis of US Health Care in a Globalized World* (Collegeville, MN: Liturgical Press, 2018), 8.
[2] Stanley Hauerwas, *Suffering Presence: Theological Reflections on Medicine, the Mentally Handicapped, and the Church* (Notre Dame, IN: University of Notre Dame Press, 1986), 71.

with them. This fresh look considers, first, the role of union with Christ through the Spirit as foundational for a Catholic and Protestant ethics of presence through the contribution of Lisa Sowle Cahill; and second, reclaiming the significance of embodied presence as a communal virtue across the Catholic-Protestant traditions with implications for moral action and our anthropology apart from mediated technology.

The Gift of Presence through Union with Christ

Considering the role of union with Christ as central for Christian ethics perhaps seems moot at first glance. Presumably, ethics forged in light of Christianity might center on the God revealed in the person of Jesus Christ. Interestingly, while theological assumptions about Christology perhaps loomed in the background, twentieth-century ethics forged ahead around debates on neighbor love and identifying obligations to such neighbors (Outka, Santurri, and Werpehowski), natural law ethics (Finnis, Pinckaers, Pope), the common good (Hollenbach, Cahill, Stiltner, et al.), and a turn toward virtue from Protestant and Catholic scholars alike (Hauerwas, Porter, Keenan, Mattison, et al.).[3] While this scholarship inevitably advanced the field, few scholars turned to the centrality of Christology or the importance of union with Christ behind these theories. While the return to virtue may be the beginning of such relational focus, given its aim at union with God, Lisa Sowle Cahill's volume *Global Justice, Christology, and Christian Ethics* makes the significance

---

[3] Gene Outka, *Agape: An Ethical Analysis* (New Haven, CT: Yale University Press, 1972); Edmund N. Santurri and William Werpehowski, eds., *The Love Commandments: Essays in Christian Ethics and Moral Philosophy* (Eugene, OR: Wipf & Stock, 1992); John Finnis, *Natural Law and Natural Rights*, Clarendon Law, 2nd ed. (Oxford: Oxford University Press, 2011); Nigel Biggar and Rufus Black, eds., *The Revival of Natural Law: Philosophical, Theological, and Ethical Responses to the Finnis-Grisez School* (London: Routledge, 2000); Servais Pinckaers, OP, *The Sources of Christian Ethics*, 3rd ed., trans. Mary Thomas Noble (Washington, DC: Catholic University of America Press, 1995); Stephen J. Pope, "Reason and Natural Law," in Gilbert Meilaender and William Werpehowski, eds., *The Oxford University Handbook of Theological Ethics* (Oxford: Oxford University Press, 2005); David Hollenbach, SJ, *The Common Good and Christian Ethics*, New Studies in Christian Ethics 22, ed. Robin Gill (Cambridge: Cambridge University Press, 2002); Lisa Sowle Cahill, *Bioethics and the Common Good: The 2004* Père Marquette Lecture in Theology (Milwaukee: Marquette University, 2004); Brian Stiltner, *Religion and the Common Good* (Lanham, MD: Rowman & Littlefield, 1999); Stanley Hauerwas, *A Community of Character: Toward a Constructive Social Ethics* (Notre Dame, IN: University of Notre Dame Press, 1981); Jean Porter, *The Recovery of Virtue: The Relevance of Aquinas for Christian Ethics* (Louisville, KY: Westminster John Knox Press, 1990); James F. Keenan, SJ, *Virtues for Ordinary Christians* (Lanham, MD: Sheed & Ward, 1996); William C. Mattison III, *Introducing Moral Theology: True Happiness and the Virtues* (Grand Rapids: Brazos, 2008).

of Christology and union with Christ central to moral theology.[4]

In her volume, Cahill unpacks the ethical implications of Christology and Christological interpretations of Christ's person and work across various strands of the tradition, including Catholic and Protestant authors as they relate to practices on the ground. Not surprisingly, her Christological focus allows her to bridge these tradition-based divides in an ecumenical spirit. Likewise, a turn to Christology and the significance of union with Christ as the gift of presence for relating to God and neighbor proves all the more important given the technological temptation to avoid, ignore, objectify, commodify, label, and "other" the neighbor. Locating union with Christ through the Spirit as love of God through beholding, serving, and being present for the neighbor challenges our eroding responsibility to one another in the twenty-first-century digital age. To consider this point, I turn to a few authors distilling union with Christ throughout the tradition as particularly noted in Cahill's work.

Union with Christ in Augustine, Thomas Aquinas, and Martin Luther

Turning to Augustine in the early fourth century is helpful for a variety of reasons. For starters, he precedes later theological categories relating to ontology and moral agency in regard to infused grace (a more Catholic category associated with Thomas Aquinas that involves a change in nature) and imputed righteousness (a more Protestant category associated with Martin Luther that involves the believer's declared legal status). Both strands of Catholic and Protestant Christianity begin with Augustine. Second, to enter into Augustine's thought-world is to enter into a thought-world deeply informed by relationships. In fact, Augustine's entire moral theory hinges upon love. Augustine's anthropology understands humans as creatures who love. The primary question rests on which objects, persons, or beings we most love and, thus, what objects in which we most place our hope, faith, and desire. To love or be present in relationship with others is a primary way of understanding human creatureliness.

While Augustine's cosmology acknowledges creaturely dependence on God since time's beginning in his *On Genesis*, his more mature work, *On the Trinity*, exposes an anthropology in which the union found in Christ's person, through both divine and human natures, remedies our injured hu-

---

[4]Lisa Sowle Cahill, *Global Justice, Christology, and Christian Ethics*, New Studies in Christian Ethics, ed. Robin Gill (Cambridge: Cambridge University Press, 2013). See Marianne Tierney FitzGerald's chapter in this volume.

manity fractured by sin.[5] As Lewis Ayres interprets *On the Trinity*, Christ's divine and human natures bring together severed wisdom and knowledge and, presumably, contemplation and virtue along with it.[6] As George Lavare affirms, "In Christ, the virtue of God and the wisdom of God, the fullness of virtue is realized concretely and made accessible to the world as a unified whole incorporating the totality of virtue."[7] Through prayer, Christ's presence is made available as wisdom through union with the Father and action (virtue). Through virtue, Christ displays the appropriate dependent posture of human nature on divine presence or Spirit-led grace.

For Augustine, our human dependence on the divine presence of spirit-led grace comes through union with Christ. While rest or union will not fully be realized until eternity, Augustine also writes on the importance of beginning love or union with God here in time, most concretely seen through neighbor love. Lavare continues, "For Augustine virtue is the very essence of Christian life, providing a clear view of the end to be achieved and the means to that end. God is love and created in love; the Christian soul returns to God in love by means of virtue, for virtue is the 'ordering of love' (*civ. Dei* 15.22)."[8] In other words, the virtue of love is the means by which individuals maintain union with God through divine presence and work on ordering their loves in time.

Eric Gregory describes neighbor love in the form of political ethics as contingent upon ordered love. Loving God first simultaneously protects the neighbor and allows the neighbor to make ethical demands on the Christian life.[9] As Tarcisius van Bavel stresses,

> In order to come to the love of God, we must begin by loving our neighbors. Although love of God comes first in the order of commanding, love of neighbor comes first in the order of performing.... This is not a denial of the absolute difference between God and the human being.... Rather, it is the conviction that we have to *participate in God's love for all human beings*. If we refuse to do so, we do not love God.[10]

---

[5] Augustine, *On Genesis*, trans. Edmund Hill, OP, and Matthew O'Connell (Hyde Park, NY: New City Press, 2002); Augustine, *On the Trinity*, trans. Edmund Hill, OP (Hyde Park, NY: New City Press, 1991), 225, 337ff.; Autumn Alcott Ridenour, *Sabbath Rest at Vocation: Aging toward Death*, Enquiries in Theological Ethics (London: Bloomsbury, 2018).

[6] Lewis Ayres, "The Christological Context of Augustine's *De Trinitate* XIII: Toward Relocating Books VIII–XV," *Augustinian Studies* 29, no. 1 (1998): 111–39.

[7] George Lavare, "Virtue," in *Augustine through the Ages: An Encyclopedia*, ed. Allan D. Fitzgerald, OSA (Grand Rapids: William B. Eerdmans, 1999), 873.

[8] Lavare, "Virtue," 873.

[9] Eric Gregory, *Politics and the Order of Love: An Augustinian Ethic of Democratic Citizenship* (Chicago: University of Chicago Press, 2008).

[10] Tarcisius van Bavel, "Love," in *Augustine through the Ages*, ed. Allan D. Fitzgerald,

Here van Bavel reflects on the embodied ways creatures participate in the love of God, beginning with presence to the neighbor. In this sense, Christian ethics is by definition social and neighbor-focused in its application.

James K. A. Smith's recent book *You Are What You Love* provides a helpful contemporary Augustinian anthropology for understanding moral agents as creatures who love by definition and act on what is most loved. In fact, for Smith all actions and habits reveal what individuals and communities most love or worship. Western cultural liturgies, such as shopping, reveal faith and hope in the temporary fulfillment of consumerism;[11] cultural liturgies associated with devices shape the way we encounter and treat one another, often as objects rather than subjects.[12] The alternative vision Smith delineates is one enveloped and marked by love of Christ. Drawing from the Apostle Paul, relational union with Christ might be personified as clothing we "put on" much like virtue.[13] The virtuous habits in which we clothe ourselves in Christ are formed not through consumeristic practices but through presence in the Christian community—the body of Christ—by participation in the love of God toward our neighbor. Thus, presence or union with Christ is directly linked to virtue for Augustine, which influences later thinkers such as Thomas Aquinas and even Martin Luther.

While reductionist critiques of Thomas Aquinas suggest he misses the transformative presence of Christ given the future focus on the beatific vision, thereby emphasizing the journey *to* God rather than the journey *with* God,[14] Cahill's *Global Justice* offers a helpful corrective. Utilizing a Spirit Christology, Cahill argues that Aquinas's theology was about Spirit-infused virtues that reflect friendship with God inasmuch as it was about natural law.[15] Christ is present to the believer through grace and the infused virtues. Grace elevates human nature through the theological virtues, allowing for "a kind of participation in the divine nature."[16] Infused grace is not immediate but set within a context of relationships in which individuals are shaped by the gospel narratives, prayer, and liturgical practices shared within the Christian community. Cahill writes,

---

OSA (Grand Rapids: Eerdmans, 1999), 512. Italics added.

[11] James K. A. Smith, *You Are What You Love: The Spiritual Power of Habit* (Grand Rapids: Brazos Press, 2016), 46–53.

[12] Sherry Turkle, *Alone Together* (New York: Basic Books, 2011), xiv; Sherry Turkle, *Reclaiming Conversation: The Power of Talk in a Digital Age* (New York: Penguin Books, 2015), 345.

[13] Smith, *You Are What You Love*, 16, 23–25, 65.

[14] James Wm. McClendon Jr., *Systematic Theology: Ethics*, vol. 1, rev. ed. (Nashville: Abingdon Press, 2002), 64.

[15] Cahill, *Global Justice, Christology, and Christian Ethics*, 178.

[16] Ibid., 171.

"For Aquinas, God always interacts dynamically in Christian existence, constantly inspiring and enabling Christians to persevere and to act. Sanctifying grace is not just a change in our 'nature,' but the presence of the Spirit 'indwelling in us.' "[17]

Cahill argues that Aquinas further describes the gifts of the Spirit as unique from virtue in that the gifts reflect "inner promptings" that come from a divine initiative. She writes, "Like habits, the Holy Spirit's gifts 'abide in' us, making us always readier to follow the Spirit's lead 'as moved by God.' The gifts do not change our natures. Instead, they testify that God is always actively *present* in the course of human lives."[18] Here, active union with Christ reflects the presence of the Spirit. Moreover, according to Cahill, for Catholics the presence of the Spirit is most manifest in the bodily presence of Christ through the Eucharist.[19]

Beyond Catholic identity, influenced by the life and work of Augustine, Martin Luther also writes of Christian presence within the believer by one's appropriation of grace.[20] While Luther is primarily known for his defense of salvation as justification by faith alone, he is less known for his focus on the moral life or moral growth, oftentimes described as the process of sanctification. However, relying on more recent Finnish interpretations of Luther, Cahill affirms Christ's presence with the believer through union with Christ.[21] While fully recognizing Luther's concern with salvation by faith apart from works, alongside his reluctance to assign anything beyond alien righteousness to the believer as simultaneously justified and sinner, Cahill emphasizes parts of Luther's work that highlight how faith unites the soul to Christ, much like the bride unites with the bridegroom.[22] Turning to Luther's *Lectures on Galatians*, and its newer Finnish interpreters, Cahill writes, "While Luther there repudiates any idea of an 'ontological change' in the natures of persons of faith, he does seem to see Christ as constantly present to and even in the believer, conforming the identity of the latter to his own in a relation of 'participation' or 'indwelling.' "[23]

Here Cahill suggest that the language of "indwelling" sounds a great

---

[17]Ibid., 172.
[18]Ibid., 175.
[19]Ibid., 177.
[20]To this day the Order of St. Augustine recognizes the order's Augustinian impact emphasizing grace on Luther's theology. See P. Alejandro Moral Anton, OSA, "Letter to the Brothers and Sisters of the Order on the Occasion of the 500th Anniversary of the Start of the Lutheran Reform," *Curia Generalizia Agostiniana*, September 28, 2017, 3.
[21]Cahill, *Global Justice, Christology, and Christian Ethics*, 187.
[22]Ibid., 184.
[23]Martin Luther, *Lectures on Galatians*, 381, as cited by Carter Lindberg, "Do Lutherans Shout Justification but Whisper Sanctification?," *Lutheran Quarterly* 13 (1999): 1–20, at 2. See Cahill, *Global Justice, Christology, and Christian Ethics*, 186.

deal like Thomas Aquinas. According to Tuomo Mannermaa, who pushed for the newer interpretation, Luther even echoed the famous phrase of Athanasius from the Eastern Orthodox tradition: "God becomes man so that man may become God."[24] However, Luther's emphasis has less to do with the language of "new nature" and more to do with "new existence" with an emphasis on "identity" in Christ.[25] Hence, the emphasis is less on the person and more on the change invoked because of "Christ's *presence* within it."[26] For Reformed figures, including Luther and Calvin, the emphasis will be on an identity received rather than achieved or merited. Because of a new identity received from Jesus (imputed) through Christ's presence with the believer, individuals are moved to love the neighbor. But beyond individual acts toward the neighbor, followers of Christ might encounter his presence through the church community as well as in serving the broader society.[27]

Such presence is not merely an individual change, but presence experienced in community through the preached word, sacraments, and service of the community to neighbors both near and far.[28] The presence and participation in Christ invoke communal practices toward the neighbor in need.[29] For Luther, the Church's preaching of the Word and sacraments are the primary way in which believers encounter God's presence as well as shape moral responsibility as seen through teaching the *Larger Catechism* in terms of ongoing moral formation. Cahill illustrates how "the experience of the Holy Spirit in the Church through word and sacraments is the experience of union with Christ. In turn, the quality of personal and ecclesial life is renewed.... Christians undergo existential change in a communal process of conversion and formation."[30] The existential change resulting from faith and regeneration involves personal, ecclesial, and political implications in loving the neighbor in need.[31]

Cahill continues, "Conformity to Christ in the Spirit requires the liturgy of the Word; it is expressed as relations of love and care among church members, in a more Christ-like fulfillment of one's worldly vocation, and

---

[24] Tuomo Mannermaa, "Justification and *Theosis*," in Carl E. Braaten and Robert W. Jenson, eds., *Union with Christ: The New Finnish Interpretation of Luther* (Grand Rapids: Eerdmans, 1998), 25–41, at 33, citing an early Christmas sermon of Athanasius. See also Cahill, *Global Justice, Christology, and Christian Ethics*, 187.
[25] Cahill, *Global Justice, Christology, and Christian Ethics*, 188.
[26] Ibid. (emphasis added).
[27] Ibid., 188–91.
[28] Ibid., 189–90.
[29] Ibid., 191.
[30] Ibid., 189.
[31] Ibid., 189–92.

in Christian advocacy for more just social practices and institutions."[32] Thus, despite maintaining Augustinian realism about the evil capacities of human nature and sin still present among believers, Luther's Christian identity also entails hope, given the presence of Christ dwelling within believers in the Church and the call to love the neighbor. Such presence is not devoid of human realism but maintains a strong theology of the cross and awareness of human suffering that benefits from a continued focus on Christ's presence. Here Anabaptist James McClendon's *Ethics* is helpful for describing the significance of presence as an embodied virtue to be lived in a thick community, especially in the realistic challenges encountered in twenty-first-century life often cloaked under the veil of technology.[33]

The Virtue of Presence and the Significance of Community in Catholic and Protestant Ethics

Turning to an Anabaptist theologian is not surprising given that Cahill's research and course offerings often included insights from the Anabaptist tradition in their shared concerns relating to concrete practices as well as peacemaking.[34] James McClendon concluded his career by writing an Anabaptist systematic theology in which he begins with ethics as opposed to apologetics, revelation, or specific doctrines. Much like Cahill's *Global Justice*, McClendon argues that theology might begin with lived practices as delineated in the realm of ethics. Further, McClendon stresses that lived theology or embodied witness in thick communities of presence are important factors for an increasingly individualistic culture.[35]

Unlike today's twenty-first-century technological culture in which we are ever connected, yet isolated from one another through the mediation of phones or tablets, McClendon begins such lived theology as "embodied ethics" formed in thick communities cultivating the virtue of presence, as displayed in the African American church as well as the life of Dietrich Bonhoeffer.[36] Here McClendon's method parallels Cahill's own approach in *Family: A Christian Social Perspective*, in which she turns to insights from the African American family for examples of concrete practices and

---

[32] Ibid., 192.
[33] McClendon, *Systematic Theology: Ethics*, vol. 1.
[34] Lisa Sowle Cahill, *Blessed Are the Peacemakers: Pacifism, Just War, and Peacemaking* (Minneapolis: Fortress Press, 2019), and Cahill's syllabus for the graduate course "Major Figures in Christian Ethics" at Boston College.
[35] McClendon, *Systematic Theology: Ethics*, 77.
[36] Ibid., 113–18, 193–212.

lived experiences through presence that translate into the work of justice.[37]

Recognizing the oppressive history in which the African American church was forged in the United States, McClendon writes of the importance of being present to one another, much like the idea of solidarity in Catholic social teaching or kinship as described in the work of Father Gregory Boyle, SJ.[38] Since the inception of separate African American churches across the southern United States, a distinctive style was integral to its identity, incorporating not only rhythm and cadence through music in the form of gospel spirituals, but also the importance of physical presence given the spirituals' themes highlighting future liberation but also hopeful freedom for the time at hand. Citing James H. Cone, McClendon notes that the gospel spiritual "Steal Away to Jesus" is ambiguous in its interpretation, perhaps simultaneously future-directed toward death, but also understood as a present "code for slave rebellion and escape."[39] McClendon argues that the African American church experience emphasized presence, responsibility, and moral action for the here and now—not only the future. This theme also appears in Cahill's *Global Justice, Christology, and Christian Ethics*, in which she opens her chapter on the Spirit of Christ as the unifying power that brings about "personal conversion, community solidarity, and the practical enactment of the kingdom of God—the reconciling politics of salvation" that will simultaneously combat racism and help "change evil hearts and social structures."[40]

Cahill quotes the following statements by M. Shawn Copeland: "The gift of God's loving Spirit creates a new basis for community. Women and men experience themselves as transformed persons who are called to live out this gift of love concretely through transformed human relations and who are knit together and empowered by that same Spirit to witness to a new reality."[41] Union through the Spirit of Christ forges new identity and new community together as the gift and virtue of presence.

---

[37]Lisa Sowle Cahill, *Family: A Christian Social Perspective* (Minneapolis: Augsburg Fortress, 2000), 111–29. On this topic, see the chapters of Mary M. Doyle Roche and Nichole Flores in this volume.

[38]U.S. Conference of Catholic Bishops, "Solidarity," http://www.usccb.org/beliefs-and-teachings/what-we-believe/catholic-social-teaching/solidarity.cfm; Gregory Boyle, *Tattoos on the Heart: The Power of Boundless Compassion* (New York: Free Press, 2010); Gregory Boyle, "Compassion and Kinship," TED Talk, https://www.youtube.com/watch?v=ipR0kWt1Fkc.

[39]James H. Cone, *The Spirituals and the Blues: An Interpretation* (New York: Seabury, 1972), cited in McClendon, *Systematic Theology: Ethics*, 88.

[40]Cahill, *Global Justice, Christology, and Christian Ethics*, 165.

[41]M. Shawn Copeland, "Knit Together by the Spirit as Church," in Colleen M. Griffith, ed., *Prophetic Witness: Catholic Women's Strategies for Reform*, Boston College Church in the 21st Century Series, ed. Patricia DeLeeuw and James F. Keenan, SJ (New York: Crossroad, 2009), 28–36, at 16, cited in Cahill, *Global Justice, Christology, and Christian Ethics*, 165.

McClendon attributes the emphasis on presence to the significance of kinship and family units in African traditional religion. Contrasting Western Cartesian dualism, in which soul or mind is separate or the soul is even viewed as superior to the body, African traditional religion, on the other hand, is closer to a biblical understanding that contrasts Gnostic dualisms dividing soul and body as well as highlights the importance of kinship tribes through the narrative of Abraham, Isaac, and Jacob in the Hebrew Bible. Sounding much like the New Testament emphases on the community as the body of Christ, McClendon argues, "In the African view there is a wholeness, an interrelatedness, a participation in the whole by every part. A tribe, or a family, or a man or woman can find peace only by such participation . . . hence also the possibility of appropriate harmony with the cosmic totality—of possession by the Spirit of holiness."[42] Community members thus find agency and responsibility located in relation to God and one another. Kinship or ties of solidarity include a thick sense of presence in which the good of individuals is tied to the good of the community, also known as the "common good" in Catholic social teaching.[43]

As Pope Francis recognizes, a thick sense of common good in which individuals are responsible to one another is dissolving under many of our technological sensibilities in which we hide behind screens.[44] Sherry Turkle and Neil Postman further recognize the power of technology to shape us, beyond being mere tools.[45] Instead, our relational bonds, capacity for empathy, responsibility to one another, and society face pressure given the erosion of what Turkle describes as the centrality of healthy solitude, friendship, and communal bonds within society.[46]

Unlike our emerging technological anthropology as beings who mediate the world through devices, McClendon's presence describes embodied authenticity as necessary for true human community. Paul's image of body is instructive for the role of presence. For McClendon, "The Christian community in its health is not a disembodied fellowship but a bodily one—it was this same Paul whose writing first gave 'body' as a metaphor of our solidarity with one another in Christ (1 Cor. 12:12 ff.)."[47] Likewise, the height of lived Christian faith originates in belief in the Incarnation, in

---

[42]McClendon, *Systematic Theology: Ethics*, 88.

[43]United States Conference of Catholic Bishops, "Seven Themes of Catholic Social Teaching," http://www.usccb.org/beliefs-and-teachings/what-we-believe/catholic-social-teaching/seven-themes-of-catholic-social-teaching.cfm.

[44]Pope Francis, Encyclical Letter *Laudato Si': On Care for Our Common Home* (2015), nos. 225, 227, 237, 102–5, www.vatican.va.

[45]Neil Postman, *Technopoly: The Surrender of Culture to Technology* (New York: Vintage Books, 1993), 20; Turkle, *Alone Together*.

[46]Turkle, *Reclaiming Conversation*, 10.

[47]McClendon, *Systematic Theology: Ethics*, 96.

which "The Word became flesh."[48] The celebration of the Eucharist and baptism are bodily events that point to Christ's presence with believers in the Spirit.

Not unlike Cahill in *Blessed Are the Peacemakers*,[49] McClendon also turns to Dietrich Bonhoeffer as an example of concrete ethics. Bonhoeffer writes on the centrality of Christ for community, affirming that "Christianity means community through Jesus Christ and in Jesus Christ."[50] He further describes the significance of union with Christ for the community as real presence together. Bonhoeffer writes,

> The physical presence of other Christians is a source of incomparable joy and strength to the believer. . . . Man was created a body, the Son of God appeared on earth in the body, he was raised in the body, in the sacrament the believer receives the Lord Christ in the body, and the resurrection of the dead will bring about the perfected fellowship of God's spiritual-physical creatures. The believer therefore lauds the Creator, the Redeemer, God, Father, Son and Holy Spirit, for the bodily presence of a brother. The prisoner, the sick person, the Christian in exile sees in the companionship of a fellow Christian a physical sign of the gracious presence of the triune God. Visitor and visited in loneliness recognize in each other the Christ who is present in the body; they receive and meet each other as one meets the Lord, in reverence, humility, and joy.[51]

Hence, for Bonhoeffer, presence with the fellow believer is a reminder of the presence of Christ.

McClendon delineates such presence *as a virtue*. He writes, "By presence is meant quite simply the quality of being there for and with the other."[52] Presence is a part of our existence by nature as embodied creatures. One can speak of not being present—like Paul, who writes to Corinth that he is absent in body but present in spirit. But the illustration does not make sense apart from our usual relation to one another as bodies.[53] Likewise, for McClendon, one can be physically present, but not emotionally or intellectually available. To be emotionally absent is the opposite of presence. Instead, presence involves intention or purposed focus—"being one's self

---

[48]Ibid., 96, 115.
[49]Cahill, *Blessed Are the Peacemakers*, 297–305.
[50]Dietrich Bonhoeffer, *Life Together: The Classic Exploration of Christian Community* (New York: HarperCollins, 1954), 21.
[51]Ibid., 19–20.
[52]McClendon, *Systematic Theology: Ethics*, 116.
[53]Ibid.

for someone else."[54] Intentional presence is the opposite of technology's pull for our attention, in which Turkle describes individuals as "loyal to a tribe of one" where we are "forever elsewhere."[55]

The distraction of technology poses the question as to whether such superficial bonds sustained through social media might withstand genuine challenges in the real world. McClendon's focus on the African American church experience serves as an example. Even when facing dehumanization, McClendon writes, the black community significantly discovered its roots in the "face of the present Christ."[56] Christ's presence with the community as the crucified Savior became an emblem of solidarity and hope in the midst of their suffering through slavery. For McClendon, "There is in the black experience a unique but in some degree communicable sense of the significance of what is suffered. 'Were you there,' asks the spiritual, 'when they crucified my Lord?' And the implicit answer of the singers is 'Yes, we were there.'"[57] The strong sense of presence in a crucified and risen Savior becomes a marker for Christ's solidarity in sorrow through a theology of the cross that is neither otherworldly nor despairing, but moves forward in realistic hope.

The cross-Resurrection narrative grounding Christian presence subsequently becomes a virtue that might be lived in communal practice, protest, and even action. Hence, McClendon links presence as virtue to the demonstration of civil disobedience during the civil rights era. He stresses,

> From presence as from any true virtue there is a path leading to other virtues. Thus we can better understand the *agape* love that led Martin Luther King's followers to *confront* their oppressors in the streets of Birmingham and Selma, rather than to flee from them (or led Clarence Jordan's Koinonia Community to *remain* in Georgia when the dynamite sticks began to explode their weathered buildings) if we interpret their action not as a "protest" but as a presence, a being there, and a being there for those who themselves shamelessly denied or oppressed their neighbor's presence.[58]

The virtue of presence through union with Christ and neighbor translates into embodied action—even while facing grave circumstances. McClendon also cites Catholic ministries of presence located in prisons across South

---

[54] Ibid.
[55] Turkle, *Reclaiming Conversation*, 4.
[56] Ibid., 17.
[57] McClendon, *Systematic Theology: Ethics*, 90.
[58] Ibid., 117.

America to be radically present to prisoners.[59] As an example, in July 2019 Catholic women religious, priests, and laity organized a "Catholic Day of Action" on behalf of separated immigrant children as a form of neighbor love through protest.[60]

Contrast such action with Turkle's description of contemporary action on social media. She uses an example of a video describing Joseph Kony's use of child soldiers in Uganda, South Sudan, the Democratic Republic of Congo, and the Central African Republic. Between March and July 2012 the video went viral and elicited over 91 million views on YouTube and over 18 million views on Vimeo.[61] The video also encouraged the use of physical signs to raise awareness around the globe. Turkle writes of a young economics graduate student named Elizabeth who was encouraged by the power of online politics and the prospect of its outcome. Turkle comments, "She was optimistic about its promise and annoyed, almost uncomprehending, at the skepticism of her African friends, who did not believe that people really cared about what was going on in Africa. They distinguished curiosity—enough curiosity to watch a video—from significant concern. And indeed, on the appointed day, few people stepped out into the physical world to put up their signs."[62] Moving from the virtual to the physical realm involved more commitment than most appeared willing to make. The young woman later explained what she learned from the experience: "You go on a website, you send in your money—that satisfies your requirement for being in the conversation. You show solidarity with a movement by going online, and then, that's it."[63] Deflated, the graduate student came to realize that solidarity operated in the virtual realm of thumbs up, likes, and Twitter hashtags—but failed to translate into a low-risk sign in one's physical yard.

Turkle writes that such phenomena reflect what sociologists label *weak ties* as opposed to *strong ties*. Weak ties belong more to the category of acquaintances, whereas strong ties are people engaged through conversation and face-to-face dialogue.[64] Turkle and political theorists still recognize the power of weak ties in their ability to generate not only awareness but even millions of dollars over the Internet, as seen through the example of the ALS Foundation ice bucket challenge. Yet despite such rapid response across the Web, Turkle cites Malcolm Gladwell, who contrasts contempo-

---

[59] Ibid.
[60] María Teresa Dávila, "Faith Is Something Best 'Lived on One's Feet,'" *National Catholic Reporter*, August 12, 2019.
[61] Turkle, *Reclaiming Conversation*, 294.
[62] Ibid., 295.
[63] Ibid.
[64] Ibid.

rary online activism with the physical activism during the civil rights era. Turkle quotes Gladwell: "If you are in a conversation with someone you don't know well—and these are most of your web contacts—the basic rule is to ask little.... Watch a video, give a thumbs-up, or buy a poster.... But if you want to take on political authority, says Gladwell, if you want to take those risks, you need ties of deeper trust, a deeper history."[65]

The pinnacle of protest as presence might be seen in the life of Dietrich Bonhoeffer. Strongly rooted in the practices of his faith community, Bonhoeffer did not find such community an enclave in which to escape or retreat from the world, but a faith community that grounded courage for his physical return and presence in Germany and that ended in his resistance to the Nazi Führer through the Confessing Church's Barmen Declaration and ultimate plot to assassinate Hitler.

An array of communities was influential for the young Bonhoeffer, including not only his family life during his early childhood and his studies of academic theology, but also his time abroad in the United States in which he encountered the African American church experience at Abyssinian Baptist Church in Harlem, New York, while studying at Union Theological Seminary.[66] As John Doberstein writes in the "Introduction" to Bonhoeffer's *Life Together*, "He was ... fascinated by Negro spirituals, and the struggle of the Negro for equality. In later years 'when the walls went up around Germany,' he introduced his students to these songs. Eberhard Bethge, Bonhoeffer's closest friend ... writes, 'We hummed "Swing Low, Sweet Chariot" twenty years before the radio and concert halls made it familiar here.' "[67] Through such spirituals, Bonhoeffer's embodied presence through worship would be transformative in his view of presence as he returned home to Germany.

In Bonhoeffer's own account in *Life Together*, his neighbor's face is transformed to him through prayer, Scripture, and conversation. This allows the neighbor to impact and change the self—as opposed to "fashioning" the neighbor in one's image.[68] Such transformed love moves one to action on behalf of the neighbor. Reggie L. Williams argues that Bonhoeffer's encounter with Jesus Christ as "vicarious representative action," its ethical mandate for followers of Christ, and his encounter with the African American community's understanding of Jesus as co-sufferer,

---

[65] Malcolm Gladwell, "Small Change: Why the Revolution Would Not Be Retweeted," *New Yorker*, October 4, 2010, cited in Turkle, *Reclaiming Conversation*, 297.

[66] John W. Doberstein, "Introduction," in Bonhoeffer, *Life Together*, 7–13, at 8–9; Cahill, *Blessed Are the Peacemakers*, 301.

[67] Doberstein, in Bonhoeffer, *Life Together*, 9–10,.

[68] Bonhoeffer, *Life Together*, 86, 93.

and hope propelled his resistance.[69] His presence in the African American community of Harlem profoundly impacted his return and presence with his fellow sufferers in Germany.

For Williams, "Bonhoeffer found that black Christians identified black suffering with Jesus' suffering. Bonhoeffer heard this connection in black preaching and in black Christian music. . . . In Harlem, African American Christians embraced the story of Jesus, the crucified Christ, whose death they claimed paradoxically gave them life, just as God resurrected Jesus in the life of the earliest Christian community."[70] Bonhoeffer's encounter with the present Jesus as embodied in the faith of the African American church of Harlem grounded him in a way that helped him in his protest when returning to his own German home full of suffering from the violence of white supremacy. Bonhoeffer's example does not reflect the weak ties formed through technology or social media, but those strong ties formed by face-to-face encounter through embodied practices of presence in a thick, living faith community. Such presence returns Christian ethics to its relational root and enlivens faith communities to practice presence with action and resistance for Catholic and Protestant communities alike in the face of the technological and ethical challenges emerging in the twenty-first century.

Conclusion

Examples such as these across Protestant and Catholic communities of presence are integral for Christian identity, ethics, and action in the twenty-first century. Lisa Sowle Cahill's life work is dedicated to such concrete practices realized in grassroots Christian communities around the globe, whether such challenges pertain to war, peacemaking, bioethics, family, gender, race, access to resources, or any other source of suffering in need of ethical response. Bridging thick theological commitments established by presence with the Spirit of Christ unifies people to God and one another. Such presence is the motivation and relational union needed in a world increasingly separated through the isolation and objectification of technology. Making explicit what is often implicit in Cahill's work, valuing the gift and virtue of presence is a complementary way that Catholics and Protestants might continue to work together in the field of Christian ethics, committed to promoting the common good.

---

[69]Reggie L. Williams, *Bonhoeffer's Black Jesus: Harlem Renaissance Theology and an Ethic of Resistance* (Waco, TX: Baylor University Press, 2014), 9–10, 19–22.
[70]Ibid., 25–26.

Living Vatican II's Vision of the Church in the World

Contributions of Lisa Sowle Cahill

Angela Senander

In a world that continues to face challenges identified in the Second Vatican Council's Pastoral Constitution on the Church in the Modern World, *Gaudium et spes*, Lisa Sowle Cahill's ethical reflection mirrors the breadth of issues found in that document.[1] Just as Pope Francis embodies the Second Vatican Council in his papal leadership, Cahill embodies the Second Vatican Council in her work as an ecumenical Roman Catholic theological ethicist. As an ethicist, Cahill has not yet written a book on ecclesiology and ethics like she has on Christology and ethics.[2] Cahill's operative ecclesiology is rarely the explicit focus of her theological writing. However, her biblically informed theological reflection not only responds to the call for a renewal of moral theology but also provides a window into the foundations of her ecclesiology and her own ecclesiological commitment.[3]

In order to better understand her operative ecclesiology, we examine her Vatican II perspective on church revealed through her retrieval of Scripture and tradition as sources for ethics and through her reading of the signs of the times in light of the gospel. To illustrate relationships

---

I am grateful for Lisa Cahill's wisdom guiding my doctoral work at the intersection of social ethics and ecclesiology, and I appreciate this opportunity to examine the same intersection in her scholarship.

[1] Among the themes addressed by *Gaudium et spes*, Cahill's scholarship engaged marriage and family life (chapter 1), the development of culture (chapter 2), economic and social life (chapter 3), the life of the political community (chapter 4), and the fostering of peace (chapter 5). See Vatican Council II, The Pastoral Constitution on the Church in the Modern World, *Gaudium et spes* (1965), www.vatican.va.

[2] Lisa Sowle Cahill, *Global Justice, Christology, and Christian Ethics*, New Studies in Christian Ethics, ed. Robin Gill (Cambridge: Cambridge University Press, 2013).

[3] Vatican Council II, *Optatam totius* (1965), no. 16, www.vatican.va.

between ethics and the Catholic Church in her work, we consider her work on the promotion of peace. This topic provides an opportunity to observe developments in both her ethical perspective and the role of contemporary Catholic faith communities in her theological reflection.

Cahill's Vatican II Perspective on Church

The Second Vatican Council had a transformative impact on Cahill's experience of the Catholic Church.[4] Cahill's high school years coincided with the Second Vatican Council. Remembering a lay Catholic woman teaching theology at her Catholic high school in Washington, DC, when *Gaudium et spes* was promulgated, Cahill notes, "Her enthusiasm for the Council and a message of lay empowerment fairly flowed from her coverage of the *Pastoral Constitution on the Church in the Modern World (Gaudium et spes)*."[5]

The lived experience of faith communities is an important point of departure for Cahill's ecclesiology. Like *Dei verbum*, she looks to the Word that animates the life of faith communities.[6] Like *Lumen gentium*, she draws on the biblical language of "body of Christ" to speak about the Church.[7] Like *Gaudium et spes*, she focuses on church as a community of disciples called to make God's reign present in our world.[8]

A Community Formed by the Word

As Sarah M. Moses describes earlier in this volume, Scripture informs Cahill's theological reflection. In particular, "The Scriptures are the voices of historical communities of faith which command the hearing of ongoing communities shaped by and shaping those Scriptures' authority."[9] Hence, for Cahill, Scripture is expressive of and formative for faith com-

---

[4]Lisa Sowle Cahill, "On Being a Catholic Feminist," *Santa Clara Lectures* 9, no. 3 (2003): 1–20, at 1–5.

[5]Ibid., 4.

[6]Vatican Council II, Dogmatic Constitution on Divine Revelation, *Dei verbum* (1965), www.vatican.va; Lisa Sowle Cahill, "A Theology for Peacebuilding," in *Peacebuilding: Catholic Theology, Ethics, and Praxis*, ed. Robert J. Schreiter, R. Scott Appleby, and Gerard F. Powers (Maryknoll, NY: Orbis Books, 2010), 300–331, at 321.

[7]Vatican Council II, Dogmatic Constitution on the Church, *Lumen gentium* (1964), nos. 1 and 3, www.vatican.va; Cahill, "A Theology for Peacebuilding," 320–21.

[8]Vatican Council II, *Gaudium et spes*, nos. 1–2. Cahill, "A Theology for Peacebuilding," 320.

[9]Lisa Sowle Cahill, *Between the Sexes: Foundations for a Christian Ethics of Sexuality* (Philadelphia: Fortress Press, 1985), 16.

munities. As she looks to the Old Testament, she remembers a covenant people formed at Mount Sinai.[10] As she looks to the New Testament, she is attentive to the diverse communities of faith that shape how Jesus's good news is presented in the gospels. Moreover, she highlights that Jesus proclaimed the good news of God's reign through teaching, healing, and inclusive table fellowship that calls for solidarity with those on the margins.[11] In fact, she notes, "If one word could be found to describe the socially transformative effect of the kingdom Jesus preached, a good candidate would be 'inclusiveness' or 'solidarity.'"[12] As she reflects on the pastoral letters, she draws attention to the effects of Greco-Roman culture on the practices of early Christian faith communities, and she highlights the call to conversion that early Christians experienced as they awaited an imminent Second Coming of Christ. Elaborating on the significance of conversion for participation in the life of an early Christian faith community, she states, "The Christian disciple was not one who was born into the family of faith, but one who heard the word of Jesus and was transformed by new kingdom life."[13] By relying on and engaging the exegesis of biblical scholars, she introduces the reader to the experiences of diverse communities living the Christian faith through liturgy and love of neighbor.

The faith community shapes both Cahill's analysis of Scripture as a source for Christian ethics and her analysis of tradition as a source for theological reflection and action. Hence, Cahill underscores the ongoing power of the Word in the faith community by stressing that "Tradition is the historical identity and self-understanding of the religious community, which is formed by the Scriptures, and which continues to inform its present and future."[14]

Cahill embodies the invitation of the Second Vatican Council's Dogmatic Constitution on Divine Revelation, *Dei verbum*, to "hearing the word of God" revealed in salvation history. Hence, Cahill's theological contributions respond to *Dei verbum*'s call that "the interpreter of Sacred Scripture, in order to see clearly what God wanted to communicate to us, should carefully investigate what meaning the sacred writers really

---

[10]Ibid., 8.

[11]For her extended systematic discussion of "kingdom of God," see Cahill, *Global Justice, Christology, and Christian Ethics*, 76–121, and Marianne Tierney FitzGerald's chapter in this volume.

[12]Lisa Sowle Cahill, *Women and Sexuality: 1992 Madeleva Lecture in Spirituality* (New York: Paulist Press, 1992), 30.

[13]Ibid., 31.

[14]Cahill, *Between the Sexes*, 6.

intended, and what God wanted to manifest by means of their words."[15] Cahill's expertise in New Testament and ethics as well as hermeneutic method in theological ethics allowed her to contribute significantly to the renewal of moral theology, honoring the observation in *Dei verbum* and *Optatam totius* that Scripture is the "soul" of theology.[16]

Biblical Images of Church

Cahill retrieves the biblical images of body of Christ and pilgrim people of God to describe the Church, as did the Second Vatican Council in the Dogmatic Constitution on the Church, *Lumen gentium*.[17] With regard to the "body of Christ" image, Cahill moves from a descriptive retrieval of Paul to a more normative claim about the Church. For instance, describing Paul's vision of life in the Christian community, she observes, "Paul responds to these controversies by reminding church members of their common life in the Spirit, and their equality in Christ's body; and by instructing them to live and act in a manner that serves the community—in short, to 'strive to excel in building the church.'"[18] Grounded in this biblical image of the Church, Cahill later uses the image of body of Christ to speak of her understanding of church: "The Christian community is the body of Christ that makes present in its life, as did Jesus in his, the reign of God."[19] Within the ecclesial context, her theological approach takes historical consciousness seriously and discerns how to contribute to God's reign, by constantly reflecting on "the ongoing and shifting circumstances of the pilgrim people of God."[20]

A Pastoral Mission to Make God's Reign Present

Cahill's operative ecclesiology focuses on the mission of the Church to make God's kingdom present in the world. She contributes to the mission of the Church with a deep understanding not only of the gospel but also of the world. Her theology demonstrates an affirmation of the Second Vatican Council's observation that "the Church has always had the duty of scrutinizing the signs of the times and of interpreting them in the light of the Gospel."[21] Reflecting on the world since Vatican II, in 2017 Cahill

---

[15] Vatican Council II, *Dei verbum*, no. 12.
[16] Ibid., no. 24; Vatican Council II, *Optatam totius*, no. 16.
[17] Vatican Council II, *Lumen gentium*, nos. 7, 21.
[18] Cahill, *Between the Sexes*, 62.
[19] Ibid., 76.
[20] Ibid.
[21] Vatican Council II, *Gaudium et spes*, no. 4.

observed that the twenty-first-century context is "more consciously global, more differentiated, more intercultural, and more interreligious than that of the four decades immediately following the Council."[22]

Cahill has been a leader in integrating global and intercultural perspectives into her theological reflection. Even in the twentieth century, she collaborated with James Keenan to edit a book on HIV/AIDS prevention with a global perspective. This book brings together cases from Catholic ministries around the world responding to HIV/AIDS as a sign of the times.[23] In the twenty-first century, she has contributed significantly to the work of a broader network of Catholic theological ethicists: Catholic Theological Ethics in the World Church. For instance, she contributed a chapter to *Catholic Theological Ethics in the World Church: The Plenary Papers from the First Cross-Cultural Conference on Catholic Theological Ethics*.[24] Just as the international conferences of this network fostered encounters among Catholic theological ethicists that informed her theology, so too participation in the Catholic Peacebuilding Network provided her the opportunity to encounter Catholic peacebuilders working in conflict situations in Africa and Latin America. This experience of encounter transformed her theological reflection on the promotion of peace.

Contributing to a Vatican II Church Promoting Peace

Cahill values the opportunity to contribute to the dialogue about war and peace as a Catholic theological ethicist, and she introduces her first book on the topic with two references to her social location.[25] In the preface of her 1994 book, reflecting on the opportunity to write an earlier essay on peace, Cahill expresses gratitude for the "chance to begin to write seriously outside of my usual areas of sexual and medical ethics (It is hard for female Catholic moral theologians to break out of a certain mold)."[26]

---

[22]Lisa Sowle Cahill, "Reframing Catholic Ethics: Is the Person an Integral and Adequate Starting Point?," *Religions* 8, no. 10 (2017): 215–22, at 217.

[23]James F. Keenan, SJ, with Jon D. Fuller, SJ, MD, Lisa Sowle Cahill, and Kevin Kelly, eds., *Catholic Theological Ethicists on HIV/AIDS Prevention* (New York: Continuum, 2000).

[24]Lisa Sowle Cahill, "Moral Theology: From Evolutionary to Revolutionary Change," in *Catholic Theological Ethics in the World Church: The Plenary Papers from the First Cross-Cultural Conference on Catholic Theological Ethics*, ed. James F. Keenan, SJ (New York: Continuum, 2007), 221–27.

[25]Lisa Sowle Cahill, *Love Your Enemies: Discipleship, Pacifism, and Just War Theory* (Minneapolis: Fortress Press, 1994).

[26]Cahill, *Love Your Enemies*, xi. See also Lisa Sowle Cahill, "Nonresistance, Defense, Violence, and the Kingdom in Christian Tradition," *Interpretation: A Journal of Bible and Theology* 38, no. 4 (1984): 380–97.

Commenting on her book's dedication, she shares with the reader, "My father, Donald E. Sowle, sought sincerely to embody his Roman Catholic faith as he successfully pursued an officer's career in the United States Air Force."[27] She has also spoken publicly about her father's witness to the Catholic faith within her family during a lecture on Catholicism and feminism, illustrating the formative nature of the domestic church that she discusses in *Family: A Christian Social Perspective*.[28]

With this experience, Cahill engages both the teaching and practice of the Catholic Church promoting peace. First, we review Vatican II's teaching on war and peace to understand her first book's focus on the relationship between discipleship and just war/pacifism. Second, we examine a development in her approach to promoting peace. Her first book—*Love Your Enemies*—highlighted Christian pacifism as an individual disciple's embodiment of the Sermon on the Mount's instruction to love one's enemy. In contrast, her second book highlights Catholic peacebuilding as an ecclesial solidarity that transforms injustice and embodies the Sermon on the Mount's beatitude, "Blessed are the peacemakers."[29]

Development in Catholic Teaching on Peace at Vatican II

The Second Vatican Council's teaching on peace in *Gaudium et spes* not only passes on the tradition of just war but also includes the possibility of conscientious objection to war.[30] Moreover, the Second Vatican Council teaches that the state has a responsibility to promote peace through justice, which could result in a just war.[31] At the same time, it accepts the witness of Catholic pacifists who heard the Sermon on the Mount as a call to renounce violence as an expression of love of enemy. This teaching on conscientious objection at the end of *Gaudium et spes* illustrates the document's earlier teaching about conscience.[32] At the same time, it underscores the obligation of the conscientious objector to contribute to the common good in other ways.[33] *Gaudium et spes* presents a soldier's participation in a just war and a conscientious objector's witness to peace accompanied by other contributions to the common

---

[27]Cahill, *Love Your Enemies*, xii.
[28]Cahill, "On Being a Catholic Feminist," 2; Lisa Sowle Cahill, *Family: A Christian Social Perspective* (Minneapolis: Fortress Press, 2000), 4, 83.
[29]Lisa Sowle Cahill, *Blessed Are the Peacemakers: Pacifism, Just War, and Peacebuilding* (Minneapolis: Fortress Press, 2019).
[30]Vatican Council II, *Gaudium et spes*, no. 78.
[31]Ibid., nos. 77–79.
[32]Ibid., no. 16.
[33]Ibid., no. 78.

good as complementary expressions of disciples acting to promote peace.

The teaching on war and peace in *Gaudium et spes* is a significant step in the development of the Catholic Church's teaching on promoting peace. Development of doctrine is an important hermeneutical key for understanding the Second Vatican Council. The practice of biblically inspired pacifism contributed to the Second Vatican Council's development of teaching on peace. These practices informing the teaching of the Second Vatican Council illustrate John O'Malley's observation: "Vatican II thus took greater account of the world around it than any previous council and assumed as one of its principal tasks dialogue or conversation with that world in order to work for a better world, not simply a better Church."[34]

Development in Cahill's Theological Reflection on the Promotion of Peace

Just as the Cold War was a sign of the times that informed the Second Vatican Council's teaching on peace, the Cold War remained a sign of the times nearly two decades later as Catholic episcopal conferences responded to the nuclear arms race with pastoral letters on peace.[35] The U.S. Catholic Bishops' pastoral letter *The Challenge of Peace: God's Promise and Our Response* relies on a foundation in Scripture and tradition to articulate Vatican II's teaching on war and peace.

Using this letter as a starting point for her writing in the post–Cold War context, Cahill's book *Love Your Enemies* provides biblical and historical insight into the development of pacifist and just war approaches in the Christian tradition, taking seriously the social histories of communities of disciples.[36] In her volume, Cahill debates whether just war and pacifism are complementary forms of discipleship that promote peace. She notes that just war is rooted in theory and Christian pacifism is an expression of a religious conversion experience.[37] Moreover, she examines the biblical roots and historical development of Christian perspectives on just war and pacifism; she appreciates the pacifist position as an expression of discipleship that loves one's enemies. Hence, she contributes to engage

---

[34] John W. O'Malley, SJ, "Vatican II: Did Anything Happen?," *Theological Studies* 67, no. 1 (2006): 3–33, at 12.

[35] National Conference of Catholic Bishops, *The Challenge of Peace: God's Promise and Our Response* (Washington, DC: United States Catholic Conference, 1983). See also James V. Schall, SJ, ed., *Out of Justice, Peace: Joint Pastoral Letter of the West German Bishops; Winning the Peace: Joint Pastoral Letter of the French Bishops* (San Francisco: Ignatius Press, 1984).

[36] Cahill, *Love Your Enemies*, 2–6.

[37] Ibid., 1–2.

the Vatican II's promotion of peace through her in-depth exposition of the development of just war theory and pacifism in the Christian tradition.

In the post–Cold War context, being aware of the strengths and limits of just war theory and pacifism, she later witnessed an approach that brought together pacifists and just war proponents to work for peace in conflict situations. From 2005 to 2010, through the Catholic Peacebuilding Network and Catholic Relief Services, Cahill had the opportunity to learn firsthand from Catholic organizations on the ground in conflict situations in the Global South. Catholic peacebuilding does not begin with a theory of just war that one might accept or reject, but rather with the concrete needs of people suffering from violence in conflict situations. Cahill considered this an advantage over just war theory, which could become an excuse to go to war rather than a means of preventing or limiting war.[38] While Cahill's 1994 perspective on discipleship as a means of promoting peace led her to see pacifism as more consistent with the gospel than just war theory, her later encounter with Catholic peacebuilders in conflict situations led her to question the adequacy of pacifism as a Christian response to conflict situations. Solidarity with those in need and working for peace in conflict situations demonstrate for Cahill the limits of both just war theory and pacifism.[39]

Cahill's experience of contemporary Catholic ecclesial practices promoting peace plays a significant role in her theological reflection on peacebuilding and provides an important opportunity for explicit reflection on her understanding of church, grounded in Catholic pastoral practices promoting peace.[40] Just as the experiences of historical communities of disciples shaped her examination of the Christian theological tradition on war and peace, so too the experiences of contemporary communities of disciples in Burundi and Colombia influenced her theological reflection in *Blessed Are the Peacemakers*.[41]

In particular, Cahill describes communities of disciples working together to transform conflict into peace. She observes, "Local agency is key to peacebuilding and its theologies; for example, traditional courts and reconciliation practices, church ministries to victims and perpetrators, initiatives to care for survivors. An asset of Catholic peacebuilding is an international network of dioceses, religious congregations, universities, and nonprofit organizations, to support and connect communities and activists."[42]

---

[38]Cahill, *Blessed Are the Peacemakers*, x.
[39]Ibid.
[40]Cahill, "A Theology for Peacebuilding," 300–331.
[41]Cahill, *Blessed Are the Peacemakers*.
[42]Lisa Sowle Cahill, "Just War, Pacifism, Just Peace, and Peacebuilding," *Theological*

This experience of encountering Catholic peacebuilders moved her reflection beyond that of Vatican II's focus on the conscience of an individual disciple as a conscientious objector to that of the peacebuilding practices of communities of disciples working to transform violent situations of conflict into the peace of God's reign. Significantly, Cahill understands her *Blessed Are the Peacemakers* as "an ethical, theological, and practical argument for Christian peacebuilding as an answer to the question: 'Where is the church?'"[43] Like *Gaudium et spes*, Cahill underscores the importance of communities of disciples entering into solidarity with those who are suffering injustice and transforming the situations to reflect God's kingdom.

Conclusion

The Second Vatican Council was a formative event in the life of the Catholic Church that Cahill experienced during her formative high school years. In a lecture at her college alma mater, she remembered learning about the Pastoral Constitution on the Church in the Modern World, *Gaudium et spes*, as a high school student. This experience shaped her understanding of the mission of the Church and its engagement with and within the world. Her research interest in the New Testament and ethics, as well as her method in theological ethics, allowed her to consider the reception of the good news of God's kingdom by diverse communities of disciples in different historical periods.

While Cahill engaged each of the topics of special urgency in the second part of *Gaudium et spes* in a historically conscious way that attends to the signs of the times, we have only considered one of them, the promotion of peace, as an example. In response to the teaching of Vatican II articulated in the U.S. context during the nuclear arms race by the U.S. Catholic Bishops, she deepened the dialogue about peace through her retrieval of Scripture and tradition on war and peace. Her starting point shifted from ecclesial teaching to ecclesial practices, resulting also in a shift from focusing on an individual disciple's conscientious objection to communities of disciples' engagement in peacebuilding. Hence, Cahill's ethical perspective developed from an appreciation of pacifism to an appreciation of peacebuilding—as a fuller expression of the transformative mission of the Church in the world making the kingdom of God present.

This chapter is a first step in unpacking the operative ecclesiology in

---

Studies 80, no. 1 (2019): 169–85, at 183.

[43] Cahill, *Blessed Are the Peacemakers*, vii.

Cahill's ethics. Since her retrieval of Scripture is shaped by the ethical issue she is addressing, some statements about ecclesial communities are distinctive and more related to one ethical issue than common across diverse ethical issues. In light of that, I hope that my analysis of her ecclesial engagement and reflection will inspire Lisa Cahill to write a book on ecclesiology and ethics, adding to her writings in Christology and ethics. Such a book would further support God's people in living Vatican II's vision of church in the world.

Christian Ethics in the Public Sphere

Grégoire Catta, SJ

Paul Ricoeur defines ethics as the search for "a good life lived with and for others in just institutions."[1] This definition is a useful first step in capturing the work and aspirations of many ethicists, such as Lisa Cahill and many of her students who contributed chapters to this book. It stresses the search for good within a social ambit that is not merely made of interpersonal relations but is also constituted of structures and institutions. The way societies are organized matters for ethicists. Now, what could be the significant features of an ethical endeavor within the public sphere as it stands at the beginning of the third millennium? And more specifically, what could be the characteristics of Christian ethics in this context? Drawing inspiration from Cahill's work and her way of engaging the world she lives in, we can start by suggesting some key elements of context that appear unavoidable in the shaping of Christian ethics today: first, globalization, liquid societies, secularization, the challenge of turning to an integral ecology; and second, some distinctive features in order to add the specific Christian qualification to ethics: listening to the poor, engaging tradition, fostering dialogue, bringing about God's kingdom.

There is no claim of being exhaustive and even less normative in this attempt at reflecting upon Christian ethics today. The few leads given here are necessarily colored by the situation and history of the author: a religious priest within the Catholic Church, brought up and educated in Western Europe, who studied several years under the guidance of Lisa Cahill at Boston College.

---

[1] Paul Ricoeur, *Oneself as Another*, trans. Kathleen Blamey (Chicago: University of Chicago Press, 1992 [1990]), 172.

Context: The Public Sphere Today

Late-modern or postmodern societies are marked by impressive challenges for ethicists aiming at pursuing the search for a good life not merely personally and in small communities but also collectively, as societies and, ultimately, as humanity within an interconnected world of human and nonhuman creatures.

Globalization

Globalization, or the consciousness to live in a global and interconnected world, is a key feature of the context for doing ethics today. The Catholic Church made a decisive step in this consciousness with the Second Vatican Council (1962–1965). Karl Rahner highlighted that the Council manifested a Church aware of becoming a "world-church."[2] Catholic social teaching (CST), through encyclicals such as *Populorum progressio,* took seriously into account that "the social question has become worldwide"[3] in the mid-1960s. Since then, the phenomenon of globalization has taken on huge proportions. Due to exponential progress in the areas of communication and transportation, more people around the world, even if separated by large distances, are nonetheless able to communicate and interact with each other and have become dependent on each other, whether they are conscious of it or not. Consciousness of the imbalance in relations, whether economic, political, or cultural, has also grown.

In the field of ethics, globalization cannot mean consecrating the expansion of the Global North worldwide through the diffusion of its modes of thinking. On the contrary, the challenge of ethics is to resist the logic of domination of some over the remainder of the world and to engage resolutely in a process of listening and dialoguing within the diversity of cultures and situations. Coming back to the example of CST, it is worth noting that fifty years after *Populorum progressio,* Pope Francis's *Laudato si'* made a significant move by not only speaking to the whole world and addressing worldwide issues but also valorizing contributions coming from various groups of bishops from all over the world. Still, as far as CST is concerned, much remains to be done.

Lisa Cahill shows an inspiring lead with regard to doing ethics in a

---

[2] Karl Rahner, "Basic Theological Interpretation of the Second Vatican Council," in *Theological Investigations* 20 (New York: Crossroad, 1981), 77–89.
[3] Paul VI, *Populorum progressio* (1967), no. 3, www.vatican.va.

global and pluralist world. She has been engaged since the early 2000s in the development of Catholic Theological Ethics in the World Church (CTEWC), a worldwide network of fifteen hundred Catholic ethicists whose main objective is to facilitate dialogue beyond the northern paradigm and to expand the collegiality of ethicists in an ever extended inclusivity.[4] She has taught seminars and workshops in many different countries in the Global South, and her writings are filled with stories and inspirations, but also concepts, discussions, and references, coming out of these experiences. To give an example, in the March 2019 issue of *Theological Studies*, Cahill's article on just war, pacifism, just peace, and peacebuilding includes a section on peacebuilding in the Global South, referring to perspectives from Argentina, the Philippines, Colombia, Kenya, and Korea.[5]

What French scholar Alain Supiot writes about the challenge of rethinking labor in the twenty-first century applies well and more broadly to the field of ethics: "To work within the perspective of globalization implies to take into account both the objective interdependency created by the common ecological, technical, and institutional challenges of today, and the diversity of national and regional situations and cultures."[6]

Liquid Society

The image of a "liquid modern society" used by sociologist Zygmunt Bauman is eloquent.[7] We live in societies characterized by accelerated changes and instability. "'Liquid modern' is a society in which the conditions under which its members act change faster than it takes the ways of acting to consolidate into habits and routines."[8] Everything changes fast. It is difficult to predict what will come next, but this also means that it is hard to make decisions about the best way to live in the present. Our modern, liquid life is marked by uncertainty.

Sociologist and philosopher Hartmut Rosa alerts us that the mechanisms of acceleration that we experience in our daily life are intertwined with the acceleration of technological innovations and the acceleration

---

[4] James Keenan, "Pursuing Ethics by Building Bridges beyond the Northern Paradigm," *Religions* 10, no. 8 (2019): 490, doi:10.3390/rel10080490.

[5] Lisa Sowle Cahill, "Just War, Pacifism, Just Peace, and Peacebuilding," *Theological Studies* 80, no. 1 (2019): 183–85.

[6] Alain Supiot, *Le travail au XXIe siècle* (Ivry sur Seine, France: Les Éditions de l'Atelier, 2019), 42 (translation mine).

[7] Zygmunt Bauman, *Liquid Life* (Oxford: Blackwell Publishing, 2005).

[8] Ibid., 1.

of social transformations.[9] One feeds the other in a self-fueling spiral. For him, it is a defining feature of modernity and modern capitalism that cannot know any form of stabilization except a "dynamic stabilization." Such a modern capitalist society needs constant material growth, intensification of innovation, and acceleration to maintain its structure.

This liquid life within a constantly accelerating world enshrines the triumph of consumerism. Everything changes. Everything and every aspect of life becomes a commodity, which one buys, uses, then throws away. The very Earth on which we are living and human beings themselves are caught up in the movement. This is the "throwaway culture" that Pope Francis regularly denounces. It is a culture that "affects the excluded just as it quickly reduces things to rubbish."[10]

For ethical reflection, the liquid feature of modern societies implies permanent adaptation because everything changes, but it also implies resisting the temptation of adopting the liberal mood of the times. It becomes obvious that the mere repetition of a few principles rooted in an essentialist anthropology cannot work in the present situation, since there is no longer a tacit agreement on this anthropology, even when people share the same religion, and there are no longer social structures unconsciously sustaining these principles. In a traditional and communitarian society, where everyone had more or less an established position, within a shared culture and many common practices, the search "for the good life" could be more easily envisaged as deductively applying in concrete situations the standard of an unquestioned morality. In a liquid and fragmented society, which so many people experience today, the ethical endeavor calls for constant dialogue and discussion about principles, always starting by taking into account specific and diverse experiences, but not being so satisfied as to stay at this level. Inductive ethics does not need to be situationist or individualistic.

Here lies the need to resist the liberal trend. If the modern liquid society tends to be shaped by what Pope Francis coined the "techno-economic" paradigm of which compulsive consumerism is a striking manifestation,[11] then ethics should not take the path of simply looking for the best way toward personal fulfillment and happiness. In the particular context of our liquid societies, it seems that the *social* qualification of ethics is all the more needed. Whatever question we are dealing with, the social dimension should never be missed. The search for "the good life" is embedded

---

[9]Hartmut Rosa, *Social Acceleration: A New Theory of Modernity*, trans. J. Trejo-Mathys (New York: Columbia University Press, 2015 [2005]).
[10]Francis, *Laudato si'* (2015), no. 22, www.vatican.va.
[11]Ibid., no. 203.

in the search for the common good in one sense or another. Lisa Cahill has repeatedly explored this path by addressing many questions such as sex, gender, and bioethics within a broader approach of social ethics.

Secularization

The global sphere in which to do ethics, and more specifically Christian ethics, is also characterized by various processes of reshaping the role of religion in society. For several decades, in many Western countries, Catholicism (the same is true for mainstream Protestantism) appears to be in decline. In terms of numbers, there is no doubt: falling numbers in Sunday church attendance and falling numbers of vocations to the priesthood and religious life. Neither is there any doubt the direct influence the Catholic Church had in shaping mentalities and public and private behaviors in areas such as sex, marriage, and family is fading away. Situations vary, of course. France and its long-lived debates over *laicity* offered nonetheless stronger resistance to the process than Quebec or Belgium. The United States remains very religious in some respects, but in a context of growing pluralism. Some observers predicted that with the end of communism and the adoption of a Western lifestyle, Poland would quickly change; however, thirty years after the fall of the Berlin Wall, Mass attendance on Sundays is still high and seminaries are not empty, although something of a slow erosion has started. Secularization is definitely at work everywhere, but it needs to be specified.

The clarification given two decades ago by sociologist José Casanova is still helpful.[12] Secularization appears as a structural trend of modern society in the sense of a functional differentiation of the sphere of religion from other spheres of human activity (state, economy, science, law, education, art, etc.). With this differentiation comes an emancipation. In short, religions have less and less capacity to impose norms that structure various aspects of social life. Nonetheless, this does not imply two other subtheses often mistakenly confused with the central thesis in a too-general approach to secularization. First, there is no ineluctable decline of religions in the modern world whose fate would be to completely disappear one day. Already in the late 1990s, Casanova was giving evidence that it was not the case theoretically and empirically. Second, privatization of religion—the reduction of religion to the private sphere—is not a modern structural claim and a necessary consequence of the differentiation and emancipation process. On the contrary, we see various phenomena of

---

[12] José Casanova, *Public Religions in the Modern World* (Chicago: University of Chicago Press, 1994), 212–16.

"deprivatization" of religion where religions maintain or regain a public character, for better—as a mobilizing resource in order to live together in society—or for worse—in cases of fundamentalism.

Christian ethics in such a public sphere marked by secularization need not necessarily hide its religious resources. Christian ethics can remain *theological* ethics and be a positive contribution to ongoing debates and the collective search for the good life. Again, the work of Lisa Cahill is a good illustration since she does not hesitate to engage in theological discussions, such as that on differing Christologies in *Global Justice, Christology, and Christian Ethics*.[13] However, acknowledging a pluralist and secularized context implies taking the path of a dialoguing and questioning approach rather than an assertive one. For example, in a recent speech addressed to Catholics in France, President Emmanuel Macron suggested that the voice of the Church "cannot be injunctive" but "it can only be questioning."[14] Thus, in a secularized country, marked by a complex and at times conflicting relationship between church and state, a role is still recognized today for religious voices, but not any type of discourse would be well received. Independent of the short-term and local political implications of such a presidential speech, the advice is worth retaining.

Integral Ecology

A final contextual feature to be highlighted in framing the public sphere in which to do ethics at the dawn of the third millennium might surprise some readers. To speak of the ecological challenges our world is facing, is it not to evoke only one specific field of ethics? If the question were reduced to environmental ethics—a field not addressed that often by Lisa Cahill—it would. However, following the path opened by Pope Francis's *Laudato si'*, one can argue that ecology is no longer a specific topic but rather an all-encompassing and integrative question shaping today's ethical endeavor.

Indeed, what is at stake with "the care for our common home," as the English subtitle of the encyclical puts it, is not merely a better stewardship of the creation but a profound personal "ecological conversion" and a collective "cultural revolution" so that all broken relationships with others, the created world, oneself, and God can be reconciled.[15] It is not

---

[13]Lisa Sowle Cahill, *Global Justice, Christology and Christian Ethics*, New Studies in Christian Ethics, ed. Robin Gill (New York: Cambridge University Press, 2013).
[14]Emmanuel Macron, *Discours devant les évêques de France* (April 9, 2018), https://eglise.catholique.fr/actualites/cef-recoit-emmanuel-macron/454837-discours-president-de-republique-devant-eveques-de-france/.
[15]Francis, *Laudato si'*, nos. 66, 70, 114, 217.

merely a *green* encyclical but a deeply *social* one, inviting all to take the path of hearing "both the cry of the earth and the cry of the poor."[16] The integral ecology that the pope is promoting envelops all dimensions of human life: economic, political, environmental, social, cultural, personal, interpersonal, and familial. Ecology is not a new field for ethics, but it reshapes ethics by integrating all its dimensions because "everything is connected."[17]

Ecological challenges also reshape ethics because, methodologically, they question any type of individualism and require collaboration. In a modern world characterized by deep, diverging individualistic tendencies, the ecological question requires work in common. "Given the complexity of the ecological crisis and its multiple causes, we need to realize that the solutions will not emerge from just one way of interpreting and transforming reality."[18] No surprise, then, that later on in the document, the pope advocates for dialogue at all levels and among all types of actors. This dialogic approach, as already noted, is not foreign to the type of ethics developed by many today and of which Cahill is a good model, but the ecological challenges make it all the more necessary.

Christian Ethics

Having framed some key features of today's context, how do we do *Christian* ethics? Again, without pretending to be exhaustive, a few characteristics of Christian ethics at the dawn of the third millennium can be outlined, drawing inspiration from the work of Lisa Cahill.

Listening to the Poor

The preferential option for the poor is a central principle in Catholic social teaching, and more generally it ought to shape ethical reasoning from a Christian perspective. Indeed, as pointed out by Pope Benedict XVI, this option is "implicit in our Christian faith in a God who became poor for us, so as to enrich us with his poverty (2 Cor 8:9)."[19] For Christians, it is primarily a theological principle rather than a political, sociological, or philosophical one. It is "a theocentric, prophetic option that has its roots in the unmerited love of God and is demanded by this

---

[16]Ibid., no. 49.
[17]Ibid., nos. 16, 70, 91, 111, 117, 138, 240.
[18]Ibid., no. 63.
[19]Benedict XVI, "Address at the Inaugural Session of the Fifth General Conference of the Latin American and Caribbean Bishops (May 13, 2007)," 3, www.vatican.va.

love."[20] Consequently, as explained by Pope John Paul II in *Sollicitudo rei socialis,* in which he enshrined in the universal magisterium of the Church a formulation first adopted by Latin American theologians and pastors, the option for the poor "affects the life of each Christian inasmuch as he or she seeks to imitate the life of Christ."[21] The Polish pope immediately added that "it applies equally to our *social responsibilities* and hence our manner of living, and to the logical decisions to be made concerning the ownership and use of goods."[22] It is a root principle for ethical discernment not merely at a personal level but also at the political, economic, or cultural levels where concern for the poor ought to guide the overcoming of the "structures of sin."[23]

Pope Francis, in his desire for "a poor church for the poor,"[24] strongly confirms the centrality of the option for the poor. "Our faith in Christ, who became poor, and was always close to the poor and the outcast, is the basis of our concern for the integral development of society's most neglected members."[25] The Argentinean pope also stresses an aspect that is crucial for ethicists, arguing that the option for the poor is not merely a matter of putting concern for the poor, the excluded, and the forgotten of our societies in first place—it is also a matter of listening to them and learning from them:

> They have much to teach us.... We need to let ourselves be evangelized by them.... We are called to find Christ in them, to lend our voice to their causes, but also to be their friends, to listen to them, to speak for them and to embrace the mysterious wisdom which God wishes to share with us through them.[26]

Listening to and learning from the poor, the excluded, the "unheard," those in the peripheries, locally and worldwide, remains a never-ending challenge for today's ethics. And it includes hearing the cry of "our Sister, Mother Earth ... [who] is among the most abandoned and maltreated of our poor."[27] The incorporation of many different voices, especially

---

[20]Gustavo Gutiérrez, "Expanding the View, Introduction to the Revised Edition," in *A Theology of Liberation: History, Politics, and Salvation,* 2nd ed. (Maryknoll, NY: Orbis Books, 1988), xxvii.
[21]John Paul II, *Sollicitudo rei socialis* (1987), no. 42, www.vatican.va.
[22]Ibid.
[23]Ibid., 36–37.
[24]Francis, "Audience with the Representatives of the Communications Media" (March 16, 2013), www.vatican.va.
[25]Francis, *Evangelii gaudium* (2013), no. 186, www.vatican.va.
[26]Ibid., no. 198.
[27]Francis, *Laudato si'*, nos. 1–2.

from the Global South, in order to address ethical questions is already a promising path. Collective edited books such as this Festschrift are a good example, and Lisa Cahill's approach in research, teaching, and writing is undoubtedly exemplary, but we are just at the beginning.

Tradition

Doing ethics as Christians implies recognizing our position as inheritors of a tradition. Christian ethics is not merely ethics referring to Jesus Christ and the Bible; it is ethics embedded in two thousand years of the history of those who followed Jesus Christ and took inspiration and guidance from him while attempting to live a good life.

To stress tradition as a key feature for Christian ethics might sound an overly Catholic concern. It is not, even if the Catholic context puts a distinctive note on it. In January 2014 the Society of Christian Ethics, under the presidency of Allen D. Verhey, gathered for its annual meeting with the theme "Retrieving the Theological Traditions." Lisa Cahill gave the first plenary address and explored the topic of Catholic feminists and traditions.[28] She masterfully drew a picture of a plurality of Catholic feminist ethics, framing them into a typology of traditions (Augustinian, neo-Thomist, neo-Franciscan, and a fourth type provisionally named "Junian"). While doing so, she exemplified an inspiring way of relating to tradition, entering into a discerning process thanks to "a threefold hermeneutics of appreciation, suspicion, and praxis: How does wisdom from the past give life today? (appreciation); how do traditions mediate dominant ideologies that continue to oppress some community members? (suspicion); and how can our traditions be embodied in just relationships now? (praxis)."[29]

Engaging traditions as a Christian ethicist is crucial since it situates ethics within an ecclesial intention. According to Lieven Bove, tradition is "the historical dynamic learning process of the whole church."[30] Taking into account traditions and inscribing one's reflection within them cannot be reduced to the repetition of doctrinal contents, whether magisterial or products of recognized figures from the past. Nonetheless, it implies thoroughly studying them in their proper context in order to then take inspiration and resources to address the present situation, and also to be

---

[28]Lisa Sowle Cahill, "Catholic Feminists and Traditions: Renewal, Reinvention, Replacement," *Journal of the Society of Christian Ethics* 34, no. 2 (2014): 27–51.

[29]Ibid., 28. See also Mary M. Doyle Roche's contribution in this volume.

[30]Lieven Boeve, "Revelation, Scripture and Tradition: Lessons from Vatican II's Constitution *Dei verbum* for Contemporary Theology," *International Journal of Systematic Theology* 13, no. 4 (2011): 416–33, at 422.

able to challenge them so as to embody the gospel more effectively.

This type of critical but consistent engagement with tradition appears all the more necessary in the liquid and secularized societies outlined previously. In her teaching and in her writings, Lisa Cahill shows considerable interest and remarkable competency in studying tradition. From Augustine to Aquinas, Luther to Calvin, and so many others, her ethical reflection never escapes the confrontation with tradition and history and finds there the means to enter into dialogue with other contemporary thinkers.

For the Christian ethicist, engaging tradition requires a capacity to enter into theological discussions. Theological ethics is more than the mere incorporation of theological arguments in ethical reasoning. As Lisa Cahill demonstrated in *Global Justice, Christology, and Christian Ethics,* there are strong and diverse interactions between ethics and theology. The social ethicist's quest for global justice impacts and nourishes systematic reflections about Christ, the Spirit, the Trinity, evil, salvation, and so on. For example, some Christologies are more helpful than others in fostering concrete commitments to tackle unjust social structures.[31]

Dialogue

As already mentioned several times, dialogue is key to ethics in the current context. It is also a feature that has a theological grounding for Christian ethics. Pope Paul VI, in 1964, at the time of Vatican II, explained at length that dialogue was the path to be taken by the Church since, indeed, dialogue has its origin "in the mind of God Himself."[32] The Italian pope then connected dialogue to the way God reveals Godself to humanity throughout sacred history as envisioned in the Bible, but also to the mystery of salvation that occurs within the dialogue between God and humanity in Jesus Christ and, finally, to the mystery of the Trinity, which is a mystery of dialogue par excellence.

For Christians, taking the path of dialogue is not a mere strategic move dictated by a specific modern context, but it is rooted in our very faith in a Triune God who, through the Incarnation, dwells in this world. Entering into dialogue and listening to other voices inside and outside the Christian faith, to other religions and wisdoms, to other sciences with their specific mode of understanding reality, is ultimately to trust that God reveals Godself in the entirety of creation and that God is at work within this world. Christian ethics, thus, cannot but resolutely take this path.

---

[31] Lisa Sowle Cahill, "*Caritas in Veritate:* Benedict's Global Reorientation," *Theological Studies* 71, no. 2 (2010): 291–319, at 292.
[32] Paul VI, *Ecclesiam suam* (1964), no. 70, www.vatican.va.

For those more embedded in the living tradition of Catholic social teaching, a strong example of dialogue as a fundamental feature of social Christian ethics appears in *Laudato si'* and the turn to integral ecology that becomes, as previously highlighted, the structural and methodological updating of CST. In the encyclical, dialogue is practiced through taking seriously into account the results of various sciences concerning the state of our "common home," but also through listening to various voices inside the Church, in other Christian denominations, and even in other religions.[33] Dialogue is also encouraged as the only practical way to tackle the challenges we are facing. As Pope Francis writes, "The gravity of the ecological crisis demands that we all look to the common good, embarking on a path of dialogue which requires patience, self-discipline and generosity, always keeping in mind that 'realities are greater than ideas.' "[34] A perfect illustration of this dialoguing path was given by the more recent Synod for the Amazon, held in Rome in October 2019, where indigenous people with their specific worldview and wisdom were welcomed and valorized; they played an important role for the purpose of envisioning "new paths for the church and integral ecology."[35]

The Kingdom of God

Christian ethics necessarily implies engagement with the Bible. Among the many biblical themes that can nourish and shape Christian ethical thinking in search of living a good life by following Jesus Christ, the kingdom of God holds a preeminent place in today's context. As a last feature for Christian ethics in the public sphere as inspired by Lisa Cahill's work, it is worth coming back to some of her thoughts on the topic.[36]

Bringing salvation to the world, Jesus preached the good news of God's kingdom or reign. This is what he came for. "After John had been handed over, Jesus came into Galilee proclaiming the gospel of God, and saying, 'the time has been fulfilled, and the kingdom of God has drawn near: repent and believe in the gospel' " (Mk 1:14—15). Other evangelists

---

[33]It is the first time that in a magisterial document of this type, explicit reference is made to a Muslim writer in support of a theological assertion (the fact that God fills the world completely and there is a mystical meaning to be found in all things) (Francis, *Laudato si'*, no. 233, endnote no. 159).

[34]Ibid., no. 201.

[35]Synod of the Bishops for the Pan-Amazon Region, *New Paths for the Church and for an Integral Ecology: Preparatory Document of the Synod of Bishops for the Special Assembly for the Pan-Amazon Region* (June 8, 2018), http://www.sinodoamazonico.va/content/sinodoamazonico/en/documents/preparatory-document-for-the-synod-for-the-amazon.html.

[36]Cahill, *Global Justice, Christology, and Christian Ethics*, 76–121.

similarly summarize Jesus's message this way (Mt 4:23; 9:35; Lk 4:43; 8:1). This is why Pope Francis, in a striking synthesis of the mission of the Church, says that "to evangelize is to make the kingdom of God present in our world."[37] God's kingdom is the heart of the salvific message of the gospel and it encapsulates what Christians are looking for when searching for the good life.

God's kingdom announced by Jesus is not yet fully present but already at work. "The coming of the kingdom of God cannot be observed, and no one will announce, 'Look, here it is,' or, 'There it is.' For behold, the kingdom of God is among you" (Lk 17:20–21). As told by many parables and the very life of Jesus, the kingdom has to do with justice, peace, inclusiveness, reconciliation of broken relations, fostering love, mercy, and overcoming evil. Most importantly, and well highlighted by Cahill, "The kingdom or reign of God is a corporate and political metaphor."[38] In fact, "Jesus' ministry of the kingdom gives content to salvation; ... Jesus saw salvation as corporate and political; and ... Jesus understood God's kingdom to be presently effective in transforming social and political life."[39] Hence, ethics shaped by Christian faith should foster not merely personal conversion but structural change.

This articulation between the personal and structural dimensions of change is certainly embedded in the notion of bringing about God's kingdom and, thus, makes of it a powerful inspiration for shaping Christian ethics. The eschatological provision included in this notion of God's kingdom is a good and necessary safeguard against the illusion of realizing it in one specific political and economic organization of the society. Its theological nature calls for both humility and unfailing hope, so necessary in uncertain times such as ours.

The option for the poor, critical engagement with tradition, dialogue, and inscription within the bringing about of God's kingdom—all four points of attention for Christian ethics exemplified in Lisa Cahill's work are particularly fitting for engaging the public sphere of the early third millennium marked by globalization, "liquid" societies, secularization, and the integral ecology challenge. Following in Cahill's footsteps, Christian ethics, whatever topic it is concerned with, will thus always be social ethics.

---

[37]Francis, *Evangelii gaudium*, no. 176.
[38]Cahill, *Global Justice, Christology, and Christian Ethics*, 76.
[39]Ibid., 77.

Postscript

Ki Joo Choi

I will always remember Lisa ending our meetings in her office with "Onward!" during my doctoral studies at Boston College. I always took her "Onward!" as a genuine word of exhortation, though I am sure at times it was her very kind way of ending our conversations and shooing me out of her office, since I often showed up unannounced to bounce off a random idea, or, more likely, to ask for an extension on a seminar paper. You start to realize how much your adviser in graduate school formed you as an academic when you find yourself saying "Onward!" as a way of signaling to students that it is time to leave your office.

I am not sure if Lisa concluded all her meetings with students with this enthusiastic declaration. But as I have been reflecting on Lisa's scholarship while working on this volume, I cannot think of a more appropriate word that captures Lisa's intellectual drive and spirit.

Lisa's scholarly production is of course something to behold, if not legendary. So it would not be hard to imagine her exhorting any one of her students to keep moving forward as a reflection of her own sense of what it means to be a teacher and scholar. At the same time, it would be totally off the mark to believe that for Lisa the goal of the scholarly life is only measured by one's scholarly productivity.

While it is true that the scholarly life by definition is an endeavor consumed with teaching and writing, what motivates such an endeavor makes all the difference. Do we teach and write because that is part of our job? Or do we engage in these endeavors because it is more than that? In other words, do we teach and write because that is how we work through the fact that truth is hardly ever a settled matter and its discernment requires ongoing inquiry? In view of that question, Lisa's remark about what she learned from her own mentor, James M. Gustafson, is particularly striking: "Gustafson taught his students not to make facile theological claims about the nature of the moral life and its possibilities, unbacked by any sort of practical evidence, and I have tried to take that lesson seriously . . . in drawing connections between Christology and global social ethics."[1] It is more than safe to say that she has taken that lesson seriously in all of her projects.

In a way, I like to think of her exhortatory "Onward!" as her way of teaching me, just as Gustafson taught her, to guard against making simplistic claims or, even worse, mistaking assertions for arguments. (I will never forget Lisa's exasperation over a book on postliberal sexual ethics for its lack of a real argument, mistaking narrative for reasoned debate.) But Lisa, like Gustafson, has never accepted the notion that even if you do make an argument for a thesis, even if it is a very good argument, you should never think that your thesis is definitive once and for all. If anything, that would ignore the complexity of the kinds of questions that frame Christian ethics. That, in turn, would trivialize the very nature of truth.

One of the recurring themes in the chapters of this volume is the sustained attention that Lisa has paid to the critical importance of dialogue, and with that, the methodological priority of expanding our circles of interlocutors and conceptual horizons. Part of this commitment pivots on the notion that truth is hardly graspable in its fullness from any one person's or tradition's perspective. While that can sound a little like St. Augustine's or John Calvin's claim, appropriating from the Apostle Paul, that as fallen creatures we can only view the truth as if looking through a mirror dimly, Lisa has never rested in such a theologically and morally pessimistic take on that metaphor. The mirror through which we view the world may indeed offer a dim view, but what we can know about ourselves and the world is revealed to us in dialogue and solidarity with one another. Truth is graspable but never alone, only through relationship.

Lisa's scholarship is without a doubt a testament to that idea, which is profoundly Ignatian and incarnational. Her work reflects a restless drive to examine and enlist the best scholarship available—from a wide-ranging, interdisciplinary field of research—to make the case for her theological-ethical commitments. Her determination to engage a broad array of thinkers and perspectives has also coincided with a resolute support of scholars from diverse and often underappreciated sectors of the theological academy, fostering networks of friendships near and far. That has included steadfast efforts to connect her advisees to emerging and established theologians within and beyond the United States. (Were it not for Lisa, I would never have had the privilege of meeting Gustafson himself and the opportunity to study with Roger Haight, the late William C. Spohn, and Roland A. Delattre.) And in all of these pursuits—in

---

[1] Lisa Sowle Cahill, *Global Justice, Christology, and Christian Ethics*, New Studies in Christian Ethics, ed. Robin Gill (Cambridge: Cambridge University Press, 2013), xiii.

listening, engaging, learning, and mentoring—Lisa has not been averse to changing her own mind; that is hardly surprising in one for whom resisting facile claims is taken as an intellectual nonnegotiable. Lisa's openness to critique and revision is in itself something extraordinary and certainly radical, especially in our present day when hunkering down on one side of an argument or political view is de rigueur, even in the academy.

But her theological scholarship is also a testament to the proposition that the relational or communal discernment of truth is imperative because, at its most basic, truth is meant to set us free. But freedom without justice is no freedom at all, and that explains in part the palpable urgency and insistence in so much of Lisa's writing, whether we are talking about her work on just peacemaking, gender equality, healthcare, participatory democracy, or the meaning of family. In all of these subjects, and many others, there is a relentless pursuit of truth that takes at its core the person of Jesus and his embodied love for the least of society. In faithfulness to this Christological shape of truth, Lisa's work is driven by a constant commitment to expanding our moral vision and in challenging us to consider whether we are relating, recognizing, and, ultimately, loving one another in the fullness of our embodied lives and not simply through a preconceived and delimiting notion of human value.

Spending time with Lisa's theological scholarship is a humbling experience. All of the chapters in this volume reflect that posture of admiration. But what is so humbling about her work goes well beyond the sheer vastness of her scholarship and the kind of insights that have made indelible marks on the field of theological ethics that we all call our intellectual and professional home. Lisa's work is humbling precisely because of the kind of humility that underlines her work. Genuine humility, especially intellectual humility, breeds an openness to self-reflection and improvement and a deep curiosity or desire to know more fully. In other words, humility calls us to never simply rest with what we know, to mistake truth for the hubris of our own thoughts. Instead, it demands that we keep moving forward—Onward!—to imagining and reimagining the moral life in community and in friendship and solidarity with those who may differ from us until our work can be called worthy of the gospel that we as theologians are called to witness in the world. For this lesson, and many more, I am—all of Lisa's students are—in her debt.

Lisa Sowle Cahill

Selected Publications

Books

Between the Sexes: Toward a Christian Ethics of Sexuality (Philadelphia: Fortress Press, and Mahwah, NJ: Paulist Press, 1985; 7th printing, 1997, Philadelphia: Fortress Press).

Religion and Artificial Reproduction: Inquiry into the Vatican Instruction on Human Life, with Thomas A. Shannon (New York: Crossroad, 1988).

Women and Sexuality (Mahwah, NJ: Paulist Press, 1992).

"Love Your Enemies": Discipleship, Pacifism, and Just War Theory (Minneapolis: Fortress Press, 1994).

Embodiment, Morality, and Medicine, ed. with Margaret A. Farley (Dordrecht, The Netherlands: Kluwer Academic Publishers, 1995).

Sex, Gender, and Christian Ethics, New Studies in Christian Ethics, ed. Robin Gill (Cambridge: Cambridge University Press, 1996).

Christian Ethics: Problems and Prospects, in honor of James M. Gustafson, ed. with James Childress (Cleveland: Pilgrim Press, 1996).

Family: A Christian Social Perspective (Minneapolis: Fortress Press, 2000).

Catholic Ethicists on HIV/AIDS Prevention, ed. James F. Keenan, SJ, with Jon D. Fuller, SJ, MD, Lisa Sowle Cahill, and Kevin Kelly (New York: Continuum, 2000).

Bioethics and the Common Good: The 2004 Père Marquette Lecture in Theology (Milwaukee: Marquette University Press, 2004).

Genetics, Theology, Ethics: An Interdisciplinary Conversation, ed. Lisa Sowle Cahill (New York: Crossroad, 2005).

Modern Catholic Social Teaching: Commentaries and Interpretations, ed. Kenneth R. Himes, OFM, with associate eds. Lisa Sowle Cahill, Charles E. Curran, David Hollenbach, SJ, and Thomas A. Shannon (Washington, DC: Georgetown University Press, 2005; 2nd ed., 2018).

Theological Bioethics: Participation, Justice, and Change, Moral Traditions, ed. James F. Keenan, SJ (Washington, DC: Georgetown University

Press, 2005). Catholic Press Association First Place Award for Theology, 2005.

Sexuality and the U.S. Catholic Church: Crisis and Renewal, ed. with John Garvey and T. Frank Kennedy, SJ (New York: Crossroad, 2006).

Global Justice, Christology, and Christian Ethics, New Studies in Christian Ethics, ed. Robin Gill (Cambridge: Cambridge University Press, 2013).

Theology and Praxis of Gender Equality (Bangalore: Dharmaram Publications, 2018).

Blessed Are the Peacemakers: Pacifism, Just War, and Peacebuilding (Minneapolis: Fortress Press, 2019). Pax Christi Massachusetts, Peacemaker Award 2019, "for distinguished scholarship on Christian nonviolence."

Concilium Series Volumes

Concilium: Aging, no. 3 (1991), ed. Lisa Sowle Cahill and Dietmar Mieth (London and Philadelphia: SCM Press and Trinity Press International).

Concilium: Migrants and Refugees, no. 3 (1993), ed. Lisa Sowle Cahill and Dietmar Mieth (Maryknoll, NY: Orbis Books).

Concilium: The Family, no. 4 (1995), ed. Lisa Sowle Cahill and Dietmar Mieth (Maryknoll, NY: Orbis Books).

Concilium: The Ethics of Genetic Engineering, no. 2 (1998), ed. Lisa Sowle Cahill and Maureen Junker-Kenny (Maryknoll, NY: Orbis Books).

Concilium: Religious Education of Boys and Girls, no. 4 (2002), ed. Werner G. Jeanrond and Lisa Sowle Cahill (London: SCM Press).

Concilium: Christology, no. 3 (2008), ed. Andrés Torres Queiruga, Lisa Sowle Cahill, Maria Clara Bingemer, and Erik Borgman (London: SCM Press).

Concilium: Human Nature and Natural Law, no. 3 (2010), ed. Lisa Sowle Cahill, Hille Haker, and Eloi Messi Metogo (London: SCM Press).

Concilium: Human Trafficking, no. 3 (2011), ed. Hille Haker, Lisa Sowle Cahill, and Elaine Wainwright (London: SCM Press).

Concilium: Gender and Theology, Spirituality, Practice, no. 4 (2012), ed. Lisa Sowle Cahill, Diego Irarrazaval, and Elaine Wainwright (London: SCM Press).

Concilium: Corruption, no. 5 (2014), ed. Regina Ammicht Quinn, Lisa Sowle Cahill, and Luiz Carlos Susin (London: SCM Press).

Concilium: Globalization and the Church of the Poor, no. 3 (2015), ed. Daniel Franklin Pilario, Lisa Sowle Cahll, Maria Clara Bingemer, and Sarojini Nadar (London: SCM Press).

Concilium: Families, no. 2 (2016), ed. Susan A. Ross, Lisa Sowle Cahill, Erik Borgman, and Sarojini Nadar (London: SCM Press).

Concilium: Mercy, no. 4 (2017), ed. Lisa Sowle Cahill, Diego Irarrazaval, and João Vila-Chã (London: SCM Press).

For a complete list of publications, see Lisa Sowle Cahill's curriculum vitae at https://www.bc.edu/content/dam/files/schools/cas_sites/theology/pdf/lcahill_cv.pdf.

Contributors

Grégoire Catta, SJ, is a Jesuit priest from France. He holds a doctorate in sacred theology from the Boston College School of Theology and Ministry. He is assistant professor of theology at Centre-Sèvres Facultés Jésuites de Paris, where he holds the Jean Rodhain Chair. Since 2018 he has worked for the French Conference of Bishops as director of the department of Family and Society. In 2019 he published *Catholic Social Teaching as Theology* (Paulist Press).

Ki Joo Choi is associate professor and chair of the Department of Religion at Seton Hall University. He is also the founding codirector of Seton Hall's medical humanities minor and faculty coordinator for the second-year University Core Program, Christianity and Culture in Dialogue. He specializes in fundamental Christian ethics, the political morality of race, and Asian American theology and ethics and is author of *Disciplined by Race: Theological Ethics and the Problem of Asian American Identity* (Cascade/Wipf & Stock, 2019). He received his BA and MDiv from Yale and PhD in theological ethics from Boston College.

Hoa Trung Dinh, SJ, lectures in bioethics and sexual ethics at Catholic Theological College of the University of Divinity, Melbourne, Australia. A graduate of the University of Melbourne (MBBS 1993) and Monash University (MBioethics 2004), he earned an STL from the Weston Jesuit School of Theology (2008) and a PhD from Boston College (2013).

Stephanie C. Edwards, MSW, PhD, is the executive director of the Boston Theological Interreligious Consortium (BTI). Her interdisciplinary research explores the intersections of traumatic experience, Christian theology, and communal practices of memory in response to suffering. Her interest in this work is rooted in extensive travel to, and living abroad in, postconflict zones, particularly the former Yugoslavia and El Salvador. Alongside her theological work, she is engaged in social work as a community organizer in her hometown of Biddeford, Maine.

Marianne Tierney FitzGerald received her PhD in theological ethics from Boston College and MDiv from Harvard Divinity School. She currently works at the University of Notre Dame in the Office of Mission Engagement and Church Affairs and also teaches students in the Moreau

First Year Experience course. She has previously taught at Holy Cross College in Notre Dame, IN. Her research focuses on the connections between theology and women's activism, and she has published essays in the *Journal of Moral Theology*, *Asian Horizons: Dharmaram Journal of Theology*, and *Commonweal* magazine.

Nichole M. Flores is assistant professor of religious studies at the University of Virginia in Charlottesville. She researches the constructive contributions of Catholic and Latinx theologies to notions of justice and aesthetics as applied in public life. She teaches courses on Latinx religion, Catholic theology and ethics, religion and democracy, and bioethics. She has published essays in the *Journal of the Society of Christian Ethics*, the *Journal of Religious Ethics*, the *Journal of Religion and Society*, and *Modern Theology*, and she is a contributing author on the masthead at *America: The Jesuit Review of Faith and Culture*. She earned an AB in government from Smith College, an MDiv from Yale University, and a PhD in theological ethics from Boston College.

Kate Ann Jackson-Meyer currently teaches part-time in the Theology Department at Boston College. In 2018 she earned her PhD in theological ethics from Boston College. Her dissertation, *Tragic Dilemmas and Virtue: A Christian Feminist View*, discusses tragic dilemmas in theology. Her research interests are virtue ethics, fundamental moral theology, and feminist theory, and she applies them to war ethics and bioethics. She received an MAR from Yale Divinity School and a BA in biology and religion from the University of Southern California. She lives in Acton, Massachusetts, with her husband and daughters.

Joseph Loic Mben, SJ, is a lecturer at the Jesuit Institute of Theology in Abidjan (Côte d'Ivoire) where he teaches bioethics and social ethics. He did his doctoral studies at Boston College. He has published articles on gender, sexual ethics, and social ethics in *Hekima Review* and *Asian Horizons*. In 2019 he edited a volume on the African theologian Jean-Marc Ela, *Jean-Marc Ela et la Recreation de l'Afrique* (Presses de l'Université Catholique d'Afrique Centrale).

Sarah M. Moses, PhD, is associate professor of religion in the Department of Philosophy and Religion at the University of Mississippi, where she teaches courses in medical ethics, aging, and comparative religious ethics. She is the author of *Ethics and the Elderly: The Challenge of Long-Term Care* (Orbis Books, 2015), and has published articles in the *Journal of the Society of Christian Ethics* and *Journal of Religious Ethics*. Sarah is an ordained priest in the Episcopal Church and has served on ethics committees of long-term care facilities and hospitals.

Jill Brennan O'Brien is an editor at Orbis Books in Ossining, NY. She holds an MAR from Yale Divinity School and a PhD in theological ethics from Boston College, where her work centered primarily on Christian environmental ethics and the writings of James Gustafson. A former freelance journalist, she occasionally publishes pieces in *America: The Jesuit Review of Faith and Culture.*

Maureen H. O'Connell is associate professor and chair of the Department of Religion and Theology at LaSalle University. She authored *Compassion: Loving Our Neighbor in an Age of Globalization* (Orbis Books, 2009) and *If These Walls Could Talk: Community Muralism and the Beauty of Justice* (Liturgical Press, 2012). She is a member of POWER (Philadelphians Organizing to Witness, Empower, and Rebuild), an interfaith coalition of more than fifty congregations committed to making Philadelphia the city of "just love" through faith-based community organizing.

Autumn Alcott Ridenour, PhD, is assistant professor in the Department of Religious and Theological Studies at Merrimack College in North Andover, MA. Her primary interests are in the areas of theological, philosophical, social, and bioethics, with attention to history and systematic theology. She is the author of *Sabbath Rest as Vocation: Aging Toward Death* (Bloomsbury T&T Clark, 2018) and has published in *Christian Bioethics, Journal of the Society of Christian Ethics, The Hastings Center Report*, and several book chapters in edited volumes.

Mary M. Doyle Roche is associate professor of religious studies at the College of the Holy Cross in Worcester, MA, where she teaches courses in Christian ethics, medical ethics, and the ethics of work and family life. Her research and writing focus on the rights and moral agency of children and young people, and she strives to be a worthy ally of LGBTQ+ persons.

Virginia M. Ryan has been at the College of the Holy Cross since 2012. From 1998 to 2012, she taught at Rivier College (now University). She received an MDiv from Andover Newton Theological School, an MA in special education from Assumption College, and a PhD in theological ethics from Boston College. Her particular areas of research and interest are bioethics, theological social ethics, and environmental theology and ethics.

Angela Senander is a research fellow at Georgetown University's Berkley Center for Religion, Peace and World Affairs and author of *Scandal: The Catholic Church and Public Life* (Liturgical Press, 2012). She taught ministerial students as a faculty member at Washington Theological Union and as a visiting professor at the Boston College School of Theology and Ministry, the University of Notre Dame, and St. John's School of Theology and Seminary.

Matthew Sherman is associate professor and chair in the Department of Theology and Philosophy at Marian University. His research areas include the ethics of friendship, marriage, and family, with a particular interest in the intersection of sacramental and moral theology. His regular course offerings cover introduction to theology, fundamental morals, social ethics, bioethics, and marriage. He lives on the south side of Indianapolis with his wife, daughter, and son.

Andrea Vicini, SJ, is Michael P. Walsh Professor of Bioethics and Professor of Moral Theology in the Boston College Theology Department and an affiliate member of the Ecclesiastical Faculty at the School of Theology and Ministry. An MD and pediatrician (University of Bologna), he is an alumnus of Boston College (STL and PhD), and holds an STD from the Pontifical Faculty of Theology of Southern Italy (Naples). He is cochair of the international network Catholic Theological Ethics in the World Church. His research and publications cover theological bioethics, sustainability, global public health, new biotechnologies, and fundamental theological ethics.

Raymond E. Ward, PhD, is director of the Wolfington Center for Civic Engagement at Cabrini University. He is the founding managing editor of *Praxis: An Interdisciplinary Journal of Faith and Justice*, a new journal with the mission of bridging the gap between scholars and practitioners. He works with the community organizing group Philadelphians Organized to Witness, Empower, and Rebuild (POWER) and the service and dialogue organization Interfaith Youth Core (IFYC), recently organizing a joint regional training for students and faculty. His academic research focuses on collective moral agency in Christian ethics.

Index

abortion and abortion rights, 75, 76, 108, 115–16, 124–25, 130
Adichie, Chimamanda Ngozi, 118
adverse virtues, 84, 85–86
Affordable Care Act, 76, 115
African American community
   Black Lives Matter movement, 95
   CST and black Catholics, 27, 79
   domestic churches, black families as, 42, 153–54
   Jesus as co-sufferer with, 185–86
   lived experiences and concrete practices, 179–81, 183
   normative ethical reflection on black families, 152–54
American-Catholic Bishops, 99–100, 193, 195
Amoris Laetitia exhortation, 97, 104, 105–6, 121
Andronicus, 49, 52
appreciation, hermeneutic of, 20, 22, 41–42, 52, 205
Athanasius of Alexandria, 178
Augustine of Hippo
   Augustinian anthropology, 174, 176
   Augustinian-influenced feminism, 20, 44, 45, 47, 205
   evil and sin, Augustinian realism on, 179
   on virtue as the essence of Christian life, 175
   war, just approach to, 91–92, 93
Ayres, Lewis, 175

Bauman, Zygmunt, 199
Baxter, Michael, 71, 82
Beauchamp, Thomas L., 157, 158
Belfield neighborhood, 17–18
Benedict XVI, Pope, 76, 135, 203
Bernardin, Joseph, 75

Bethge, Eberhard, 185
Beyer, Gerald J., 28
Biden, Joseph, 108
bioethics
   Cahill, influence on field, 108–9, 110, 118, 172
   Catholic bioethics, 112, 114–15, 117
   Christian participation in bioethics discourse, 129
   CST methodology applied to, 78
   feminist approach, 41
   gospel-based bioethics, 119
   healthcare for the poor, 75
   the marginalized, taking into account, 47, 116, 156–58
   moral agency in, 111
   PDE, over-reliance on, 85–86
   proportionalism *vs.*, 113
Boff, Leonardo, 137
Bonhoeffer, Dietrich, 89, 90–91, 179, 182, 185–86
Bourg, Florence Caffrey, 104
Bove, Lieven, 205
Boyle, Gregory, 118, 180
"Bridge Burners" (Kaveny), 113
Brooten, Bernadette, 50–51
Brown, Brené, 118
Burggraeve, Roger, 105
Burke, Raymond, 108

Cahill, Lisa Sowle
   common ground, dedication to finding, 110, 120, 124, 161
   on community recognition of practices, 155–56
   dialogical/dialectical model, preferring, 4, 10, 11, 15
   embodiment, on the psychosocial dimensions of, 23

221

essays, articles, and lectures
   "Abortion, Sex and Gender," 75
   "Abortion and Argument by Analogy," 129
   "'Abortion Pill' RU 486," 124–25
   "Bioethics, Theology and Social Change," 11
   "Just War, Pacifism, Just Peace, and Peacebuilding," 199
   "Moral Theology," 43
   "Natural Law," 13
   "Nature, Change, and Justice," 10
   "Reframing Catholic Social Ethics," 118
   "Toward Global Ethics," 4, 134
euthanasia, dissertation on, 110
intellectualizing, warning against, 21, 22
irreducible moral dilemmas, grappling with, 87–89, 92
middle axioms approach, 97, 101, 112–13, 122, 127, 132
operative ecclesiology of, 187, 190, 195–96
participatory bioethics, framing, 156–58
peacebuilding work, 72, 79, 84, 94–95, 191
plenary address, 20, 40–41, 44, 49, 205
provisionality of truth, stress on, 11–12, 14
publications
   Between the Sexes, 96
   Bioethics and the Common Good, 172
   Blessed Are the Peacemakers, 90–91, 182, 194–95
   Building a Bridge, 52
   Christian Bioethics, 109
   Family, 60, 96, 107, 151–54, 172, 179–80, 192
   Love Your Enemies, 192, 193
   Public Theology and the Global Common Good, xvii
   Sex, Gender, and Christian Ethics, 7–8, 48, 96
as a realist, 45, 144
scholarship from the margins, advocating for, 149–51
sin, understanding of, 26–27, 46–47, 85–86, 135, 140, 143
socio-historical methods, embracing, 55–56, 63, 65–66
South and East, giving preferences to voices from, 116–17
transversalism, suggesting, 163
See also Global Justice; Theological Bioethics
Callahan, Sydney, 98
Calvin, John, 178, 210
cantineras, liturgical participation of, 155–56
capability theory, 98
Caritas in Veritate encyclical, 76, 135
Casanova, José, 201
Catholic Action and social engagement, 80
Catholic Bioethics and Social Justice (Lysaught), 172
Catholic casuistry, 101
Catholic culture wars, 76, 108, 121–23, 132
Catholic ethics, 24, 44, 49, 78, 162
Catholic Peacebuilding Network, 191, 194
Catholic Social Teaching (CST)
   in bioethics, 172
   common good, on the duty to participate in, 111, 131–32
   as communal praxis, 81–82
   compassion, offering a blueprint for, 117
   cross-cultural communication, valuing, 9–10
   dialogue, finding common ground through, 73–75
   environmental justice and, 137–38
   on the family, 100, 153
   integral ecology, turn to, 207
   on the kingdom of God, 99
   modernity, response to, 71
   participation, considering as a right and duty, 169
   power of anti-blackness in, 27
   preferential option for the poor as a central principle, 203

principle of subsidiarity, 112
shared action, promotion of justice through, 79–81
solidarity concept in, 180
structural change, advocating for, 76–79
theology of reversal in, 115
UN, moving away from sole reliance on, 135
wicked problems, transforming response to, xv
world-church, awareness of becoming, 198
Catholic Theological Ethics in the World Church (CTEWC), 43, 117, 191, 199
The Challenge of Peace pastoral letter, 193
Chan, Lúcás, 38
Childress, James F., 157, 158
Christian ethics
  authenticity, Cahill, prioritizing, 25–26
  characteristics of, 203–8
  Christological foundation, establishing, 37
  commonality, search for, 163–64
  communal identity as essential to, 57
  contemporary practices, 58–59, 63
  death of Jesus, lessons and insights offered by, 32, 33
  descriptive and normative tasks, engaging, 64–65
  key elements shaping, 197–203
  the marginalized, engagement with, 150, 158–59
  marriage and, 97
  middle axioms as practicable, 101
  overlapping identities, contending with, 66–67
  participatory Christian ethics, xiv–v, 132
  Scripture, informing, 38, 54–55, 60, 62–63, 67, 189
  secularization, challenge of, 202
  as social and neighbor-focused, 176
  as suspect in the postmodern world, 162
  unexpected conditions, applied in, 136
Chrysostom, John, 50, 99, 100
civil rights era, 183, 185
climate change, 13, 133, 134
Cloutier, David, 106–7
Cold War as a sign of the times, 193
Commentary on Genesis (Luther), 99
common good, 48, 76, 102
  bioethics and, 117, 157, 172
  Cahill's contribution to, 24, 46, 72, 121
  Catholic promotion of, 74, 111, 131–32, 171, 186
  commitment to, strengthening, 113
  common ground, substantiating search for, 161
  conscientious objectors, obligation to contribute to, 192
  contributive justice, participating through, 165–66
  ecological crisis and, 207
  engagement as fulfilling the meaning of, 127
  the excluded, keeping the perspective of in mind, 20
  family participation in, 100
  global ethics of, in need of revision, 116
  for HIV/AIDS sufferers, 130
  love of neighbor as part of, 152
  neo-Thomist pursuit of, 44
  in political arrangements, 170
  positive dialogue as contributing to, 124
  promotion of peace and, 192–93
  rights and duties in relation to, 123
  scholarship on, 173
  search for the good life, linking with, 200–201
  thick sense of, as dissolving, 181
  Thomistic view of, 129
  threats to, 43
  true and useful friendships, locating in, 168–69
  universal common good paradigm, 24, 27
  war, justifying on the basis of, 92
Cone, James H., 180

conscientious objection, 192, 195
contributive justice, 165–66
Copeland, M. Shawn, 27–28, 180
Cosgrove, Charles, 62
the cross, theology of, 32–35, 37–39, 179, 183
Cruz, Jeremy V., 29
Curran, Charles, 86, 111

Day, Dorothy, 89, 90, 91
Deane-Drummond, Celia, 134
Dei verbum dogmatic constitution, 188, 189–90
Dinh, Hoa Trung, xx
distributive justice, 165–66
Doberstein, John, 185
domestic church, 42, 97, 100, 102–4, 153–54, 192
Doyle Roche, Mary M., 102

Economic Justice for All pastoral letter, 99–100
Edwards, Stephanie C., xx
Elizondo, Virgilio, 137
embodiment
  communal embodiment of resurrection life, 26
  embodied love of Jesus for the poor, 211
  in feminist theology, 20, 98
  in human agency as nonnegotiable, 1
  human embodied life as ambiguous and incoherent, 48
  in method of Cahill, 22–24, 29
  reign of God, Jesus embodying, 30–31, 32
  theological beliefs, practices embodying, 154
  universal claims and particular realities, connection between, 27
environmental ethics
  ambiguity as inherent in, 140
  Cahill, level of engagement with, 133, 202
  Christian environmental ethics, 141
  CST and gender, intertwined with, 137–38
  hopefulness as aspect of, 142–45
  prudence, key role in, 134
  suffering, moral obligation to reduce, 139
Epp, Jay, 51
Ethics (McClendon), 179
evil
  human nature, evil capacities of, 10, 179
  material evil, direct causation of, 85
  moral evils, not excusing, 128
  principle of double effect and, 84
  reality of, 164–65
  reduction of as an ethical obligation, 140

Familiaris consortio exhortation, 100
family ethics
  Amoris Laetitia and the task of, 105–7
  Cahill, central theological ideas on, 97–101
  Christian social tradition, privileging, 99
  common human needs, rooted in, 104
  ecclesiology of justice, applying to, 96
  hermeneutic of transformation, reflecting, 61
  the margins, family ethics from, 151–54
  methodology of CST, extended into, 78
  shared experiences of body relationship, reliance on, 98
Farley, Margaret, 44, 137, 159
feminism, 10, 12, 33
  Cahill's feminism, 6–9, 172
  Catholic feminist ethics, 40–41, 44, 45, 47
  cooperative social action, ahead of the curve on, 43
  experience, feminism anchored in, 14, 20–22
  feminist ethics, 9, 48, 62, 74–75, 78, 96
  feminist hermeneutics, 20, 42, 97–98

feminist methodology, Cahill's commitment to, 60
  inter-cultural engagement in, 152
  Junian feminism, 45–46, 49–51
  just anger of, 16
  marginalization, recognizing potential for, 101, 150, 156
  natural law, feminist approach to, 3, 13, 15
  as a necessary vantage point, 1
  new feminist theologies, 109
  Thomas, feminist perspective on, 8
Finnis, John, 3, 173
FitzGerald, Marianne Tierney, xvii
Fletcher, Jeannine Hill, 27
Forming Consciences for Faithful Citizenship (USCCB), 115
Francis, Pope
  Amoris Laetitia, 97, 104, 105–6, 121
  on the common good, 181, 207
  kingdom of God, making present, 208
  moments of encounter, encouraging, 81
  option for the poor, support for, 204
  polarized responses to exhortations of, 72
  on the techno-economic paradigm, 200
  throwaway culture, denouncing, 200
  Vatican II, embracing in papal leadership, 187
  See also *Laudato si'* encyclical
Franciscan theological tradition, 40, 45, 47, 49, 205
Friends and Other Strangers (Miller), 159
friendship, analogy of, 168–69
Fullilove, Mindy, 17–18, 20, 29

Gaudium et spes pastoral constitution, 187, 188, 192–93, 195
Gaventa, Beverly Roberts, 49
gender ethics, 13, 16, 44–45, 47–48
Georgetown Mantra, principlist approach of, 157

Gladwell, Malcolm, 184–85
Glendon, Mary Ann, 44
Global Justice, Christology, and Christian Ethics (Cahill)
  Christology and union, on the centrality of, 173–74
  differing Christologies, exploring, 202
  ethics and theology, on the interactions between, 206
  grounded ethics in, 172
  marginalized voices, engaging, 151
  moral reasoning, emphasizing, 7
  Pineda-Madrid, drawing on the work of, 154–55
  pragmatism, Cahill claiming as a cultural heritage, 12
  on redemption, 30
  on the Spirit of Christ as a unifying power, 180
  theology and practice, on reciprocity between, 156
globalization, effect on Christian theology, 198–99, 208
grace, 44, 47, 96, 174, 175, 176–77
Gregory, Eric, 175
Grimes, Katie Walker, 27
Gustafson, James
  Cahill, building on thoughts of, 111, 142, 144, 209–10
  Christian ethics' lack of works on Scripture, lamenting, 54, 63
  culture in ethical methodology, viewing as significant, 150
  ecological future, little hope in, 133
  environmental ethics, ambiguity in approach to, 140
  human limits, recognizing, 141
  prophetic and narrative modes of discourse, focus on, 110

Haight, Roger, 32, 210
Hall, Pamela, 4
Hauerwas, Stanley, 66, 90, 173
healthcare ethics
  bridge building in the healthcare system, 114–15, 117–18
  Catholic healthcare and moral discourse, 121–23

dialogue, commitment to, 127–29
four principles of medical ethics, 112
healthcare access, 28, 75, 78
healthcare activism, call for, 131–32
healthcare studies, Cahill's contribution to, 7, 118
"middle way" approach, 120
social dimensions of healthcare, 80, 111
hermeneutics
　Cahill, hermeneutic method of, 190
　hermeneutical keys, 97, 99, 193
　major themes and, 97–101
　threefold feminist hermeneutic, 20, 22, 41–43, 97, 205
　of transformation
　　as applied, 59–62
　　contributions and questions, 62–67
　　defining features, 55–59
hierarchy of goods, 84, 85
HIV/AIDS, 43, 103, 130, 170–71, 191
Hollenbach, David, 168, 173
Hursthouse, Rosalind, 88

Imperatori-Lee, Natalia, 25
infused virtues, 144, 176
integral ecology, 102–3, 207, 208
Interfaith Center for Corporate Responsibility (ICCR), 158
Interfaith Youth Core (IFYC), 80–81
irreducible moral dilemmas, 87–89, 92, 94
Isasi-Díaz, Ada María, 46, 149, 159

Jackson-Meyer, Kate Ann, xix
Jenkins, Willis, 134, 135–36, 139, 142
Jesus Christ
　African American community, as co-sufferer with, 185–86
　anti-family sayings of, 60–61
　Christian community as the body of Christ, 190
　evil, overcoming, 164
　injunctions, Paul's call to extend or limit, 98
　justice, working for in the image of Jesus, 37–38
　marriage as sacramental communion with Christ, 104
　nonviolence, Jesus's example of, 89, 90
　reign of God, proclaiming, 30–32, 207–8
　resurrection of, 35–36, 143–44
　two sides of the coin, reading of, 19
　union with Christ, 173–74, 174–79
　victims of injustice, solidarity with, 32–35, 189
John Paul II, Pope, 106, 125, 130
　on the common good, 169
　economic and development questions, deferring to others, 77
　Familiaris consortio, 100
　marriage, viewing as an eschatological sign, 105
　Sollicitudo rei socialis, 76, 99, 204
　theology of the body and ethics of reproduction, addressing, 44
　Veritatis Splendor, 121
　war, defending in light of the common good, 93
John XXIII, Pope, 76, 77, 82, 135
Junian theology
　Junia, 41, 46, 49–51, 52
　Junian feminisms, 44–47
　Junian school of thought, introducing, 40, 205
　marginalized women, relying on the experiences of, 20
jus ad bellum ethics, 91
Just Mercy (Stevenson), *xi*
just war theory
　Cahill, cross-cultural approach to, 75
　inherent ambivalences in, 88
　irreducible moral dilemmas, ignoring, 83
　just war and pacifism, 89–93
　in *Love Your Enemies,* 192, 193–94
　peacebuilding and, 94, 199
　sinfulness, role in, 47, 95
justice, types of, 165–66. *See also* social justice

Kaveny, Cathleen, 108, 113, 159
Keenan, James F., 173, 191
Kelly, David F., 113
Kelly, Gerald, 111
Kennedy, John F., 71–72
Kerry, John, 108
kingdom of God
  as already/not yet present, 89
  call to make present in this world, 188
  in Catholic social teaching, 99
  Christ's vision for, 18, 189, 207–8
  embodiment of, 30–31, 37, 38
  generosity as characterizing, 101
  as inclusive, 126
  peacebuilding, role in, 94, 195
  pilgrim people, contributing to God's reign, 190
  preferential inclusion of the poor, 37, 118
  present availability of, 31–32
  Spirit of Christ as bringing about, 180
Knieps-Port Le Roi, Thomas, 105
Kohlhaas, Jacob, 102, 106, 107
Kony, Joseph, 184

Laudato si' encyclical
bishops' contributions, valorizing, 198
dialogue on Christian ethics, featuring, 207
ecological/environmental focus of, 77, 202
women, providing an opportunity to uplift, 137–38
world authorities, on not solely relying upon, 135
Lavare, George, 175
Lectures on Galatians (Luther), 177
Leo XIII, Pope, 73, 116
liberation theology, 10, 31, 33, 36, 125, 143
Life Together (Bonhoeffer), 185
liquid modern society, 199–201, 208
Lumen gentium dogmatic constitution, 188, 190
Luther, Martin, 99, 109, 174, 176, 177–79
Lysaught, M. Theresa, 172

Macron, Emmanuel, 202
Mannermaa, Tuomo, 178
Martin, James, 52
Mary Magdalene, 36
Massa, Mark S., 8
Massey, Julie Donovan, 103
Massingale, Bryan N., 26
McCarthy, David Matzko, 102–3
McClendon, James, 179–80, 181–84
McCormick, Richard, 110, 111
medical ethics. *See* healthcare ethics
Meeks, Wayne, 66
middle way concept
  Cahill, middle axioms of, 97, 101, 112–13, 122, 127, 132
  in Catholic Social Teaching, 73, 74, 77, 104
  in healthcare debates, 120–21
  in theological bioethics, 114, 119
Miller, Richard, 159
Miller-McLemore, Bonnie, 101
moral dilemmas, 86–89
moral truth, contingency of, 163
Moses, Sarah M., 188

natural law
  Cahill, reliance on theory of, 3–4, 12, 44, 47, 166–168
  in Catholic social teaching, 73, 78
  common ground, search for, 43, 161
  feminist approach to, 13–16
  Greco-Roman natural law, 106
  justice, as pervaded by the concept of, 165
  in medical ethics, 113
  natural law ethics, 167, 173
  neo-Scholastic accounts, 6
  Thomist approach, 3–8, 11–12, 74, 124, 166, 176
Niebuhr, Reinhold, 93, 109
Nussbaum, Martha, 24, 98

O'Connell, Maureen, *xviii*
O'Malley, John, 193
On the Trinity (Augustine), 174–75
Optatam totius decree, 190
option for the poor. *See* preferential option for the poor

Pacem in terris encyclical, 76, 77
Patel, Eboo, 50
Paul, Apostle
 Christian community, vision of, 190
 communal priority, 98
 greetings from, community contemplation of, 52
 image of body and the role of presence, 181
 Junia and, 41, 46, 49, 50, 51
 new moral pattern, seeking to encourage, 56–57
 present in spirit, on being, 182
Paul VI, Pope, 76, 80
peace and pacifism
 Cahill, contribution to peace studies, 47, 75
 just war tradition and, 83, 88, 89–93, 193–94
 peacebuilding
  Cahill, contributions to field, 47, 72, 94–95, 131
  Catholic peacebuilding, 194–95
  in the Global South, 199
  just war theory and, 83
  nonviolent witness, importance of, 27
  social transformation as linked to, 79, 84
 peacemaking, 60, 69, 179, 186, 192, 211
 Vatican II, promoting, 191–93, 194, 195
Peppard, Michael, 50
personalism, 113
Peter, Apostle, 34
Phan, Peter, 11
Phoebe, 50, 52
pilgrim people of God, 190
Pineda-Madrid, Nancy, 155–56
pluralism, ethics in the face of, 161–64
Pontius Pilate, 34
Pope, Stephen J., 82, 173
Populorum progressio encyclical, 76, 198
Porter, Jean, 7, 12, 173

Postman, Neil, 181
praxis, 1, 57, 61
 communal moral praxis, 56–57, 59, 63, 65–66, 67
 CST as communal praxis, 81–82
 hermeneutic of, 20, 22, 41, 42–43, 52, 205
 narrative as a central praxis, 25
preferential option for the poor
 in Catholic social teaching, 77, 203
 centrality of, 204
 in Christian ethics, 49, 208
 emphasis on, 171
 as the foremost principle, 116
 in a global context, 47
 global health justice, recognizing, 132
 Jesus's preference for the poor, 27–28
 moral priority of, 37
principle of double effect (PDE), 84–86, 88
Principles of Biomedical Ethics (Beauchamp/Childress), 157
privatization of religion, 201–2
proportionalism, 91, 93, 110, 111, 113, 121

Rahner, Karl, 198
Ramsey, Paul, 93, 110
Ravizza, Bridget Burke, 103
reign of God. *See* kingdom of God
Reimer-Barry, Emily, 103
Rerum Novarum encyclical, 73, 76–77, 80, 116
Ricoeur, Paul, 197, 206
romanticism, magisterial teaching on, 100
Rosa, Hartmut, 199–200
Rubio, Julie Hanlon, 103, 104
Ryan, Virginia, xx

Schiavo, Terri, 116, 123
secularization, 201–2, 208
see-judge-act approach, 78
sexual ethics, 44, 47–48, 78, 191, 201, 210

Shannon, Thomas, 73
Sherman, Matthew, *xix–xx*
signs of the times, 77, 187, 190, 191, 193, 195
sinning bravely concept, 84, 85, 86
Smith, James K. A., 176
Sobrino, Jon, 31–32, 36
social justice, 52, 78, 157
   basic equality, recognizing, 166
   call in/call out, use of terms, 109
   Church's commitment to, 82
   defining, 165
   hierarchical approach to, 114
   trauma-informed practices of, 23
social location, importance of, 150
Society of Christian ethics (SCE), 40
Sollicitudo rei socialis encyclical, 76, 99, 204
Sowle, Donald E., 192
stem cell research, 125, 126
Stevenson, Bryan, *xi, xiii*
subsidiarity, principle of, 103, 169–70
Summa Contra Gentiles (Aquinas), 99
Supiot, Alain, 199
suspicion, hermeneutic of, 20, 22, 41, 42, 47, 52, 205
Synod for the Amazon, 207

techno-economic paradigm, 200
Theological Bioethics (Cahill)
   common good, on working towards, 113
   concrete communities, ethics grounded in, 172
   major themes of, 112
   marginalized voices, engaging with, 151
   moral discourse, on the participatory mode of, 110–11, 156
   particularistic theological discourse, arguing for, 7
Theological Studies (periodical), 52, 116, 199
Thomas Aquinas, Saint
   basic spheres of morality, identifying, 166
   hierarchy of goods as a Thomistic strategy, 85
   on hope as an infused virtue, 144
   infused grace concept, 174, 176
   just war theory, supporting, 91, 92–93
   language of "indwelling" as common to, 177–78
   marriage as a servile relationship, against, 99
   natural law, approach to, 3–8, 11–12, 74, 124, 166, 176
   particularity of moral norms, supporting, 7
   PDE, relying on the strategy of, 84–85
   prudence, on the virtue of, 5
Thomistic tradition, 45
   Aristotelian-Thomistic ethics on injustice, 9
   common good, Thomistic view of, 129
   embodiment in Thomistic thought, 23
   engagement and learning, high priority on, 44
   feminist theology, Thomistic heritage of, 98
   marriage, Thomistic view of, 105
   neo-Thomistic paradigm, Cahill's place in, 20
   peacebuilding, applying Thomistic thought to, 94
   Thomistic epistemology, Cahill reinterpreting, 14
   Thomistic theological tradition, 40, 47
Tobin, Joseph Cardinal, 122
"Traditioning: The Formation of Community, the Transmission of Faith" (Pineda-Madrid), 155
transformation, four traits of, xi–xiii
transversalism, 163
Tuck, Eve, 21–22
Turkle, Sherry, 181, 183, 184–85

United States Conference of Catholic Bishops (USCCB), 108, 115, 128

van Bavel, Tarcisius, 175–76
Vatican II
    activist approach in CST, validating, 77
    church in the world, vision of, 188–91, 196
    divisions in the wake of, 78, 121
    Gaudium et spes, 187, 188, 192–93, 195
    global consciousness, embracing, 198
    peace, promotion of, 191–92, 194
    proportionalism, post-council move to, 111, 113
Verhey, Allen D., 205

Veritatis Splendor encyclical, 121
La Virgen de Guadalupe, 155, 156

war. *See* just war theory
Ward, Raymond E., *xix*
weak ties *vs.* strong ties, 184–85, 186
West, Traci, 136
Westburg, Daniel, 4
Whitman, Gordon, 22, 23, 82
Williams, Bernard, 87
Williams, Reggie L., 185–86

Yoder, John Howard, 90
You Are What You Love (Smith), 176